Cinema and Society Series
General Editor: Jeffrey Richards

Published and forthcoming:

To Gifford and Kamila, to Tom and
Alice, with love

The great cities are false
Jean-Luc Godard

FROM MOSCOW TO MADRID
Postmodern Cities, European Cinema

Ewa Mazierska and
Laura Rascaroli

I.B. TAURIS
LONDON · NEW YORK

Published in 2003 by I.B.Tauris & Co Ltd
6 Salem Road, London W2 4BU
175 Fifth Avenue, New York NY 10010
www.ibtauris.com

In the United States and Canada distributed by Palgrave Macmillan
a division of St. Martin's Press, 175 Fifth Avenue, New York NY 10010

ISBN 1 86064 850 9 (hb) 1 86064 851 7 (pb)

A full CIP record for this book is available from the British Library
A full CIP record for this book is available from the Library of Congress

Library of Congress catalog card: available

Set in Monotype Garamond by Ewan Smith, London
Printed and bound in Great Britain by MPG Books, Bodmin

Contents

Illustrations

General Editor's Introduction

The cinema has from its earliest days been fascinated by the city – as setting, subject and symbol. The city has featured as a living organism in a wide variety of genres – comedy, drama, science fiction, documentary – from *Metropolis* to *Night and the City*, from *City Lights* to *A City Speaks*, from *While the City Sleeps* to *Blade Runner*. We are now in the era of the postmodern city, an era that has seen the overthrow of communism, the expansion of the European Union, the simultaneous rise of nationalism and globalization and the return of war to Western Europe.

In their absorbing and wide-ranging study, Ewa Mazierska and Laura Rascaroli explore the postmodern city in the context of European cinema. They divide their study into three parts: 'Old Europe' where their focus is on the Latin countries, Italy (Naples), Spain (Madrid) and France (Marseilles); 'Postcommunist Europe' which takes us to Russia (Moscow), Poland (Warsaw) and Germany (Berlin); and 'Great Britain' which features the capital (London), the northern seaside (Blackpool) and the Celtic city (Edinburgh, Swansea).

In each section, after carefully establishing the social, political, architectural and artistic histories of particular cities, they give close textual readings of key films set in those cities, films such as *The Flower of My Secret*, *Luna Park*, *Trainspotting*, *Bye-Bye*, *Girl Guide* and *Bhaji on the Beach*. They also analyse the distinctive urban visions of such significant directors as Pedro Almodóvar, Pavel Lungin, Juliusz Machulski and

Michael Winterbottom. In so doing, they examine the issues of reality versus artifice, modernism and postmodernism, fragmentation and alienation, ethnicity and gender, place and space. The whole adds up to a fascinating, thought-provoking and ground-breaking study which is essential reading for anyone interested in contemporary European cinema, the city and the postmodern condition.

Jeffrey Richards

Acknowledgements

We wish to express our gratitude to Professor Jeffrey Richards of Lancaster University for reading the manuscript and for his kind support and encouragement; to Philippa Brewster at I.B.Tauris for believing in our project and for assisting us throughout our work with her editorial advice; and to Susan Lawson at I.B.Tauris for her help in preparing the final version of the book. Our special thanks go to Tom Carroll and to Gifford Kerr for helping us with the editing of the book.

Many colleagues, friends and relatives have helped us in various ways, and we wish here to give them credit: Grzegorz Balski, Grazyna Grabowska and Adam Wyzynski at the National Film Archive, Poland; Andrzej Kolodynski at *Kino* magazine; Elzbieta Ostrowska at Lodz University; David Young at Manchester Metropolitan University; John Walton, Susan Burnett and Helen Jones at the University of Central Lancashire; Luca Rascaroli at the Politecnico of Milan; Mary Noonan and Aisling O'Leary at the National University of Ireland, Cork; and Alba Bariffi at Reader's Digest, Milan.

The authors and publishers wish to thank the following for their permission to reproduce illustrative material: BFI Stills, Posters and Designs for *Trainspotting*, *Wonderland*, *Kika*, and *L'amore molesto*; MK2 s.a. for *Taxi Blues*; the Polish Film Archive for *Girl Guide*, *Kiler*, *Night Shapes*, *Life is a Building Site* and *Luna Park*; Dacia Films for *Nenette et Boni*. The authors and publishers would also like to thank the following for permission to use copyright material: El Deseo s.a. for *Kika* and *The*

Flower of My Secret; Teatri Uniti for *Morte di un matematico napoletano*, *L'amore molesto* and *Teatro di guerra*; Dacia Films for *Nenette et Boni*; Studio Filmowe Zebra for *Girl Guide* and *Kiler*; Peter Rommel Productions for *Night Shapes*; X Filme for *Life is a Building Site*; MK2 s.a. for *Taxi Blues*; IMA Films/UGD-DA for *Luna Park*; FilmFour Ltd for *Trainspotting*; Universal Studios for *Twin Town*.

Research for Chapter 3 was funded by the Faculty of Arts Research Fund of the National University of Ireland, Cork.

A preliminary version of Chapter 5 was published with the title, 'Any Town? Post-communist Warsaw in Juliusz Machulski's *Girl Guide* (1995) and *Kiler* (1997)' in the *Historical Journal of Film, Radio and Television*, 19: 4 (October 1999).

Introduction

The City-text

In the introductory notes to a special issue of *Screen* on Space/Place/ City published in 1999, editor Karen Lury pointed to the emphasis on the concepts of 'space' and 'place' that has emerged in film and television studies in recent years. With particular reference to the relationship between the cinema and the city, Lury wrote:

> An expanding body of literature ... uses historical and critical material related to the 'city' and discusses the way in which certain films have represented the modern or postmodern city. Further- more, in relation to early cinema, for example, such work has also attempted to understand the representation of the city by cinema as a fundamental part of the construction of actual cities them- selves, and the lived experience of individuals who inhabit these particular places. The 'city', or the characteristics of city life, then becomes a way of interpreting identity and living practices within the modern and/or postmodern world. (Lury and Massey 1999)

This ever more diffused critical and analytical practice is, on the one hand, an example of that growing interest in interdisciplinarity and in cultural studies that has become a characteristic feature of film studies among other disciplines; on the other hand, it can be seen as a response to Henri Lefebvre's seminal work on the concept of space (Lefebvre 1974), and specifically to his call for 'a new kind of spatial imagination capable of confronting the past in a new way and reading its less tangible secrets off the template of its spatial structures – body, cosmos, city' (Jameson 1991: 364–5).

A number of volumes and essays have established the pair city/cinema as an object of scientific inquiry.[1] Together they form a body of work that is significant but at the same time deficient, considering the paramount importance and complexity of the history of the relationships between film and city – a history that for the most part still has to be written. From this perspective, David B. Clarke rightly lamented, only two years before the publication of *Screen*'s special issue, the scarcity of academic reflection on the cinematic city: 'Despite the immediately perceptible cinematic qualities that cities frequently seem to possess, and despite the uncredited role played by the city in so many films, relatively little theoretical attention has been directed towards understanding the relationship between urban and cinematic space' (Clarke 1997: 1).

Though different approaches are adopted, the existing (and expanding) literature on the relationship between city and cinema is dominated by the study of the city as a text and as a representation, a perspective that is common in much contemporary writing. This is because 'city' is not only a built environment, but also 'the space produced by the interaction of historically and geographically specific institutions, social relations of production and reproduction, practices of government, forms and media of communication, and so forth' (Donald 1992: 422). Furthermore, the same built environment can hardly be conceived independently of the concept of representation, since 'spatial, building and architectural practices are representations, as also are the material, physical and spatial forms that result' (King 1996: 5).

This book situates itself within this scientific framework, and consequently addresses the 'city' as an ever-shifting text, as the mutating product of a complex series of relations and of representations, one that can be investigated by means of specific discursive regimes. Accordingly, when discussing the cinematic representations of a city we refer not only to the 'real' city, (semi)permanently sited and described by its map, but also, and more interestingly, to the city-text (the product of countless and intermingled instances of representation), and to the lived-city (the experience of urban life and of its representations that an inhabitant or a visitor may have). Adopting these perspectives, we hope to find ourselves beyond the edges of the map.

Beyond the edges of the map we enter the localities of the vibrant, everyday world and the disturbance of complexity. Here we find ourselves in the gendered city, the city of ethnicities, the territories of different social groups, shifting centres and peripheries – the city that is a fixed object of design (architecture, commerce, urban planning, state administration) and yet simultaneously plastic and mutable: the site of transitory events, movements, memories. This is therefore also a significant space for analysis, critical thought and understanding. (Chambers 1994: 92–3)

Cities–Cinemas

Though much of the cinematic city's history is as yet unwritten, past and recent research has shed some light on it. Far from aiming at a detailed description of the relevant literature, our concern here is to draw attention to some examples of this work and to some of the principal images that shape it. The following account will therefore be only partial and generic.

Reaffirming the importance of the city both as a setting for and as a protagonist of early cinema, in his essay on the city in film from the origins of cinema to 1930, Helmut Weihsmann (1997) remembered how pioneering filmmakers such as the Lumière brothers, Skladanowsky, Edison, Friese-Green and Notari regularly positioned their cameras before the urban spectacle. 'The first film shows were primarily "big city" affairs ... Nearly all early film documents present a *mise en abîme* of audiences filling vaudeville halls from busy city streets in order to see projected on the screen – busy city streets' (Gunning, quoted in Weihsmann 1997: 8).

Enthusiasm for the elating spectacle of modernity vanished rapidly, however: 'After 1918, the metropolis is no longer a place for the idler searching for amusement, excitement and diversion, but a horror-scenario for its frightened and threatened inhabitants' (p. 12). German Expressionism epitomizes the changed attitude towards the city and urban life. Films such as Wiene's *Das Kabinett des Doktor Caligari* [The Cabinet of Doctor Caligari, 1919], with its uncanny and distorted architectures; Boese and Wegener's *Der Golem* (1920), with its archaic ghetto; and Lang's *Metropolis* (1927), with its dystopian cityscape, reflect an era's 'haunted, darkened atmosphere of apocalypse and unchained fear' (p. 12). Also the 'street films' genre of 1923–25 in Weimar Germany mirrored and exploited the concrete fears of an ill-fated democracy, at a time when 'the streets of German cities actually were the setting for terror and violence' (p. 13).

A different, more optimistic view of modern urban life was offered in the 1920s by a new genre, the 'city symphonies', in which 'the individual contributions of millions of people (working with technologies that have developed over centuries) are subsumed within the metropolis's mega-partite movement through the day' (MacDonald 1997–98: 4). This genre's foremost examples are Strand and Sheeler's *Manhatta* (1921); Alberto Cavalcanti's *Rien que les heures* [Nothing but the Hours, 1926]; Walter Ruttmann's *Berlin, die Sinfonie einer Großstadt* [Berlin, Symphony of a Big City, 1927]; and Dziga Vertov's *Chelovek s kinoapparatom* [Man with a Movie Camera, 1929]. Despite the significant differences in style and approach, all of these films took as their subject the big city seen as the incarnation of progress and of modernity. The 'city symphonies' celebrated the rhythm and fascination of the fast-moving metropolis; a similar view of the city is also found in many Dada and Surrealist films.

A classical way of looking at the representation of the city in film is through the study of specific genres, a perspective that applies primarily to Hollywood cinema. Film noir, gangster film and *film policier* have consistently been discussed with reference to the representation of the city. These, in fact, are typically urban genres, whose narratives and characters stem from a particular urban milieu – that of the night, of crime-plagued streets, and of the city's underworld. Its expressionist urban iconography is an essential component of film noir, so much so that dark and wet streets, reflecting surfaces and city lighting are its trademark and represent much of its fascination.[2] As for the gangster movie, one of its forging tensions is the contrast between city and countryside; the same contrast has been traced by Colin McArthur (1997) in many Hollywood films belonging to different genres, from *The Barkleys of Broadway* (1949), a musical with Fred Astaire and Ginger Rogers, to Capra's *Mr Deeds Goes to Town* (1936) – both examples of films which, according to the author, are representative of America's reflection on its transition to modernity and to urbanization.

Science fiction, with its utopian and, more often, dystopian urban visions and readings of modernity, is another genre that has often given rise to discussions about the cinematic city. The films that best represent the debate are *Metropolis*, an icon of the apocalyptic vision of modernity;

and Ridley Scott's *Blade Runner* (1982), epitomizing the postindustrial decay, vast immigration and architectural pastiche of the postmodern metropolis. The discourse on the postmodern cinematic city, both in science fiction and in films set in contemporary times (such as *Falling Down*, Joel Schumacher, 1992), has concentrated mainly on Los Angeles, the metropolis that has come to epitomize the urban discontents of our society.

It is not difficult to identify in utopia/dystopia the dichotomy ruling the critical discourse on the city, not only in science fiction but also in all the films and genres quoted above. The idea of the city as spectacle, clearly connected to a utopian vision of modernity, can be traced in discussions of early cinema, of the 'city symphonies' of the 1920s, as well as of specific films, such as *Lost Horizon* and *The Fountainhead*. A dystopian vision of modernity underlies discussions of German Expressionism, of the 'street films' genre of 1923–25, of film noir and, of course, of science fiction.

Other ways of looking at the cinematic city have also been employed, for instance an attention to the contrast between the centre and suburbs. Pierre Sorlin (1994) has traced a history of the city in Western European cinema from 1930 onwards. He has distinguished a first phase characterized by the lack of distinction between the centre and the outskirts; a second phase, beginning in 1930, when this distinction becomes very clear; and, finally, a phase in which the image of cities blurs altogether.[3] An article by Chris Darke (1997) applies Sorlin's idea to the 'blurring' of Paris in the cinema of the *nouvelle vague* and of Godard in particular, showing how a dystopian vision of the city is, once again, at the core of Sorlin's thesis. For Darke, it is the modernist urban projects of the 1960s that obscure and blur 'Haussmann's rationally planned centre. It is just such a fear that informs *Alphaville*'s image of an architecturally brutal future world in the heart of the city' (Darke 1997: 12).

The Borders of New Europe

The focus of our attention is the contemporary European city as represented in European films of the last two decades. This period is associated with abrupt changes in Europe's economy and its politics, notably the end of communism and the disintegration of the Soviet Union and the Eastern European bloc; the move from a totalitarian system to modern democracy in Spain, facilitated by the death of Franco in 1975; Thatcherism and the shift from Fordism to post-Fordism in Britain; devolution in Scotland, Wales and Northern Ireland; the dissolution of Yugoslavia and the Balkan conflicts. While the European Community strives for political and economic strength and credibility, two opposite tendencies are observed in the socio-political life of this continent: on the one hand globalization, the shedding of national differences and the acquisition of uniform, transnational or postnational identities; on the other hand, a surge in nationalism and even regionalism, particularly in those countries in which the nation-state aspiration was thwarted, such as the former Yugoslavian republic, the former Soviet Union and Scotland. These and other momentous changes are deeply influencing life in European countries, and their effects are often best seen in the cities, where new ideas, aspirations and contradictions are concentrated and erupt. In this book, we examine whether and how these mutations have been mirrored by recent European urban cinema.

Several aspects of this work touch on problematic issues that must be identified and discussed in this Introduction. One of these is the extent and meaning of what we call 'Europe'. Frequently, and also in the context of 'European cinema', this term is used to refer to a relatively small number of Western countries that form a part of post-imperialist Europe, identified with democracy and the market economy: Germany, France, Great Britain, Italy and Spain. These countries are perceived as stable (despite the many political, social, economic and cultural changes that they have undergone, even in recent years), and are usually associated with 'high culture', to the detriment of other European countries, marginalized by this vision. As the title of our book suggests, we adopt instead a broader concept, according to which Moscow, Warsaw and Sarajevo are as integral to Europe as Paris and London. This conception is not unproblematic. The reality of the continent has transformed dramatically in the last twenty years, so much so that its identity has changed and is constantly shifting. One novel element is the strengthening of the European Union, and the term 'Europe' today is often used to refer to the states that comprise it. To see Europe simply as the set of member-states of the European Union is, of course, highly unsatisfactory; such a criterion does not necessarily explain what Europe is and what being European means in this postmodern, post-Berlin Wall era of increasing globalization and cosmopolitanism. On the other hand, the idea that Europe has changed completely is also easily challenged. Considering that the borders of Europe are shifting and that communism has ceased to be the Other against which the European identity was shaped, David Morley and Kevin Robins set out to identify contemporary Europe's new Others: America, seen as the intolerable future or the Satan of anti-culture; and particularly the Islamic world, since '"The Turk" and "The Moor" have always provided [Europe with] key figures of difference, or of "threat" (and indeed, dread)' (Morley and Robins 1993: 21). Against this backdrop, the authors' discussion of the reactions to Turkey's application to join the EC highlights the perhaps surprising persistent centrality of Christianity in the definition of contemporary Europe's identity and culture.

Without underestimating the thorny question of a contemporary European identity, but with the aim of indicating the transformations that this continent is undergoing, and of highlighting the existence there of different cultures, aspirations and lifestyles, this book includes the cinema of countries that are often neglected – such as Poland – or whose belonging to 'Europe' is problematic – such as Russia. For cognate reasons, rather than privileging the capital cities, which have come to embody the essence of a country in the global imagination but often represent a small or special section of a nation's population and lifestyle, in this book we include studies of cities and towns that are often out of the limelight, for example Marseilles, Naples, Swansea, and Blackpool. We nevertheless have had to be selective for reasons of space and have omitted many other countries and cities that would have offered interesting examples.

We devote one section of the book to France, Italy and Spain, referring to them collectively as 'Old Europe' for their place in the backbone of nineteenth-century Europe, of 'Christendom' Europe. A second section, entitled 'Postcommunist Europe', includes Russia, Poland and Germany, the latter having in Berlin a prominent and controversial symbol of post-'iron curtain' Europe. The blatant absentee in this section is Yugoslavia. It seemed important to us to discuss recent cinematic representations of postmodern Sarajevo, but we found that these almost invariably offer the image of a city torn by war, which with deeper analysis turns out to be, more than anything, an absent city. Sarajevo in recent European film does not seem to have an existence of its own, but frequently becomes a metaphor for an existential condition, as is evident in the portrayals of foreign filmmakers, such as Michael Winterbottom's *Welcome to Sarajevo* (1997); Robert Guédiguian's *À la place du coeur* (1998); and Mario Martone's *Teatro di guerra* (1998; see Chapter 3).

Perhaps cities such as Sarajevo and Belgrade are best represented in these years by the televisual images that show them to us as torn, bombed and, most recently, in revolt.[4]

With a view to highlighting the differences that exist even among cities of the same country, the last section of the book focuses on a case study. Great Britain was chosen for a series of reasons. It has undergone momentous economic, political and social changes in its recent history, in particular with Thatcherism and the passage from a Fordist to a post-Fordist society on the one hand, and political devolution on the other. Thanks to London, Great Britain belongs, more than any other country in Europe, to a globalized, late-capitalist economy. Furthermore, since Thatcherism, British cities, according to observers such as Bianchini and Schwengel (1991), show remarkable contradictory tendencies (for instance, urbanism and anti-urbanism; Europeanization and Americanization).

The Cinema of the Postmodern Condition

Whereas in several cases academic work on North American metropolises in film has been influenced by theories of postmodernism, research on the European filmic city has often been linked to discourses on modernism.[5] In this book, in contrast, concepts coming from the literature on postmodernism and the postmodern condition are, for the first time, systematically applied to the investigation of contemporary Europe's cinematic 'city-texts'. Our discussion is developed against the backdrop of ideas and instruments of analysis deriving from several disciplines: postmodernism theory, urban theory, sociology, geography and socio-political history are required, separately or jointly, both to define the postmodern city, and to support the analysis of specific urban films; film theory and criticism are used in the examination of all those aspects of the *mise-en-scène* that contribute to the construction of a cinematic city-text. In this sense, the *mise-en-scène* is broadly considered as being that set of interrelated filmmaking choices that result in the signifying 'being' or 'body' of the film. A precise analysis of such a 'body', with the backdrop of theories of the postmodern city, is our ultimate objective.

We must clarify at this point what is meant in this book by the expressions 'postmodernism', 'postmodernity' and 'postmodern cinema'. 'Postmodernism' is a problematic term, in the same way as is 'Europe' but even more so. This is not the place to offer a history of the numerous and even contradictory meanings that have been attached to this term, nor of its various incarnations in different areas of the critical discourse.[6] Nevertheless, it is important to clarify the position of this book in the debate. By 'postmodernity' we mean Western society's current cultural, economic and socio-political condition. This condition is characterized by such interrelated phenomena as an increasingly postindustrial and service-oriented economy, with its characteristics and consequences: the growth of hi-tech and entertainment industries; the increase in social polarization; the fragmentation of the urban habitat; the compression of space and time produced by the information revolution; the increasing cosmopolitanism and multi-ethnicity of our living environments; the globalization of culture and the shedding of barriers that once existed between 'high' and 'low' culture. Whereas in the course of this work we refer, directly or indirectly, to postmodernism theories such as those of Lyotard, Baudrillard, Deleuze and Guattari, the general theoretical framework is the thought of Fredric Jameson and his use of the term 'postmodernism' to refer to the cultural discourse of the third stage of capitalism, that is, late or multinational capitalism.

The other expression that requires clarification is 'postmodern cinema'. Much of the debate has been shaped by Fredric Jameson's ideas on postmodern films as characterized by an obliteration of the historical past and by a strong sense of nostalgia, hiding an inability to understand the past behind the reproduction of stereotypical images (see Jameson 1991). David Harvey has concentrated on ideas related to time–space compression in his analysis of postmodern icons such as *Blade Runner* and *Wings of Desire* (Harvey 1989). An emphasis on time is also present in Norman Denzin's analysis of *Blue Velvet*, whose narrative, according to the author, is impossible to place in time; the film effaces the boundaries between past and present and the viewer is placed in an eternal present (see Denzin 1988). The debate has also extensively focused on the key-words 'pastiche', 'self-reflexivity' and 'intertextuality'. On this front, a distinction between modern and post-modern cinema becomes problematic, as these elements can be seen as characteristic of both. For John Orr, in fact, these are merely 'neo-modern inventions' (Orr 1993: 3). For Maureen Turim postmodernism is often, in cinema as well, 'an unconscious repetition of many principles already used within various forms of modernism' (Turim 1991: 178). Tony Wilson tried to disentangle the question by suggesting a distinction between modernism's investigation of the transparency of the image and postmodernism's undermining of the image's reference to reality (see Wilson 1990).

Pastiche; a metalinguistic attitude; intertextuality; the abolition of boundaries (between past and present; 'high' and 'low' culture; visible and invisible); an experimental approach to the narrative; and a passion for the surface of the image (for instance, the use of detail shots devoid of a narrative purpose) are all elements that can be attributed to postmodern as well as to modern cinema. The distinction is challenging, all the more so because postmodernism is not a school, and there is a great difference, for instance, between Lynch's postmodernism and Almodóvar's.

By 'postmodern cinema' we intend a cinema that comes after – after the momentous changes of western society specified above, such as the progressive deindustrialization of the economy, the increasing globalization of culture, the decline of the communist ideology and the falling down of the 'iron curtain'. As is clear, there is no inaugurating date, but a long sequence of changes that matured into a new socio-cultural condition. When it learns from modernism, and imitates its characteristics, the cinema linked to such a postmodern condition unavoidably does so with an attitude that can be seen either as more playful or as more sceptical, as is appropriate for a post-ideological, post-'grand narratives' age. Furthermore, we wish to suggest the importance of distinguishing at least between a more marketable form of postmodern cinema, that which absorbed the lesson of modernism, but also of the society of franchising (a cinema of which *Blade Runner*, with its mix of commercial focus and modernistic visuals, is a good example), and a radical form that resumes and continues, within a new milieu and atmosphere, the project of certain modernist filmmakers. Contemporary directors such as Derek Jarman, Atom Egoyan, Abbas Kiarostami and Wong Kar-Wai derive from modern directors – chiefly Godard and Antonioni – such characteristics as a radical self-reflexivity; a political attention to the nature of the cinematic apparatus and the audiovisual language; an unorthodox approach to narration and its parameters, in particular space and time; and a polemical attitude towards modern capitalism and its features, for instance media saturation, political apathy and loss of freedom and authenticity.

Our work, nevertheless, does not engage exclusively with postmodern cinema, but with cinematic representations of postmodern cities. An important objective of our book is precisely that of investigating the complex relationship between postmodern cinema and the postmodern city. We consider whether cities that can be regarded as postmodern (for example very cosmopolitan, ethnically mixed, with a postindustrial economy and landscape, full of graffiti and franchising logos) are always represented as they are, or whether they tend to lose their postmodern character when shown in films. Furthermore, can the postmodern style of the filmmaking make a city look more postmodern and, conversely, does a postmodern urban setting tend to influence the narrative, characters and style of a film? What role does cinema play in defining the character of contemporary European cities?

With the postmodern city as its subject matter, this work employs postmodernism theory as an instrument of inquiry, and postmodern metadiscourse as a methodological approach. Each chapter adopts a different perspective, uses a different tactic and concentrates on different issues. We do not propose to follow all paths and exhaust all meanings; rather than aiming towards comprehensiveness, we lean towards multiplicity and eclecticism.

The City in Focus

Of the main objectives that guide our work, the principal one is that of understanding whether or not the European cinema of the 1980s and 1990s has mirrored the many transformations that affected European cities in the past twenty years. Do recent European films construct city-texts that carefully try to reflect the social, human and geographical 'reality' of a place, or do they tend to forge cinematic urban habitats that have little in common with an inhabitant's or a visitor's perception of 'reality'? With this question in mind, we intend to explore the complex relationships between Europe's economy and its politics and the cinematic portrayal of European cities, from the viewpoint of postmodernism theory. The objects of our inquiry are a number of European cities and their filmic representations. The approach to each city varies, depending on the issues with which we chose to engage in each chapter. In some cases we concentrate on the portrait of a city given by a number of films by the same filmmaker. For example, Madrid is analysed through the films of Pedro Almodóvar, in particular *Kika* and *The Flower of My Secret*; in the chapter on Moscow we discuss two films by Pavel Lungin: *Taxi Blues* and *Luna Park*. In other cases, we instead consider the portrayals of the same city in films by different filmmakers. Examples are the chapter on Marseilles, where Robert Guédiguian's *Marius et Jeannette*, Karim Dridi's *Bye-Bye*, and Claire Denis' *Nenette et Boni* are analysed; in the chapter on London, we examine the representation of this city in Roger Michell's *Notting Hill*, Peter Howitt's *Sliding Doors*, Jasmin Dizdar's *Beautiful People* and Michael Winterbottom's *Wonderland*.

Despite these different approaches, the analysis of the filmic representation of each city tries to establish whether the city's reality is prevalently mirrored, ignored or altered by the filmmakers. This objective is pursued, for instance, by comparing different representations, both cinematic and non-cinematic, of the same city; by referring to the social, political, architectural and cultural history of a city; and by studying all the relevant elements of the *mise-en-scène*. Our conclusions on this point are, of course, partial as we work on a limited number of European films, all of which engage with contemporary issues, even if they cannot always be called 'realist' in the traditional sense of the term. They are all films that, openly or indirectly, offer insights on life in the city in which they are set, on the way in which that city is perceived and represented by its inhabitants and/or by visitors, immigrants and external observers. Nevertheless, the films analysed in this book cover a wide spectrum. Some are regarded as prominent examples of postmodern cinema, such as Almodóvar's films; others belong to mainstream production, as does *Notting Hill*, or, at the opposite extreme, to a regional and 'artisanal' cinema, for example *Marius et Jeannette*. We hope that our work will help to accomplish a better understanding of the socio-political and aesthetic values of contemporary European cinema, through this limited but variegated sample.[7] At the same time, we strive to offer useful and accomplished analyses of the films considered, based firmly on postmodernism theories and film theory in general. The study of the representation of cities in this sense is not an end in itself, but becomes a vehicle for reaching a full understanding of the films. Not only the settings, but all aspects of the *mise-en-scène* in the broad sense (cinematography, costumes, narrative structure, characters, dialogues) are considered.

A Postmodern European City?

The last objective that we set for our study is that of establishing whether or not the expression 'postmodern city', which in the contemporary imagination and in the relevant literature is strongly connected to the North American metropolis, can be safely borrowed and used in the context of European urban design and city life. This is a moot point, for at least two reasons: because North American cities are widely regarded as the 'home' and natural site of postmodernity; and because most academic studies on the 'postmodern city' refer only to North American metropolises (and chiefly to Los Angeles and Las Vegas).[8] At the same time, many observers of the development of cities in the United States agree that the changes connected to the new postmodern society 'are happening not only in Los Angeles but, in varying degrees and, to be sure, unevenly developed over space and time, all over the world' (Soja 1997: 20). What interests us is reaching an understanding of the sense and the degree to which such changes apply to the European conurbation. The opening chapter, 'From the USA to Europe: Development of a New City', is devoted to this question.

1

From the USA to Europe: Development of a New City

The contentious character of the concept of postmodernity, and in particular of its application to the description of contemporary urban life and fabric, necessitates a discussion of the city in contemporary Europe. Whereas it is customary to refer to North American metropolises in terms of postmodernity, the question of whether a similar perspective can be applied to the European conurbation, and to what extent, is still open. Furthermore, observers even disagree on the existence of a European City:

> Today, any attempt to identify the common traits of the European city would seem a risky exercise. The influence of states has structured various urban forms. Urbanisation has been through a series of movements, and the city no longer constitutes an integrated and relatively closed system. A portion of the research being done on cities no longer bothers with ... nuances and presents models that are relatively universal, or then again, the diversity within Europe appears in such a way as to rule out any kind of generalisation. (Bagnasco and Le Galès 2000: 8)

Although it may be a risky exercise, it is necessary to identify some common elements in the development of European cities in the past twenty years, in order to lay the foundations for our work on the cinematic postmodern city. This does not mean that we ignore diversity, but that we look for a model against which particular urban situations can be compared and evaluated.

Whereas the temporal limits of the modern and the postmodern are a thorny issue in many cultural and artistic fields, including cinema, there is greater consensus when it comes to architecture and urban design. Charles Jencks goes so far as to date the symbolic end of modernism and the passage to the postmodern as 15 July 1972 at 3.32 p.m., when the Pruitt-Igoe housing development in St Louis, Missouri, a prize-winning version of Le Corbusier's 'machine for modern living', was dynamited as being an uninhabitable environment for the low-income people it housed (Jencks 1981: 9). This event symbolically marks the end of the modernist dream of a highly rational, planned city, consisting of distinctive zones, each fulfilling a single social function.

In spite of the differences and even disagreements that emerge from their analyses, urban theorists, sociologists and geographers concur in reading the new North American metropolis as a locus of difference and fragmentation, the opposite of the modernist city. Whereas the modern cityscape was architecturally, socially and environmentally dominated by the factory, the postmodern city is characterized by diffusion and dispersion. The growth of telecommunications and the passage to a late-capitalist, global society have produced a more flexible, decentralized and dispersed economy that remodelled the city, now a network of scattered services and subjects.

In a post-Fordist era, the decline of the manufacturing industry and the shift to a service economy have forced the deindustrialized city to develop technologically advanced urban areas and specialize in the production and provision of services. The changed economy of the global city has had a clear impact on its social structure. A strong tendency to polarization has widened the gap between the affluent, upper-middle classes linked to management, to high-quality services and hi-tech industry, and the lower blue-collar class. The middle class, composed of the salaried employees of bureaucracy and commerce and of skilled labourers, is noticeably regressing and becoming impoverished. Sociologists documented the rise of new social classes or groups, such as yuppies, the truly disadvantaged, the working poor and the upper professionals.

Cosmopolitanism is another salient feature of the North American postmodern city. Whereas in the modern city different social and ethnic groups generally dwelled in different areas, in the postmodern city the most varied lifestyles exist side by side, in a chaotic and fragmented manner. Even areas such as the Village in New York are no longer homogeneous, but present a segmented and mixed population. Also in this sense, the city has become a kaleidoscope, an 'emporium of styles' (see Raban 1975). The massive immigration of Third World workers, combined with the parallel exodus of the local population to the suburbs, has changed the aspect of the North American inner city. Neither do the suburbs fit the image that we had of them in the past; these, once purely residential areas devoid of other functions, have become 'highly heterogeneous agglomerations of industrial production, employment, commerce, cultural and entertainment facilities, and other character-istically "urban" qualities such as gangs, crime, drug-dealing and street violence' (Soja 1997: 25–6). In other words, the city can no longer be thought of in terms of the duality inner city/suburbs. Numerous observers see suburbia as a true new city, for which names such as 'exurbia', 'outer city' and 'technoburb' have been suggested. This idea has challenged sociologists and geographers to find new ways of des-cribing the North American city. Robert Fishman, for instance, believes that this is now better illustrated by the expression 'techno-city', which designates a whole metropolitan area retaining the name of its principal city, but whose economic and social life more and more bypasses its alleged core (see Fishman 1987).

The modifications of the urban economy, social life and physical structure have also influenced the way in which cities are viewed. Paris and New York, the quintessence of the modern city, have been replaced by Los Angeles and Las Vegas, which typify the postmodern metropolis. Baudrillard described LA as a network of unreal circuits, devoid of dimension (see Baudrillard 1981); Las Vegas, with the 'roadside eclectic-ism' of its Strip, epitomizes the apotheosis of communication (see Venturi et al. 1985). It is significant that the idea of the modern city has been embodied by a European capital and by the most European of the North American metropolises, whereas postmodernity is better repres-ented by two extremely American cities that could never exist in Europe.

Undoubtedly, the European city greatly differs from the North American metropolis in its architectural, social and economic history. Nevertheless, urban theorists often do not clearly distinguish between European and American cities when describing the changes in the urban fabric that have taken place during the past thirty years. Many of these changes, which began as early as the mid-1960s, are linked to the diffusion of the private car as the population's principal means of transport: the vast percentage increase of those urban areas devoted to streets and parking; the decentralization of industry; the development of malls and shopping centres; the rise of office parks distant from the city centre; the birth of residential areas devoid of other functions; and a distribution of services that does not respond to real needs, but rather to abstract principles of urban organization. The difference between the North American and European city seems to be one of proportions more than of substance; in the USA all the above-mentioned changes have been much more extreme and extensive.

The argument of dimensional disparity, though, is not sufficient to explain the incontrovertible difference between the North American and European city. Clearly, there is a historical factor for this difference – on the one hand we have the recent past of America, and on the other the centuries or even millennia of history that lie behind many European conurbations. As the loss of historicity is one of the main postmodern themes, it is clear why postmodernity has become directly associated with the North American metropolis. Furthermore, whereas the United States of America share a relatively common, homogeneous past, the European countries have heterogeneous histories and are today at different levels of development – even if the European Union is attempting to homogenize as much as possible the economic and social status of its member-states.

Irrespective of these differences, the history of each European conurbation is usually represented and illustrated by its centre. Three different urban areas are commonly distinguished in the European city: the 'historical centre', which works as a constant remainder of the past and as a gravitational pole for the whole city, and is therefore exemplified in the critical discourse by the figure of continuity; an external area exemplified by the figure of the fragment; and an even more external and peripheral area, characterized by the dispersion of countless fragments. In the modern European city power and wealth decreased as one moved from the centre to the suburbs; in the contemporary European city they are instead 'disseminated in an aggregate, which is immense, polycentric, moderately structured, undoubtedly dominated by the figure of dispersion, and in which innumerable fragments of city, of cultures, of local economies, float ... among these are fragments of the ancient town, the old centres and parts of the modern city, and the suburbs' (Secchi 1999; our translation).

In other words, despite its long history and the presence of a gravitational heart, the European city too can be described in terms of postmodernism, as a place of fragmentation and difference. The historical centre, which for centuries granted the community its sense of continuity with the past and its distinctiveness, in most cases is no longer a sufficiently strong point of reference for a population that is dispersed over a large area. Furthermore, the city centre today has often become an assembly point for immigrants who, in its squares, avenues and galleries, meet, do business and spend their leisure time. Thus, the historical centre, which once differentiated and characterized a conurbation, has today become the city's most cosmopolitan and international area. As a consequence of both its fragmentation and its cosmopolitanism, the city partly loses its individual identity, and looks more and more like any other city in the world – or, at least, in Europe.

Cosmopolitanism and fragmentation are not the only indicators of the postmodernity of urban life in contemporary Europe. Most big cities are characterized by a postindustrial landscape. Graffiti extensively cover the walls of both the centre and the suburbs, despite the efforts of the local authorities; and the historical centres are dominated by commercial images – neon signs, familiar franchising logos and gigantic posters invite the consumption of well-known goods and services. These highly recognizable visual elements homogenize the cityscape. Irrespective of the country in which they happen to be, European consumers can shop in the same chain store, purchasing their favourite goods; they can eat the same food in the same restaurant; and buy the same newspaper that they read at home.

Regardless of all these factors, the European cityscape is – if postmodernity is quantifiable – less postmodern than the North American one. The dramatic changes brought to American urban life by the mall, by theme parks, by a model of urban organization that constructs the city as an entertainment hub (cf. Hannigan 1998), are still very distant from the European urban experience. In substance, the particular character of each European city centre is, in most cases, preserved. A European Las Vegas is hardly conceivable; or, to put it in another way, it is difficult to imagine Philip Johnson 'discussing the Chippendale frieze of his AT&T tower with the planning officers of the city of Turin' (Amendola 1997: 4; our translation) or of almost any other European city. This is because the centre of a European conurbation, regarded as the city's historical patrimony, is usually extremely and deliberately resistant to change.

As a result, Europe can claim only a limited number of buildings that may be called postmodern. France is particularly at the forefront as regards postmodern architecture; examples range from Piano and Rogers's hi-tech Centre Georges Pompidou (1970–77) in Paris, to Ricardo and Emilio Bofill's Les arcades du lac, an extensive neo-classical housing development in Marne-la-Vallée (1978–83). Further examples of European postmodern architectures, of various size and importance, include: James Stirling's Neue Staatsgalerie (Stuttgart, 1984); Hans Hollein's Abteiburg Museum (Mönchengladbach, Germany, 1972–82); Carlo Scarpa's Brion-Vega Cemetery (San Vito d'Altivole, Italy, 1970–72); Hans Hollein's Haas Haus (Vienna, 1987–90); and Erik Gunnar Asplund's Villa in Djursholmen (Djursholm, near Stockholm, 1917–18).

Notwithstanding the scarcity of buildings capable of representing and interpreting the postmodernity of contemporary urban life in Europe, in many cases the cityscape is noticeably modified, in order to keep pace with the requirements of the changing world. The reorganization of the urban fabric in Europe is catalysed by some crucial constituents of the contemporary, late-capitalist economy and society: the networks and connections, both virtual and physical; and the hi-tech, mass media and entertainment industries.

The need to move people and goods and to communicate in the fastest way possible is a distinctive feature of the postmodern world. Many European cities are altering their image and are becoming more competitive by completing new systems of communication: Dublin, with its urban ring-road; Lisbon, with a new railway and a 12 km-long bridge on the Tagus; Athens, with an international airport; London, with the underground Jubilee Line; Paris, with the new RER line for 170,000 passengers per hour, and the connection of the stations of Austerlitz and Lyon by means of a bridge on the Seine; Colonia, with the high-speed railway for London, Paris and Amsterdam; Copenaghen and Malmö, which will be connected by a great bridge (see Roma and Dominici 1997: 21–2). The Channel Tunnel, which links France and England, is the prototype of all these new, rapid inter-city and international connections.

In addition to roads, airports and railways, the city is being transformed into a network of virtual connections. The revolution in the communication system is becoming slowly apparent to the citizens of many European cities who can sometimes obtain computerized certificates and documents; read information of general interest (for instance about the traffic situation) on electronic panels; and access the Internet at home or in cafés. The possibility of working from home using a personal computer connected with those of other working partners has changed the way in which some European citizens live the city. Also, many cities small and large are becoming virtual municipalities, by developing Internet sites that offer interactive information of public interest.

Another transformation of the urban fabric that is characteristic of a late-capitalist society is the renovation of ex-industrial spaces, such as factories and warehouses, which are then converted to other uses. Principally, these spaces are either turned into residences for single people and couples without children, as happened in Manchester and elsewhere in England; or they become headquarters for the new service, hi-tech and mass media industries, or even cultural and/or recreational areas, such as theatres, libraries, universities and parks (but also cafés and discos, in agreement with the postmodern tendency to assimilate low and high culture). Two examples of these trends are the exhibition hall Lingotto Fiere in Turin, which is located in the former buildings of the FIAT factory, converted for this purpose by architect Renzo Piano; and the Parc André-Citroën in Paris, created in the area that hosted, until the 1970s, the Citroën factory. The Lingotto is described in the promotional literature as 'one of the largest and most futuristic multi-functional structures in Europe'; the Parc André-Citroën is defined in the tourist literature as 'a futuristic park'. It is significant that two dismantled car factories – remains of the modern cityscape – have been recycled and transformed into sites for commerce and recreation that are viewed as futuristic and ultramodern.

A third way in which the European urban fabric is being modified is a consequence of the gentrification of the central areas of the city. This phenomenon is very clear, for instance, in the most North American of the European capitals: London. The concentration of corporate activities in central London has caused an increase in speculative building that resulted in the gentrification of the City and the old docks area of East London. Similarly, in other European conurbations the centres or other areas have been upgraded to attract upper-income residents, modifying not only the urban fabric, but also the quarter's original social composition. These areas are usually those previously populated by artists and therefore considered as Bohemian and fashionable, such as the Rive Gauche in Paris, or Brera in Milan. The gentrification of certain urban areas has often given rise to operations of superficial make up, or beautification, instead of responding to sound criteria of urban planning.

The urban landscape is being modified in yet other ways. As in the United States, also in Europe the city wants more and more to please its users – inhabitants and visitors – through the beautification of its landscape. Whereas the modern city, in the name of science and rationality, chose to be functional, the postmodern city aims to be enchanted, and to please all. Instead of heading towards standardization, universality and efficiency – the key concepts in the dreams of modernist urban planners – the contemporary city points towards difference, individuality and pleasure. The city too becomes a product, which has to be beautified and promoted accordingly among the citizens/customers.

The city centre, for instance, at least in the most affluent European countries, often aspires to imitate the mall, and to intensify its lure for consumers by closing its streets to traffic and by furnishing them as if they were interiors, with carpets, plants, lights and diffused music. The American mall, for its part, tries to resemble an (imaginary) European city centre, by reproducing streets complete with fashion boutiques, street lighting, cafés and restaurants. These attempts to imitate each other tend to a common ideal, that of an elegant, alluring street in which the consumer can stroll in comfort, protected from distractions and worries. In other words, the enchanted city tries to shelter its customer from the other city – the city of poverty, of drugs, robbery and prostitution. The citizen who promenades in the beautified city centre is the contemporary version of the modern *flâneur*, who enjoyed looking at the crowds and goods, but always maintained a safe distance – like the narrator in Edgar Allan Poe's short story 'The Man of the Crowd' (1845), who sits at the window of a London café and observes the passing people. The postmodern *flâneur* renounces that distance and seeks to *experience* the enchanted city, to play (or have the illusion of playing) an active role on the kaleidoscopic urban stage. The postmodern 'city-experiencer', a follower of short-lived fashions and compulsive shopper, lives the city as if this were Disneyland, as a virtual simcity (see Soja 1997), a more-than-real place offering many possible stories and roles to play.

Along with the idea of 'experience' goes that of 'event'. In the European postmodern city culture, art (both low and high) and leisure activities are presented, promoted and lived as 'events'. Each event – an art exhibition, a concert, a trade fair – is organized as a skilful marketing operation, and is consumed intensely but rapidly, in order to progress quickly to the next event. Beauty and pleasure have become a right for the masses and, at the same time, a demanding and expensive duty.

This tendency to the enchantment and beautification of the city, and to the hedonistic experience of the events that the city produces, is in contrast with the material and social realities of many European urban areas. The other face of the postmodern urban experience is an increasing non-habitability, due to an unmanageable traffic and parking situation; to the distressing daily contact with the inhuman living conditions of countless immigrants; to the constant bombardment of commercial messages urging a fast consumption of products, events, experiences. Underneath the enchanted city is the city of widening income gaps; of growing social inequalities; of areas devoid of urban meaning and quality; and of the rise of intolerance and urban violence. The growth of the protest against undesired intrusions emphasizes how the gap between the citizens and those who are perceived as illegitimate citizens or, even, as non-citizens (non-EC foreigners and travellers) is wide, and is exacerbated by the failure of local governments to cope with the multi-ethnic reality of the new city. As a result of deindustrialization, many urban areas have been or still are in a regressive crisis, even though the tendency for a high polarization of the urban classes is often hindered by the social and welfare policies of the national governments and unions.

Whereas most of the above characteristics of postmodern urban life may be applied, with varying degrees of accuracy, to the majority of European cities, it is crucial to distinguish between Western Europe and the postcommunist countries. The end of communism and the problematical and sudden shift to a market economy have had deep effects on life in the former Soviet Union and in the Eastern European bloc. The postcommunist countries have been thrust towards a postcapitalist culture and economy, in an abrupt and improvised manner. Western lifestyle models, after having been for many years the forbidden aspiration of a large part of these countries' populations, have suddenly become available to them, at least in theory, or in a revised form. In the case of some postcommunist countries, elements of the enchanted postmodern conception of life, which have penetrated their urban life, are in strident contrast with a difficult national and individual financial situation and, in some cases, with a reality of internal conflict or even war.

Differences and variations not only concern the countries of Western and Eastern Europe, considered as two separate blocs characterized by some uniformity. Each European country has a particular history that defines and determines its current situation. It is precisely these many differences that, in our opinion, are characteristic of postmodern urban life in Europe, and distinguish it from the canonical American one. Undoubtedly, a comparison between the postmodernity of different North American cities reveals the presence of variations: Las Vegas differs from Chicago, but they both unmistakably belong to the same culture. In Europe, almost each city seems to have developed its own, particular postmodernity, in accordance with its specific and original economic, cultural, social and ethnic history. Moscow, London, Warsaw, Blackpool, Naples, Marseilles, Madrid, Berlin are all profoundly different and original, even if they all belong to the same global, late-capitalist society that has produced the postmodern condition.

I

Old Europe

Old Europe's Cities: Between Tradition and Transition

The first section of the book focuses on 'Old Europe', an expression that seemed to us to be more eloquent than the prevalent 'Western Europe' and that hints at the changing political geography of the continent. Europe no longer identifies solely with these countries, which once formed its backbone, but they are none the less influential in the construction of the continent's new identity.

Postimperialist Europe in its trappings of democracy, market economy and 'high culture' is generally perceived as being politically and socially stable and resilient to abrupt changes and, at the same time, as being technologically advanced and economically competitive. Tradition and progress, stability and development are qualities widely associated with the image of Old Europe. This vision is obviously incorrect. Western European countries have undergone momentous political, social and cultural changes in the last two decades, among which are the shift from a totalitarian system to modern democracy in Spain after the death of Franco (1975); the passage from Fordism to post-Fordism, with particularly deep repercussions in Britain; the reunification of West and East Germany after the fall of the Berlin Wall (1989); the end of the First Republic in Italy, with the obliteration of a whole political class; devolution in Scotland, Wales and Northern Ireland. Stability has been endangered by various forms of terrorism – bombs have exploded for instance in Belfast, London, Paris, Florence, Milan, Venice, Bilbao and Madrid. The protest against globalization has also violently hit European cities, as was the case in Genoa during the summer 2001 G8 summit. Furthermore, despite their aura of cosmopolitanism, economic power and widespread wealth, western countries present vast internal contradictions, such as widening gaps between affluent and poor social classes; the economic decline of whole geographical areas and the concentration of capital in others; the resurgence of regionalisms; the rise of racism and intolerance.

The cities of Old Europe reflect the contradictory state of this part of the continent and the consequences of the deep structural and social changes it has undergone in the passage to a postindustrial, globalized economy. In contrast with the prosperity of capital cities, of important metropolises and of provincial towns that are situated in wealthy regions, many cities have declined as a result of the shift from an industrial to a service-oriented economy. This is the case in former mining towns or industrial cities, especially in Britain, as well as in once vital commercial ports, such as Marseilles.

Whereas Great Britain will be taken as a case study that will occupy the last section of the book, Spain, Italy and France have been chosen to represent Old Europe. These countries have had relatively quiet histories in the past twenty years; even the transition to democracy in Spain has been peaceful, despite an attempted military coup in 1981. All three countries present areas of emergence of separatist nationalism: the Basque region and Catalonia in Spain; the so-called Padania in Italy; and Brittany and Corsica in France. They have also seen the rise of extreme-Right parties and movements, most importantly Le Pen's Front National, for which one-third of France's industrial workers voted in the 1995 presidential elections, perhaps as a result of a long phase of rising unemployment and inflation.

The three diverse cities that will be considered below are Madrid, Naples and Marseilles. Each is characterized by a long history and by strong local traditions, but also by recent attempts to modify its structure and economy and to re-launch its image. Madrid, Naples and Marseilles are analysed as different versions of Europe's multiform postmodernity.

2

Stratified Madrid:
Layers of Realism and Artifice
in Almodóvar's Cinema

Madrid is the backdrop to all Almodóvar's films, with the single exception of *Todo sobre mi madre* [All about My Mother, 1999], which is set partly there, but primarily in Barcelona. The Spanish capital is the necessary milieu for Almodóvar's stories, and is almost the main character of his films. Almodóvar's is unquestionably an urban cinema, and not simply because the countryside figures sparingly in his films. His characters are city-dwellers, and his stories can be envisaged only in an urban environment.

The importance of Madrid in Almodóvar's cinema has often been noted. For instance, critics concur in thinking that Almodóvar's early films are linked to the Madrid of the late 1970s and early 1980s in a direct and almost historical manner. They are, in fact, considered to be a product of and a testimony to the *movida*, the movement that flourished after Franco's death in 1975. During this period Madrid saw a blossoming of underground life and hippie counterculture, as testified by a proliferation of art exhibitions, rock concerts, fashion shows and film shooting. *Pepi, Luci, Bom, y otras chicas del montón* [Pepi, Luci, Bom and Other Girls on the Heap, 1980]; *Laberinto de pasiones* [Labyrinth of Passion, 1982]; and *Entre tinieblas* [Dark Habits, 1983], are the films for which Almodóvar has been cited as the quintessential chronicler of contemporary Madrid, for instance by novelist and columnist Francisco Umbral (Smith 1992: 169).

The most coherent and focused study of Madrid in Almodóvar's cinema is, to the best of our knowledge, Marvin D'Lugo's essay 'Almodóvar's City of Desire' (D'Lugo 1995), concerning Almodóvar's first seven films, from *Pepi, Luci, Bom* to *Mujeres al borde de un ataque de nervios* [Women on the Verge of a Nervous Breakdown, 1988]. According to D'Lugo, as he writes apropos of *La ley del deseo* [Law of Desire, 1987], Madrid in these films 'constitutes a privileged space in which individual desires freely circulate' (p. 128). The city thus becomes 'a cultural force, producing forms of expression and action that challenge traditional values by tearing down and rebuilding the moral institutions of Spanish life: the family, the church, and the law' (p. 125). Despite Almodóvar's denial of a relationship between his cinema and Francoism, D'Lugo maintains that in his films Almodóvar 'appropriates the social constructions of Francoist culture – the family, the church, the police – and mobilizes them into the emerging expression of new cultural "desires"' (p. 129). The city is therefore represented as the space in which private and social desires can be expressed and both personal and national new identities achieved. For instance, in *Dark Habits* and *¿Que he hecho yo para merecer esto?* [What Have I Done to Deserve This?, 1984] Almodóvar's Madrid is for both female and gay subjects 'the place of liberation from the tyrannical sexual and social codes of patriarchy' (p. 134).

Such a reading of a liberating Madrid, which is most convincing when applied to the early films, is shared by other authors, particularly those attentive to articulations of lesbian and gay desires in Almodóvar's cinema. Paul Julian Smith, though, has rightly observed that Almodóvar's early films 'show little interaction between lesbian and gay characters and the institutions which shape their lives: the family, the workplace, the legal and medical establishments. They tend to take place in a utopian, asocial place: the post-punk *movida*, the convent, the demi-monde of cinema and theatre' (Smith 1992: 200).

Though the city undeniably mobilizes desires and offers spaces for new identities to be forged, Madrid in Almodóvar's cinema is not at all a delightful paradise, a place where happiness is easily achievable. Almodóvar himself contradicts and mocks this myth: 'Three and a half years ago I made a film whose premise was that "Madrid is the centre of the universe and everybody comes here to have fun" (*Labyrinth of Passion*). A lot of people believed it and now there are tons of magazines that talk of nothing else' (Almodóvar 1991: 132). As this witty quote suggests, reinventing Madrid is one of the co-ordinates (as well as one of the extra-diegetic effects) of Almodóvar's work. Another is to show Madrid for what it is: a multifaceted, difficult metropolis that presents many negative signs of its belonging to a postmodern society. This is why the idea of Almodóvar as chronicler of contemporary Madrid is paradoxical and convincing at the same time – paradoxical because his narrative universe is deeply personal and, one would say, artificial; convincing because his films are always realistically symptomatic of present problems and lifestyles. This combination of realism and artifice, social analysis and references to Hollywood, location shooting and studio sets, is a fundamental characteristic of Almodóvar's work and, in our opinion, is also the key to an understanding of the representation of Madrid in his films. The question, then, is to clarify the nature and form of this combination.

What Have I Done? is realistically set in the working-class area of la Concepción, 'a neighbourhood of high-rise, cheap housing built in the sixties as a demonstration of Franco's modernization of living conditions in Spain' (D'Lugo 1995: 133). The strong social characterization of the film has been discussed both in the context of this lower-class urban area of Madrid and in that of Spanish neorealist cinema of the 1950s and 1960s. Whereas most commentators discussed the realistic aspects of the film, others, like Víctor Fuentes, noted that in *What Have I Done?* realism coexists with artifice in a postmodern way:

> The artificiality of the studio sets, an inheritance of the Hollywood dream factory's dominion over time and space, is also appropriate to the postmodern exaltation of artifice that serves to create a space of heterotopia, an access zone where diverse worlds coexist without transition. In *What Have I Done?*, we move from Madrid's M-30 freeway to the Berlin superhighway and back to the working-class Concepción quarter, an exterior setting that could just as well be the desolate urban landscape of *Blade Runner* – as the director himself notes – and that will return in *Tie Me Up*. (Fuentes 1995: 160)

Fuentes thus proposes the model of a postmodern space 'where diverse worlds coexist without transition'. The result is a mosaic-like Madrid, which loses its individuality and can even resemble *Blade Runner*'s Los Angeles. Similarly, Smith wrote, with reference to the sequence of the attempted rape in a Madrid street at the beginning of *Matador* (1986), that 'although the location is authentic, the effect is as distancing as any studio set. As Almodóvar says of this sequence, he has made the "concrete location" a "metaphorical space", transforming the single city into a thousand cities' (Smith 1994a: 69). Other critics have argued that *Matador* marks the beginning of Almodóvar's distancing from real locations, a distancing that has been read as a progressive decontextualization of his cinema. 'Madrid continues to be the privileged, or even exclusive background of his films. Nevertheless, references to the city become increasingly less explicit. It is not insignificant that, starting with *Women on the Verge of a Nervous Breakdown*, all his films will be almost exclusively shot in studio' (Aronica 1993: 16; our translation).

Aronica's monograph stops with *Kika* and thus does not consider Almodóvar's renewed interest in real settings and location shooting, which emerged powerfully with his subsequent films *La flor de mi secreto* [The Flower of My Secret, 1995], *Carne tremula* [Live Flesh, 1997], and *All about My Mother*. Even setting these films to one side, we find it difficult to agree with Aronica and those who distinguish the 'prominent realism' of *What Have I Done* from the artificiality of other films. Realism and artifice, as we said above, cohabit and merge in each of Almodóvar's films, even if the result of this mix may vary from film to film.

Women on the Verge, for instance, is widely considered to be the film in which artifice most clearly prevails over realism. Most of the action is set in Pepa's (Carmen Maura) penthouse apartment, an undisguised set, whose artificiality is increased by the clearly fake view of the roofs of central Madrid visible from Pepa's balcony. Fuentes traced the intertextual presence in this film of Irving Rapper's *Now, Voyager* (1942) and so commented on the borrowing of a luxurious balcony in Rio from that melodrama:

> Almodóvar transposes that tropical Hollywood balcony to post-modern Madrid, thus creating one of the most striking 'zones-collages' found in postmodern cinema. In the leafy and luxuriant vegetation of Pepa's penthouse balcony, smack up against an impossible, idealized Madrid skyline, there meet several realms of incompatible 'reality': Rio de Janeiro, as imagined by Hollywood; Hollywood of the fifties and sixties; and eighties postmodern Madrid. (Fuentes 1995: 161)

The example of Pepa's penthouse balcony with its layers of 'realism' offers in our opinion a perfect model for reading Almodóvar's Madrid which, despite being sometimes transformed by the shooting 'into a thousand cities', also always remains very much itself. Madrid never disappears underneath the several layers of the *mise-en-scène*; it resembles many other cities (European, but not only) without ever losing its individuality. This effect is achieved by maintaining the importance of the location, despite its internationalization through the 'metaphoric' transformation of space described above, as well as through the use of music, objects and intertextual quotations referring to a global culture. Madrid is still Madrid, because each film makes use of clearly recognizable locations; because of the many references to Spanish culture (cuisine, music, folklore); and because the characters often comment on life in the capital and compare it to that in the pueblo from which they come. We are never allowed to forget for too long where we are, and Almodóvar reminds us of this by also making frequent use of real-life Madrid topography: his characters often utter the names of streets, civic numbers and even floor numbers.

It could be argued that, if Almodóvar's Madrid looks like any city, and at the same time only like itself, this is not exclusively an effect of the cinematography, but also comes from the postmodernity of Madrid. Madrid's cityscape is a mix of diverse spectacles such as a city centre characterized by a net of avenues adorned by fountains at each intersection; suburbs marked by a disorderly development; ultramodern glass and steel skyscrapers along the Paseo de la Castellana; and working-class houses in pink or red brick in the southern, industrial areas. Different urban landscapes and opposing lifestyles are sometimes postmodernly contiguous, as is best seen in Almodóvar's *Live Flesh*, with the prefabricated houses of the area of la Ventilla that survive alongside modern skyscrapers. Madrid also shows all the negative signs of life in a contemporary metropolis: drug abuse, violence, traffic, acoustic pollution (one of the highest readings in Europe), smog and high social polarization. Madrid is also postmodern in that it is historically a city of immigrants – even today it is common to hear that natives of Madrid do not exist, and that Madrid is an artificial, constructed capital, not representative of the rest of Spain.

Many of these themes are present in Almodóvar's cinema, thus confirming it to be – perhaps despite its appearance – a cinema attentive to social reality, and grounded in an urban experience which is at the same time European, global and specifically Spanish. For example, one of the recurrent problems for Almodóvar's city-dwellers is the quality of life in Madrid, a problem that emerges in their desire to leave the city, either to go back to their pueblo, or to move to other places. This desire can be dictated by a difficult relationship with the metropolis; by a wish to go back to a simpler, better life in the country; or by the need to change one's life. One of the clearest instances is to be found in *What Have I Done to Deserve This?*, with Chus Lampreave's provincial character of the mother-in-law who hates Madrid and dreams of going back to her village in the country. Her obsessive desire – she is confined during the cold Madrid winter in the horrible apartment building in la Concepción – is shared by one of her grandchildren, who takes her to see *Splendour in the Grass* and, at the end of the narrative, will spend the profits of his drug business to buy a ticket back to the pueblo for himself and his grandmother. Another character, Cristal, the nice prostitute who lives next door, dreams instead of moving to Las Vegas. Two parallel and contrasting desires are shown in *What Have I Done*: the return to the simpler, better life in one's native village, and the jump towards an exotic land that belongs to the global imagination. These are the two poles between which many of Almodóvar's films oscillate: national traditions and preoccupations on the one hand, and gravitation towards global society on the other.

As Almodóvar once said of himself: 'I'm a man of many pieces' (Almodóvar 1991: 105). His Madrid could similarly be defined as 'a city of many pieces', and in the following pages we are going to examine some of them, parts of the mosaic of a postmodern city. We chose to discuss two recent films that could not be more different in their representation of Madrid: *Kika*, shot almost completely in studio, and *The Flower of My Secret*, shot instead on location. We hope to show how layers of artifice and realism coexist in these films and contribute to Almodóvar's portrayal of a postmodern, stratified Madrid.

Kika: The City as Voyeuristic Spectacle

Kika lives with Ramón, a photographer and a collage artist whose mother committed suicide a few years before in Casa Youkali, her villa outside Madrid. Ramón's stepfather, Nicholas, returns to Madrid penniless to write a new novel on a serial killer. Ramón offers to accommodate him in his studio above the apartment that he shares with Kika in central Madrid. The action takes place partly in Madrid (principally in the protagonist's apartment), and partly in Casa Youkali. The film is set mainly in interiors that were re-created in studio.

1. *Kika* (1993), dir. Pedro Almodóvar

Kika and Ramón's city-centre apartment is colourful, decorated in an original and tasteful way, and reflects both Ramón's prosperous financial status and his passionate interest in images. The apartment's walls are covered in posters, pictures and Ramón's photographic collages. Ramón and Kika do not have financial worries, and seem to work more for personal interest than for need. They have a devoted live-in maid, Juana, and Ramón can easily afford to lend his studio to Nicholas and rent another one in a nearby apartment block. Casa Youkali, which was closed after the death of Ramón's mother, is an elegant villa with a vast garden; Ramón clearly states that he never thinks about it in financial terms, as opposed to Nicholas, who is penniless and would like them to sell the house and share the profits.

The main characters in *Kika* all work in advertising, in the mass media or in the entertainment industry generally, which is symptomatic of their belonging to a postindustrial, late-capitalist society. Kika is a beautician who once worked in television; Ramón is a fashion photographer; Nicholas is a journalist and a writer, occasionally for television. The fourth main character, Andrea 'Caracortada', is the presenter of a TV reality show. *Kika* is clearly a film about the postmodern society of the spectacle, which as presented is ruled by voyeurism. Elements of the *mise-en-scène* itself testify to this, such as the various eyes gazing at us during the film: those drawn on the walls behind Kika during a make-up lesson; those forming the pattern on Kika's professional make-up case; and the flower vase in the shape of an ocular bulb in Ramón and Kika's apartment. Even the religious procession, broadcast by Andrea's show, is meaningfully set in Villaverde De Los Ojos. Furthermore, intertextual quotations from films on voyeurism abound. *The Prowler* (Joseph Losey, 1951) is shown on television during a pertinent dialogue between Ramón and Nicholas; and a poster of *Peeping Tom* (Michael Powell, 1960) is visible in Ramón's studio. A classic on the relationship between images and reality, Michelangelo Antonioni's *Blow Up* (1966), is quoted twice, first by the photographic session during which Ramón invites his model to mimic an orgasm (a very similar scene is found at the beginning of *Blow Up*, with David Hemmings in the role of the fashion photographer). The second reference is when Andrea, watching over and over again the stolen images of Nicholas and his lover Susana, comes to believe that his stepfather has killed the woman with a vase – similarly, Hemmings becomes convinced that the photographs that he took while hidden hold the secret of a murder.

The most relevant cinematic reference, though, is Hitchcock's *Rear Window* (1954), where James Stewart is the prototype of Ramón, a photographer who spies on his neighbours through his apartment's windows. As is *Rear Window*, *Kika* is a film about the relationship between voyeurism and the visual media. Both films, through their main characters, unmask photography as exploitative of the model and of the public. Both films also carry out a metadiscourse on cinema as a medium that is activated by and founded on human curiosity and the desire to see. Furthermore, *Rear Window* and *Kika* both focus on the relationship between voyeurism and the city. Almodóvar recognized that his sets have the same significance as those in Hitchcock's masterpiece: 'They are a portrait of the town' (Strauss 1994: 147). In this respect, nevertheless, there is a fundamental difference between the two films. In *Rear Window* the city is represented almost as a village: it is epitomized by a self-contained courtyard, all of whose inhabitants we come to know. *Kika*'s city is, instead, anonymous and unknowable. Besides Ramón, who films his girlfriend from his studio's windows, and gets excited only when looking at a woman through the camera lens, *Kika*'s second, more insidious voyeur is the person who filmed Nicholas's night with his lover, and Kika's rape by her maid's retarded brother, Paul Brazzo.

This person could be Andrea, who displays a sick interest in her ex-lover Ramón's private life, and can also be considered as a voyeur for her prying TV show. Nevertheless, Almodóvar chose not to disclose the identity of the video-maker, thus avoiding his or her humanization, and reinforcing the impression of anonymous and threatening gazes that arise from and hide in the city.

Madrid in *Kika* is thus characterized as a hostile, frightening, unknowable metropolis. Despite a cheerful protagonist, the prevalent tone of comedy and a hopeful ending, *Kika* is Almodóvar's darkest film. It brims with aggression, with perverse gazes and a violent and deregulated televisual industry that penetrate the protective domestic walls. This aggression concentrates on oppressed and fragile subjects, on women and children. Women are the objects of most of the film's physical violence – that reported by Andrea's show, that of the serial killer Nicholas and that of the voyeurs' gazes. It suffices to think of the model in Ramón's photographic session, spied through a keyhole and through a camera lens; of Kika, photographed by Ramón during sexual intercourse; again of Kika being raped while observed by her partner and filmed by a mysterious voyeur; of Susana, filmed naked by the same voyeur; and of course of all the women killed by their lovers (Susana), or husbands (Ramón's mother; the woman in Andrea's programme).

Kika's cynicism has often been associated with the crisis in the hedonistic optimism of the 1980s (see Aronica 1993: 109; Triana Toribio 1996: 187). This prevalent opinion has strengthened the reputation of Almodóvar as a chronicler of Madrid: 'Ever sensitive to the mood of the moment, Almodóvar's latest feature offers evidence of a new pessimism clouding a famously sunny outlook; the erstwhile muse of Madrid now proclaims the city to be "unliveable", swamped by drug-related crime' (Smith 1994b: 6). Whereas we will see the streets of night-time Madrid effectively swamped by drug addicts and dealers in *Live Flesh*, *Kika* shows very little of 'real' Madrid. Almodóvar has suggested in an interview that it is very difficult to shoot in Madrid, since the city council does not want to exacerbate the already serious traffic congestion. Another, more subtle, explanation for this choice was also put forward by the filmmaker:

> *Kika* is about the sickness of big cities. I wanted to show this sickness as if it were something one breathed in the air. Which is why I hardly ever show the city in the film, in the same way one

never sees Los Angeles in *Barton Fink*, even though the film is about the hell the lead character experiences living there. You don't see any streets in *Kika*. When you do see the city, it's only a representation of the city, such as in the set of Andrea's reality show. But the aggression is there all the same, in spite of it not being expressed in concrete form. (Almodóvar in Strauss 1994: 126)

The 'sickness of big cities' is, in fact, expressed in *Kika* in 'concrete form' via the town's configuration: a set of apartment buildings facing one another, and punctured by the 'holes' of countless windows, openings through which people look in and look out, spy on each other, and feel threatened by hidden gazes. From the balconies and windows of Ramón and Kika's apartment we can see other houses, other apartments, other windows. This idea of the metropolis is epitomized by a large picture in Ramón and Kika's bedroom, showing a series of tall buildings at night-time, with lightning against the dark sky and naked female bodies in the foreground.

'*Kika*'s a film where all the doors and windows are open, where all the characters are open even though they all have something to hide' (Almodóvar in Strauss 1994: 129). The idea of the urban apartment as a semi-transparent space through which we look and are looked at, and in which we find no privacy or protection from external (or internal) aggression, is fundamental in the film, and is strengthened by a constant framing of the characters not only through windows, but also through frames of all types, as the circular skyline in Ramón and Kika's kitchen door, or their see-through pieces of furniture, behind which the camera is sometimes placed. Television itself is presented as a window, not as in the old metaphor of the window opened on to the reality of the world, but in the sense of an opening in private walls through which we look, but sometimes are looked at and exposed, as happens to Kika. The television set is equated with a window in a particularly effective manner in the close-up of Nicholas sitting in front of it, looking at Ramón's tapes. The man is so near the screen, and the television is so big behind him, that it truly looks like a window, a sensation accentuated by the images on it, which are those of a domestic Kika filmed precisely from behind a window. The presence of the television set in the house is also multiplied, as Almodóvar recognized, by the many colourful and shiny tiles to be found in the apartment: 'they are a direct visual metaphor for a television screen' (Strauss 1994: 145).

2. Andrea Caracortada in *Kika* (1993), dir. Pedro Almodóvar

In most of his films Almodóvar introduced comments on the visual
media, and on television in particular. Many humorous televisual inserts
are present in his work, from the characteristically surreal mock ads, to
the news programmes in which public and private often merge. As
Aronica has noted, whereas the television that we see in Almodóvar's
previous films is still a 'domestic animal', whose pervasive nature is
neutralized by Almodóvar through parody, in *Kika* we witness a mon-
strous metamorphosis of the medium (Aronica 1993: 118). The television
exposed in *Kika* is a voracious medium exploiting people's curiosity,
their taste for gossip, interest in private lives and misfortunes, and
predilection for gory and violent spectacles.

Andrea's reality show, *Lo peor del día* (The Worst of the Day), is
paradoxically sponsored by a brand of milk. Wearing vampire-like clothes
and bloody make-up, Andrea recites with a stony face a litany of crimes
from the local news – a daily gallery of ordinary horrors, among which
are rapes, prostitution of children, murders and so forth. The crucial

component of the show is the broadcasting of images, filmed by Andrea herself or by voyeurs. Her biggest scoop is Kika's rape; according to Andrea, it significantly boosted her show's ratings. Andrea's reality show is pure junk television, mocking many American but now also European programmes (for one, the local versions of *Big Brother*) deriving their strength from, and at the same time nourishing, people's voyeurism and their curiosity for morbid or violent spectacles.

Through Andrea, its frightful embodiment, television is unmasked in its abusing attitude, disguised behind a vocation to serve and impartially inform the public. This television, on the contrary, has no respect for the public, as the empty red chairs in Andrea's studio testify. Andrea's bizarre and futuristic outfit, which includes arc lights in the shape of breasts and a helmet-camera, transforms her into television itself, and provides the film with an important statement on contemporary visual media. During the first programme that we are shown, Andrea broadcasts a video of a man murdering his wife in a cemetery. The scene was filmed by Andrea herself, who recorded images and sounds with her helmet-camera and her body gear, so that parts of her limbs are always visible, strongly suggesting her physical, subjective presence in the frame. Andrea's video, as well as her whole programme, uncovers the false objectivity and naturalness with which televisual images offer themselves to the viewers, and demonstrates the often disguised mix of technical apparatus and human intentionality that is always the source of broadcast images.

Andrea's programme is typically urban, not because aggression and curiosity do not exist in the country, but because the city capitalizes on them thereby becoming a voyeuristic spectacle. *Kika*'s first, abstract image meaningfully resembles a piece of tarmac lit by a spotlight. This image soon turns out to be a screen with an aperture in the shape of a keyhole, through which Ramón takes pictures of a woman undressing for a lingerie ad. The resemblance of this screen to asphalt is confirmed by an identical image seen in the sets of *Lo peor del día*: 'The floor of the set is the potholed tarmac typical of Madrid streets' (Almodóvar in Strauss 1994: 143). The set in Andrea's show recalls a city, with a series of panels that stand for tall buildings. The rough backside of the panels is shown: 'One therefore has the constant impression of looking at the city sideways as well as seeing what's behind the walls of the buildings' (p. 143). In Andrea's set, Madrid's skyline is dominated by television sets that resemble eyes gazing on the city.

The city is almost invisible in *Kika* precisely because it has turned itself into a voyeuristic spectacle, one that is exploited by a deregulated televisual industry. Streets and public places either do not figure, or are transformed by the filmmaking into interiors to be voyeuristically searched, as the following example indicates. Nicholas and Andrea meet one evening at the Circulo de Belas Artes. The camera is placed in a car in the street right outside the café's wide windows, and performs a slow horizontal sweep from the right to the left, showing the customers sitting at their tables, absorbed in their conversations. The camera's position and its deliberately slow searching movement are suggestive of a voyeuristic human gaze.

Private places are also filmed in a similar manner that puts the spectator in the place of a voyeur. After Nicholas has moved into Ramón's photographic studio, directly above Ramón and Kika's apartment, we are shown Ramón and Kika's bedroom from outside the window, where Kika wakes her partner and runs to get dressed. Immediately afterwards, thanks to a vertical movement of the camera, we are shown from a similar perspective Nicholas's bedroom, where he and his lover are also dressing after spending the night together.

The most evident effect of the opening of *Kika*'s interiors to outside gazes is that the private becomes public. The camera movement on the windows of the Belas Artes stops on Andrea and Nicholas sitting at their table. With a sudden change of perspective, the camera is then placed in front of the table from inside the room, and frames the actors from a perspective that 'pushes' the table out in the street, eliminating the interior effect and making what is private public. Another evident example is the escape of Paul Brazzo from Kika's bedroom after raping her. The man, who is interrupted by the police before reaching his fourth orgasm, jumps on Kika's windowsill to masturbate, turned towards the city, thus highlighting the thin barrier between interior and exterior, between private and public in *Kika*'s postmodern city-spectacle.

The Flower of My Secret: Melodrama Suits the Postmodern City

The Flower of My Secret, as Almodóvar has stated in more than one interview, is a drama and not a melodrama. In fact the film, according to Almodóvar and to several reviewers, does not make any concessions to sentimentality, nor does it dramatize or lend itself to excess. As one reviewer has commented: 'Almodóvar has here subordinated his auteurist identity to an overall reality-effect: a repression of basic instinct that he never before dreamed of inflicting on his characters' (Matthews 1996: 40). The film itself wishes to clarify its position on this point, and immediately states that it will not be overacted and will not indulge in the excesses of melodrama. At the end of the seminar on organ donation that opens the narrative, in which two doctors must convince a woman to agree to the transplant of organs from her dead child, the nurse acting as the mother asks her colleague Betty whether her performance 'wasn't a bit overacted'. 'Not at all,' Betty answers her. 'You are a better actress each time.'

Hence, strictly speaking, it is not possible to label *The Flower of My Secret* as a melodrama. It lacks many of the essential components of the genre, so effectively summarized by Peter Brooks in his seminal study *The Melodramatic Imagination*: 'the indulgence of strong emotionalism; moral polarization and schematization; extreme states of being, situations, actions; overt villainy, persecution of the good, and final reward of virtue; inflated and extravagant expression; dark plottings, suspense, breathtaking peripety' (Brooks 1995: 11–12). On the other hand, genres in Almodóvar are never faithfully reproduced in all their characteristics, but are continuously, and postmodernly, mixed, modified and transformed. Drama and melodrama do meet and merge in *The Flower of My Secret*, a film that combines some elements of the latter with more numerous characteristics of the former.

In a weak (and modern) sense, melodrama in *The Flower of My Secret* is present through the film's absolute conception of love. Almodóvar, for instance, has described *Dark Habits* as a melodrama on account of its conception of 'love as a source of inspiration, as engine, as energy that pushes you to do the most extraordinary things, and it does not matter whether they are the most outrageous or the most sublime' (Vidal, quoted in Aronica 1993: 43; our translation). The protagonist's love for her husband in *The Flower of My Secret* is in this category. Leo, the author of successful sentimental novels under the pseudonym of Amanda Gris, is suffering from a marital crisis. Her husband Paco, who works at NATO in Brussels, asked to be sent to Bosnia in order, according to Leo, to avoid facing their problems. Leo still loves her husband deeply, and hopes to save their marriage, but his lack of attention and love generates a state of extreme insecurity and pain in Leo that also affects her work. When Paco finally leaves her, Leo is so distraught that she attempts suicide – even if her behaviour never reaches the melodramatic intensity of Antonio's in *Law of Desire*.

Also in a strong (and classical) sense *The Flower of My Secret* exhibits elements of melodrama. The first of these elements is the dramatic use of song, of which Chavela Vargas' apparition on television after Leo's attempted suicide is a prime example. The second element is the sacralization of private pain. Brooks has read melodrama as the response of a post-sacred era to the loss of the tragic vision: 'melodrama represents both the urge toward resacralization and the impossibility of conceiving sacralization other than in personal terms' (Brooks 1995: 16). Almodóvar meaningfully comments on *The Flower of My Secret*: 'When I film pain, I see it in an almost mythical fashion, as if I were genuflecting in front of the altar of pain in order to pray ... Pain moves me, it's like a religion to me' (Strauss 1994: 164). The third melodramatic element in *The Flower of My Secret* is the polarization of values. The film is built around three cardinal polarities: life/death; reality/artifice; country/city.

The film presents the first two polarities in its opening sequence. Two doctors tell a woman that her son has died, but she does not want to believe them, because she just saw him breathing. The doctors tell her that a machine is oxygenating his body, while his brain is already dead. When she finally accepts this fact, they try to persuade her to donate her child's organs. Soon, we realize that we are watching a simulation, a role-playing part of a seminar on organ donation. Betty, who is leading the seminar, turns towards her medical audience, but also towards the film's spectators, and looks straight into the lens, uncovering both the diegetic artifice and, at a wider level, that of the filmic fiction.

Almodóvar will develop his idea of the seminar on organ donation in *All about My Mother*. Even so, *The Flower of My Secret* highlights the concepts put forward by this first sequence, so much so that the pair life/death is a touchstone of the film, and always with physical, almost medical connotations. Looking for Betty, Leo enters the conference room during the seminar at a moment in the dialogue that stresses her resemblance to the relative of a dead person, one who does not want to accept the idea of death – in precisely this way Leo rejects the idea of the end of Paco's love. Almodóvar meaningfully said that the pain of abandonment is 'a pain which I believe one feels as physically as a death. No matter that for the rest of the world the person who has gone continues to live. For us, the relationship is the same as if they had died' (Strauss 1994: 164).

Dialogues on organs recur elsewhere in the film. Just before Leo

arrives at *El País* to propose herself as a literary critic, the director of
the literary supplement, Angel, compares the printing presses to the
heart and arteries of the newspaper, because if they don't work *El País*
does not work. Leo's mother could undergo an operation to correct her
eyesight, but she opposes the idea vigorously, and asserts that she does
not want to be operated on while she is alive, but adds 'do to me
whatever you want when I am dead'. These references, along with Betty's
job, create in the spectator an awareness of the thin line between life
and death, which Leo crosses twice during the film – once during her
attempted suicide, once in her mother's story on her birth. Leo learns
from her mother that she was not breathing when she was born, after
forty-eight hours of labour, and was saved by her grandmother, who
took her out of the house and into the freezing cold to revive her.

The second polarity, reality/artifice, is fundamental to Almodóvar's
cinema. Whereas in *Kika* it was articulated with particular reference to
the visual media, here the discourse focuses mainly on literature, and
the distinction is between a literature that contains real pain and emotion,
and a literature that does not. The question, thus, is not one of natural-
ism but, as always in Almodóvar, of grades of a combination of reality
and artifice. As the director commented: 'This is my most realist [sic]
film, with the proviso that my realism is very personal and that there is
always a touch of artifice there' (Smith 1996: 24). In another interview
Almodóvar drew parallels with Italian neorealism – the neorealism that
was happy to use narrative devices coming from genres such as comedy,
drama and melodrama itself (see Strauss 1994).

City/country is the polarity in *The Flower of My Secret* that interests us
most, and on which we intend to concentrate. Leo's family comes from
Almagro, a pueblo in La Mancha. Her sister Rosa lives with her husband,
an unemployed and often drunk man whom we never see, in an apartment full of kitsch, tasteless objects, symbols of that search for a petit
bourgeois status typical of many who come from the provinces without
the cultural and material means to become middle-class city-dwellers.
Whereas Rosa seems comfortable in these environs, Leo is clearly out
of place, belonging to a much more refined, and affluent, milieu. Their
mother too is out of place, and calls Rosa a gypsy because of her taste
for 'all that gold'. She does not like 'this Madrid', she does not want to
go out because she does not want to be killed by a skinhead or run over
by a car, and she threatens all the time to go back to the pueblo, despite
her partial blindness. When she and Leo do return to Almagro, after

Leo's attempted suicide, we realize that her wish was more than just a whim. Here she has her roots, and she is really herself, finally at ease in a strongly communal and matriarchal culture (no man is ever seen), in which women sit together in the courtyard to do traditional embroidery, gossip about common acquaintances and sing popular songs. Even her house clearly suits her better, with its furniture that is simple but in good taste, its traditional dimensions, its harmonization of interior and exterior. As she tells Leo, when a woman is 'like a cow without a cowbell', having lost her husband, either because he died or because he left her for another woman, she must go back to the pueblo, and pray in the chapel even if she does not believe. Like Kika at the end of the previous film, Leo and her mother need 'some pointing in the right direction'. Nevertheless, they look for it not in a new relationship, as Kika did, but in a return to their roots, even if one woman intends to stay and the other to go back stronger to Madrid. Leo returns from Almagro with the belief that she does not belong to the pueblo, and that the city is somehow her destiny, if not her ideal environment.

Madrid in *The Flower of My Secret* is a multifaceted city, where different lifestyles coexist: Rosa's kitsch, petit bourgeois life; Leo's and Angel's refined apartments; junkies and skinheads in the street; an experimental theatre; graffiti on the walls; a cosy restaurant; a courtyard full of playing children; a monumental square. It is a cosmopolitan city, where discourses on Bosnia alternate with the memories of a trip to Athens, but also with returns to rural origins. Above all, the Madrid of *The Flower of My Secret* is a city suited to melodrama.

In 'Almodóvar's Melodramatic *Mise-en-scène*: Madrid as a Setting for Melodrama', Núria Triana Toribio maintains that Almodóvar in his films tries to transform the real Madrid into a melodramatic city, 'more emotionally expressive, and able to accommodate the repressed pointers of desire and passion' that are typical of melodrama (Triana Toribio 1996: 183). Madrid, though, according to the author, 'is not easily compatible with the relationships and passion that are the stuff of melodrama' (p. 188), and is 'inadequate as a melodramatic space unless it is altered' (p. 183). For the author, such alteration in Almodóvar is mainly achieved through the excesses of the *mise-en-scène*: 'It even becomes parodic in that every single object can be seen as a sign expressing information which the action itself cannot accommodate' (p. 187).

While this may perhaps be true in other films by Almodóvar, Madrid in *The Flower of My Secret* is on the contrary a truly melodramatic city. In

3. *The Flower of My Secret* (1995), dir. Pedro Almodóvar

keeping with the rest of the *mise-en-scène*, Madrid is not filmed with hyper-emphatic tones – though the emergence of melodrama in the film strongly influences the way in which the city is viewed.

As Brooks writes about melodrama, the 'description of the surfaces of the modern metropolis pierces through to a mythological realm where the imagination can find a habitat for its play with large moral entities' (Brooks 1995: 5). Madrid in *The Flower of My Secret* is described precisely through surfaces that are either translucent or reflecting. Whereas the main filmic figure in *Kika* was the frame, which evoked both the window and the television screen, *The Flower of My Secret* is dominated by the mirror. Leo's face is reflected countless times by mirrors, lamps and other shiny objects, such as glass or ceramic. The characters are sometimes filmed through translucent matter, such as a shower curtain or a piece of embroidery. Occasionally, the reflections are doubled, as when we see Leo's image multiplied many times by the glass doors of Angel's office, or reflected by several mirrors in the toilets of *El País*. Leo and Paco's faces also are multiplied, and fragmented at the same time, by the numerous small mirrors that decorate their entrance wall, in the scene of the kiss at Paco's arrival from Brussels.

This fundamental sequence shows that the function of the film's many reflections is that of fragmenting the subject, and in particular

Leo, who is splintered by her pain and somehow emptied by it, becoming almost a ghost.

Leo's states of mind are also reflected by the urban exteriors and thus Madrid becomes, as in Brooks's phrase, the habitat for Leo's imagination to play with large moral entities. The city, in fact, often seems to embody and amplify Leo's larger-than-life pain, transferring it to a sort of mythical plane, as if hers was an unavoidable, almost inhuman destiny. In this, above all, the Madrid of *The Flower of My Secret* is a melodramatic city.

One morning, the wind blows Leo's window open and turns the pages of a book, until it stops almost deliberately at the underlined sentence: 'Defenceless against the lurking madness.' From her window, Leo sees a courtyard full of playing children, a subtle reminder of the sterility of her marriage, an idea confirmed when Leo, who is outside her sister's house waiting for the door to be opened, smiles at a passing child. The constant presence of these happy children outside her window highlights Leo's solitude. When Leo leaves her house panicking because she cannot take off the boots that Paco gave her some time before, it begins to rain on her, as if to increase her pain and anxiety. The huge poster of a tropical beach that frames Leo's confused face in the bar in which she looks for shelter emphasizes the effect of the rain. After her attempted suicide, Leo is once again in the same bar. First she is psychologically assaulted by an unnerving and absurd screaming competition on television; when the barman changes channel, the words of a song by Chavela Vargas pitilessly epitomize her present condition. Disorientated, Leo leaves the bar, and finds herself in the middle of a medical students' protest rally, hopelessly trying to go against the flux of young marchers, and submerged by a snow of pieces of paper. Lost in this sort of human tempest, Leo even sees on a shop window a slogan advertising bathroom furniture ('*Te quiero, Roca*'), which Paco and herself used as a coded phrase to say that they loved each other. The camera leaves Leo fainting in the arms of Angel, and looks up towards the sky with a lyric movement, once again giving the impression of a fate that pitilessly looks down at the protagonist. Leo wakes in Angel's central penthouse apartment, and from the panoramic windows she sees the side of a tall building covered by a huge poster advertising Amanda Gris's latest book – once again, the city seems to amplify Leo's pain and almost persecute her.

The city is not only a source of intensification of Leo's pain and

4.   Angel dancing in Plaza Mayor in *The Flower of My Secret* (1995), dir.
Pedro Almodóvar

confusion, but also of her happiness and excitement. One night Angel
phones Leo to tell her that he has read her essay and novel and that he
liked them very much, and to offer her a collaboration with *El País*. This
warm, surprising and exciting conversation, both at a professional and at
a human level, is filmed in a way that makes the screen look split, with
Angel on the left-hand side talking on the phone and, on the right-hand
side, a stream of cars, seen from above, forming the fascinating night-
time traffic of an important road, probably the Gran Vía. These images,
which alternate with those of Leo talking on the phone in her apartment,
speak about the thrill of living in Madrid, a city that never sleeps ('It is
never late in Madrid,' Paco says acerbically to Leo on the phone a few
minutes later), about the opportunities for work and new relationships,
and about the beauty of the metropolis and the charm of its night life.

Madrid in *The Flower of My Secret* is a postmodern metropolis that Leo
lives in as if it was a stage on which to play her role in between drama
and melodrama. She wears her clothes like costumes, bright red for
hope and love, electric blue for despair and discomfort – in general,
colours echo the mood of the scene. Her life is like the stirring flamenco
show seen in the film, in which the woman, drenched in a deep red

light, is strong and fragile at the same time and dances with an aggressive and domineering man. The city is a theatre in which Leo melodramatically fights against polarized forces. 'I have to learn to live without Paco, and without alcohol,' she says gravely to Angel after the man, with his intense albeit mock flamenco performance, has just transformed night-time Plaza Mayor into a stage, exposing once again the city's theatrical nature.

Almodóvar's Postmodern Madrid: Not a Fake City

At the end of his essay on urban landscape in Spanish film noir, Alberto Mira discusses the representation of the city in two postmodern films, *Beltenebros* (Pilar Miró, 1991) and *Todo por la pasta* (Enrique Urbizu, 1991). According to the author, in these films 'urban landscapes are offered to us in all their grittiness, but somehow they are not "our" urban landscapes … Madrid and Bilbao are explicitly cities of the imagination, and excess in representation is possible because the connection with real cities never really comes true' (Mira 2000: 136).

Postmodern Madrid in Almodóvar's cinema is sometimes part of an excessive *mise-en-scène*, but it is not a fake city and never disappears beneath the several layers of its representation. In the films that we have discussed, the connection with the real city does come true, even if in contrasting ways. In *Kika* and *The Flower of My Secret* the movement goes respectively from the postmodern any-town to the Spanish capital and vice versa. Madrid in *Kika* is represented as a threatening metropolis in which voyeurism, aggression and violence are both exploited and aggravated by deregulated television. So little is seen of the city that Madrid even becomes a metaphor for the western metropolis turned into a voyeuristic televisual spectacle. Nevertheless, Madrid underlies *Kika*'s postmodern, standardized any-town, so much so that some critics have suggested that the film be read in the context of the effects of the economic recession on the Spanish capital. Furthermore, Almodóvar's discourse is not only directed towards global television, but also towards the Spanish media. As Smith wrote: 'in the very week of *Kika*'s release, a Spanish family who were victims of a kidnapping complained of the "disgusting" exploitation of their case by a private television channel. And the newly hostile press coverage of Almodóvar himself has revealed hitherto unplumbed depths of that combination of unhealthy curiosity and ghoulish delight known in Spanish as *morbo*' (Smith 1994b: 8).

Unlike *Kika*, which was almost completely shot in the studio and set in interiors, *The Flower of My Secret* was shot on location. The Spanish capital is very much visible and present, through its bars, restaurants, apartment buildings, streets, night-time traffic and monumental squares. References to contemporary Madrid are numerous, we even witness a protest rally against Prime Minister Felipe Gonzáles. In *The Flower of My Secret*'s various layers of *mise-en-scène*, though, Madrid also becomes a postmodern any-town, resembling Jonathan Raban's soft city (see Raban 1975), both in the sense of a metropolis in which many different lifestyles coexist, and of a theatrical city-stage, on which the protagonist plays her role. The show staged is a mix of drama and melodrama, in which the city becomes a mythical space embodying the great polarities of life.

3

A Present and a True City? Naples in Mario Martone's Cinema

The cultural and artistic rebirth of Naples in the 1990s, a rebirth encouraged by a period of enlightened and courageous administration, saw a flourishing of filmmaking, thanks to which Naples has today become the most interesting production centre in the Italian cinematographic industry. Critics talk of a new Neapolitan school, formed by filmmakers such as Mario Martone, Pappi Corsicato, Antonio Capuano, Antonietta De Lillo and Giuseppe M. Gaudino. Although they have never presented themselves as a compact movement, and have frequently asserted their individuality (Capuano, quoted in Gariazzo 1995: 38), these directors do share experiences, technicians and actors, and they produce films that, albeit with different styles and aims, pay particular attention to the representation of contemporary Naples.

Naples is one of several Italian cities, such as Rome and Florence, which have been frequently used as film sets. Many films, belonging to several genres, together construct the cinematic image of Naples; among these films are: early, realistic melodramas such as Gustavo Sereni's *Assunta Spina* (1915); the empathic visions of an almost primitive land offered by Roberto Rossellini in the Neapolitan episode of *Paisà* [Paisan, 1946] and later in *Viaggio in Italia* [Voyage to Italy, 1953]; the comedies of the 1950s centred on the character of Totò, among which are *Napoli milionaria* by Eduardo De Filippo [Naples Millionaire, 1950], *47 morto che parla* by Carlo Ludovico Bragaglia (1950), *Miseria e nobiltà* by Mario Mattoli [Poverty and Nobility, 1954], and De Sica's *L'oro di Napoli* [Every Day's a Holiday, 1954]; the courageous denunciation of the links between the camorra and local politicians in films by Francesco Rosi *La sfida* [The Challenge, 1957] and *Le mani sulla città* [Hands Over the City, 1963]; the trash cop-thrillers made in the 1970s that construct a melodramatic and simplified image of a violent Naples, dominated by the rule of the camorra, such as: *Camorra* by P. Squitieri (1972), *Napoli violenta* by U. Lenzi (1976), and *Napoli … serenata calibro nove* by A. Brescia (1978); the overemotional melodramas (*sceneggiate*) of the 1970s and 1980s starring the Neapolitan singers Mario Merola and Nino D'Angelo; and the fresh, bitter-sweet comedies by Massimo Troisi on being a young Neapolitan in the 1980s.

Some of these films have contributed to the creation and diffusion of one of the strongest images of Naples – that of a poor, popular, superstitious albeit beautiful city, short of jobs and opportunities, in-habited by resourceful people endowed with a restless vitality, who survive only by means of an underground economy. This representation has frequently been accompanied by the well-known stereotypical Nea-politan imagery – colourful rooms packed with people, objects, candles, saints, photographs, souvenirs; and vibrant alleyways full of carts, street traders, sacred statues and shouting and gesticulating people. Such an image of Naples alternates and combines with that of a corrupt and violent city, ruled by the camorra and the word of honour, and that of a decaying peripheral city, at the borders of European society, devoid of reliable services (water supply, public transport and sewage dispersal) and with habitations in an appalling state of preservation.

Seeing that it simultaneously presents so many different faces, and that its complex rules and languages (social, body and verbal) seem indecipherable to the outsider, Naples has often been described as an enigmatic city.

In the years from 1993 to 1997 the city authorities inaugurated a politics of urban renovation that has partly changed the appearance of Naples. A symbol of this renovation is the closure of the central piazza Plebiscito to traffic and its repaving with volcanic paving stones. The new image of the city was promulgated by means of the G7 summit that took place in Naples in 1994, and was endorsed by Bill Clinton's jog in via Caracciolo. Yet despite these recent urban developments, and the signs – which are clear to the visitor – of its belonging to a postmodern, global society, contemporary Naples is still afflicted by old plagues. A recent report on Italian cities places Naples in the category of 'cities far from development' (Roma and Dominici 1997: 48–50). These are the cities where, between 1981 and 1991, the industrial sector has suffered a recession far more dramatic than that in the rest of the country; the percentage of employees in service industries is lower than the national average; production has decreased and public services have not improved substantially; the levels of general and of youth un-employment are almost double those of the average Italian city. At the same time, the level of income per inhabitant is, paradoxically, only slightly below the national average. Contemporary Naples seems to be perceived by observers as in the old riddle: 'Its crumbling historical core toasting in the sun has also been abruptly interrupted by the modern skyline punctuation of a Japanese-conceived commercial and adminis-trative centre. With its violent mixture of antiquated street rites and global design capital, Naples confronts us as an enigma' (Chambers 1994: 104–5).

The films of the new Neapolitan auteurs have often been presented as showing a novel and realistic portrait of the contemporary city. Capuano, for instance, offers 'slices of life in a unique city'; his films' protagonist is 'the soul of Naples, a city that Capuano succeeds in capturing and recounting like few others have' (Chiacchiari 1996: 75; our translation). *Vito e gli altri* by Capuano, *Morte di un matematico napoletano* by Martone and *Libera* by Corsicato 'immerse themselves in the city, in its alleyways, in its streets, in its lights – in the extended and luminous body of the city' (Gariazzo 1995: 38; our translation). The vividness of the representation of Naples, a Naples far from the tourist routes and the familiar clichés, is one of the most outstanding characteristics of these directors' films.

In particular, the importance of Naples in Mario Martone's cinema has frequently been highlighted by his films' reviewers. A recurrent comment on Martone's filmic portrayal of Naples is that it is non-stereotypical, innovative and realistic. One reviewer comments as follows on *Morte di un matematico napoletano*: 'If it is true that Naples dies in the imagination precisely because of the excessive number of times it has been portrayed – portrayals which, in their overlapping, delete it – in this instance the danger has been avoided' (La Capria, quoted in Ranucci and Ughi [n.d.]: 42; our translation). This opinion is shared by Áine O'Healy, according to whom Martone's films 'offer a complex construction of the familial, social and spatial mappings of Naples, defying previous cinematic stereotypes' (O'Healy 1999: 256).

In this chapter, we analyse the three full-length feature films made to date by Mario Martone: *Morte di un matematico napoletano* (1992), *L'amore molesto* (1995), and *Teatro di guerra* (1998). Our intention is to demonstrate that Martone's films offer a novel perspective on this enigmatic and much portrayed city, and that they mirror the changes in the urban fabric and, above all, in recent city life in Naples.

Modern Naples: *Morte di un matematico napoletano* and *L'amore molesto*

A tormented middle-aged man dressed in an old, smudged, white raincoat who roams the streets of the Naples of 1959 and a nervous, self-conscious young woman who rambles contemporary Naples wearing a bright red, skin-tight dress – these are the two most remarkable bodies that Martone's cinema has 'produced' up to now. The protagonists of, respectively, *Morte di un matematico napoletano* and *L'amore molesto*, they stand out for their paradoxical combination of symbolism and extreme physicality. His waning body, dilapidated by alcohol and the anguish of living, is transformed by the white raincoat into a metaphysical object. Her restrained, uneasy body becomes, via the close-fitting red dress, a metaphor of the burden of sensuality. These two characters exemplify different aspects of a troubled relationship with the city and the urban community that are characteristic of a modern sensitivity.

Morte di un matematico napoletano (1992) focuses on the last week in the life of Renato Caccioppoli (Naples, 1904–59). A mathematical genius, a communist who on account of intellectual scepticism never joined the party, a bohemian dandy and an alcoholic, Caccioppoli committed suicide by shooting himself in his apartment at Palazzo Cellammare, at the age of fifty-five. Caccioppoli was a significant and nonconformist figure in the Naples of the 1950s; he was well known not only to his fellow intellectuals and to his students – on whom he exerted a great influence – but also to ordinary people. He always went on foot and it was common to see him roaming the streets, dressed in his old raincoat. He was politically active, and his audacious and mordant civil courage landed him in a fascist prison. Martone's film does not intend to be a faithful reconstruction of Caccioppoli's last seven days, but reinvents them by fusing the memories of those who knew him and the director's imagination.

During his last week, Renato Caccioppoli gives a lecture, holds exams, goes to the theatre, and meets people: Don Simplicio, his assistant and closest friend; his students; his brother Luigi, who has just married an ex-partner of his; the comrades of the Communist Party; Anna, his never-forgotten ex-wife, who wants to abort the baby she is expecting, and seeks Renato's help; and his old aunt Maria Bakunin, daughter of the Russian anarchist Mikhail Bakunin. In between these encounters, Caccioppoli constantly and frenziedly roams the streets of Naples, day and night, as if chased by his own death (and by the camera), while drinking, thinking, writing mathematical formulae on the walls, talking to bar-owners and to homeless people, to a concièrge and a group of transsexual prostitutes, the *femmenielli*.

It is precisely in the scene of the meeting with the *femmenielli* that one of the most important aspects of Caccioppoli's character emerges. The transsexuals believe that he is not from Naples, that he is a foreigner. Renato, in fact, is a stranger at home, he belongs to his city and, at the same time, he is an outsider. When in the company of his students, of the comrades at the Party, or of members of his family, Caccioppoli looks as if he both belongs to these circles and at the same time is apart from them. This paradox is due to his unique, outstanding personality, and to his suicidal tendencies. It is not clear in the film when the decision to commit suicide is made, but Caccioppoli from the very beginning seems to be already dead, as if lingering in this world only to have a look at it from his position of outsider. The first sequences of the film, with Renato sitting at night in the grimy waiting room of the train station of Roma Termini, which looks like the anteroom of hell, can be read as a metaphor of the character's peculiar condition. His relationship with the urban community is also marked by his paradoxical position of outsider at home. He is inside and outside institutions at the same time. He is a professor at the University of Naples, but falls asleep during a meeting of the Academic Council, uninterested as he is in the interminable, unruly discussion. He takes part in activities organized by the Communist Party, without being officially a member. He goes to the Teatro San Carlo for a concert, and talks rudely to a lady with whom he shares a balcony. The offspring of one of the best Neapolitan families, he is far more sympathetic towards ordinary people and those at the fringes of urban society than to his peers, and favours talking to bartenders, concièrges, cleaners, homeless people and prostitutes.

Many of the interiors of *Morte di un matematico napoletano* look

5. Caccioppoli in *Morte di un matematico napoletano*
    (1992), dir. Mario Martone

dilapidated, while still showing signs of their previous splendour: Renato's apartment at Palazzo Cellammare, with its crumbling plasterwork;
the lecture rooms and the professorial offices at the university; and
Maria Bakunin's house. The Caccioppolis' former, elegant apartment in
viale Calascione is being emptied by the movers, who are removing
paintings from the walls and carrying around pieces of furniture. The
other two apartments in the film either look unfinished, like Luigi's
house, which is full of suitcases and boxes; or are places of passage:
Renato's former wife, Anna, who comes from Rome to see Renato,

stays at her brother's place. Furthermore, we are told that one of Renato's young friends, Leonardo, sleeps in the headquarters of an organization for peace, as he hasn't enough money to afford accommodation. The instability and decay of the living spaces emphasize the film's (modern) motif of the frailty of the human presence in this world, as does the protagonist's status of man who loiters before leaving the scene for ever.

Even though his apartment is tastefully furnished and full of personally selected objects, Caccioppoli uses it in a distracted, albeit intense, manner. He sleeps on an unmade bed, furiously plays the piano without taking off his raincoat, drinks from bottles hidden in the bookcase and in the record player. With the same distracted intensity he lives the city, continuously, day and night. In its streets and alleyways he talks, drinks, thinks and works. His city is old, central Naples; he lives at Palazzo Cellammare; walks in the area of via Chiaia; eats with his friends in an *osteria* close to the university; falls asleep in an elegant bar in via Partenope, with a view over Castel dell'Ovo; he rambles the lanes of Quartieri Spagnoli at night; he is at the port at sunrise. He often drinks in modest taverns and eats in open-air restaurants.

His walking is tense, animated by sudden accelerations. Once he believes that he is being followed and starts running. When he stops and turns, the road is empty behind him. It is as if the city itself was chasing him – a city that is often empty, absent, a curious but invisible spectator of Caccioppoli's agony. This impression is intensified by the recurrent presence of a character who, mostly unseen, looks at Renato from above – Renato's landlord, the marquis of Palazzo Cellammare, who is often to be seen gazing down from his balcony. It is only after Renato has died that the city comes out to manifest its opinions on its complex and talented child. During the open, fluid scene of the funeral, Caccioppoli's friends, colleagues, relatives and acquaintances comment, with varying degrees of benevolence, on Renato's suicide, on episodes of his life, but also chat, talk about matters that concern them, discuss political or personal affairs.

The Naples of *Morte di un matematico napoletano* is a changing, decaying city, in which a whole generation of intellectuals has lost its former ideals and its integrity. In politics, intellectual life and private relationships, compromise dominates. Society is still strongly influenced by the past; one of the characters is said to have compromised himself through association with fascism. The new, widespread system of achieving success is to use unfair means – acquaintances, relations, recommendations. Members of the leadership of the Italian Communist Party mention the imminent alliance with the Christian Democrats, which will come to be known as the Historic Compromise. At a lower level, we learn that an ordinary member of the Party has accepted a job at Pirelli in Milan, a symbol of the new capitalism – after all, 'one has to live'. Only Caccioppoli's youngest friends – among whom are Leonardo and Leo – continue to struggle to preserve their ideals of a fairer society, but are left only with the project of a trip to Lapland, a place where 'nothing resembles us'. In this society, Caccioppoli leaves a gap that will be hard to fill. Caccioppoli's exceptional personality, his torment, his appearance of former dandy, his intellectual sharpness and his cynicism make him a modern urban myth, both at a filmic and at a historical level.

As is Caccioppoli, so too the protagonist of *L'amore molesto* [Molested Love, 1995], Delia, is a sort of outsider at home, as she left Naples years before and moved to the northern city of Bologna. It is understood that the cause of her departure was an urge to escape a past of domestic violence. Delia is still distressed by her family, as well as by her native city. In fact, when her mother Amalia visits her in Bologna, Delia is clearly disturbed by her presence, and not only because Amalia upsets her minimalist routine. Amalia, unlike her daughter, is a very physical person, at ease with her sexuality, a quality that clearly unsettles Delia.

After Amalia's dead body is found floating naked in the sea, Delia returns to Naples seeking an explanation for her mother's end. Her approach to her native, carnal city resembles her reaction of revulsion towards the loved/hated figure of her mother. In Naples, surrounded by the chaotic traffic and touched by anonymous bodies in the crowded streets, she shrinks and shivers at the physicality of her city.

As does Caccioppoli, Delia moves through Naples mainly on foot. Her tour of the city is marked on a map reproduced at the beginning of the published screenplay (see Martone 1997). The map is entitled '*Il cammino di Delia*' – Delia's itinerary (literally, Delia's walk). She covers various areas of Naples, including those crossed by Caccioppoli, and once drives to Pozzuoli with Antonio, her childhood friend.

Investigating Amalia's last days, Delia goes to the hill of Vomero and the shop in which her mother bought the brassiere that she was wearing when she drowned, and a red, tight dress that she was bringing to Delia as a birthday present. In the shop, Delia tries to gain time by claiming

6.   Delia in *L'amore molesto* (1995), dir. Mario Martone

that she wants to change the dress, which is too small for her. After being invited to try it on, she is thrown out of the shop by the owner, who is annoyed by her intrusive questions. Wearing only the skin-tight red dress, Delia is forced out of the shop, into the rain. Her outfit exposes her to the looks and the comments of men, in a way that first distresses her, then slowly forces her to begin to confront her inhibited sensuality. Delia's journey is, in fact, twofold: in space, she traverses Naples in her mother's footsteps; in time, she travels back to her childhood, digging into her memory. This inner process of discovery, which accompanies Delia's investigation of both her mother's recent and distant past, culminates in the recollection of a repressed childhood memory of sexual violence, which finally frees Delia from her ghosts and reconciles her with her mother and her city.

In both *Molested Love* and *Morte di un matematico napoletano* the photography is by Luca Bigazzi. In *Molested Love* contemporary Naples is photographed in colour. The Naples of the 1950s shown in the flashbacks of the same film is close to black and white, without ever being quite black and white; grey and blue are the dominant colours. In *Morte di un matematico napoletano* the city is mostly plunged in a warm, ochre light. A yellow tint can be as much suggestive of a past epoch as black and white. Nevertheless, the idea that the Naples of *Morte di un matematico napoletano* is a past city is principally rendered by the choice of settings. Martone's words on this subject are revealing:

> We were making a film set in 1959, but we could not, and did not want, to re-create anything. We did not have enough money, and the last thing I wanted to do was a period film. With the architect Giancarlo Muselli, we did a stencil job. We cut out, within the existing city, a portion of it that subsists unchanged, that survived the transformations and devastation that took place from the 1960s onward. (Martone 1997: 135; our translation)

As this quote suggests, the Naples in *Morte di un matematico napoletano* is a city within a city, more precisely a modern city within the contemporary city. This urban duplicity is even more evident in *Molested Love*. Delia's memories of the past materialize in a series of flashbacks that alternate with sequences set in the present. The two Naples in *Molested Love*, the past and the contemporary, are distinguished not only by the different quality of the photography, but also by the use of sound. While old Naples is almost a quiet rural town, the present Naples is incredibly noisy – the clamour of the traffic and of shouting voices is intensified by a soundtrack full of piercing trumpets. The streets are chaotically invaded by cars, and the motorbikes even drive on the footpaths. The contemporary Naples of *Molested Love* is, in the words of Luca Bigazzi, 'a molesting city devastated by illicit property development' and by traffic, a noisy, infernal, foul-smelling city: a present and a true city' (Ranucci and Ughi [n.d.]: 58; our translation).

The contrast with the Naples of the 1950s is strong. The latter is a dream city, altered by the filter of private memory and by the lens of childhood. This city is contemporaneous with the Naples of *Morte di un matematico napoletano*, but nevertheless is very different from it. Delia spent her childhood at the peripheral area of Gianturco, whereas Caccioppoli lived near the historical centre. His Naples was simultaneously animated by intellectuals, by a politically active youth and by the fringes of the urban society; working people trying to earn a living, sometimes on the borders of legality, populate Delia's memories of her city – a society psychologically still influenced by the war and by the memory of recent poverty. Delia's family had to work hard to maintain its achievements, such as a decent apartment and a bit of money – Amalia sewed and her husband painted commercial portraits that were sold on the streets. Their life and that of the people around them was strongly

7. Amalia and Delia as a child in *L'amore molesto* (1995),
    dir. Mario Martone

marked by primary needs and instincts, among which sex and jealousy played a fundamental role. The popular city of Delia's childhood was affected by ignorance and by male authority and control; Amalia stood out in this environment as a strong female figure, who partly played with male authority and its sexual pressure and partly succumbed to it. When Delia many years later pays a visit to the Gianturco, she finds that, in Martone's words, 'the rural air that had belonged to it, with those whitish, four-storey buildings erected in the middle of the dusty countryside, over the years had transformed into those sallow outskirts besieged by skyscrapers, choked by traffic and by decelerating trains, which run alongside the houses like snakes' (Martone 1997: 98; our translation).

In *Molested Love* contemporary Naples is portrayed as a city of our times, plagued by traffic, vulgarity and noise and tempted to sort out its own long-standing troubles by resorting to authoritarian solutions. In the streets, walls are covered in posters for the imminent election of the city mayor. Many of these posters promote Alessandra Mussolini, a descendant of the Duce and a member of MSI (Fascist Party), who actually ran for mayor in 1993 and lost. Old central areas such as the Galleria Umberto I, where Amalia lived, have lost their former fascination; suburbs like the Gianturco have been urbanized and now are plagued by the same problems as the city centre. Nevertheless, this Naples shows only in part signs of belonging to a postmodern era. This is principally due to the protagonist's perspective, one that reduces the difference between old and new Naples. Delia roams through the contemporary city reading it as if it was the city of her childhood, or a direct descendant of it; each place, each encounter, each route brings her back to the past, and activates almost oneiric memories. Contemporary Naples and the Naples of the late 1950s are intertwined in Delia's mind. Slowly but surely, she regresses to her past sensations, experiences and fantasies. A softening of her manners, of her state of mind, and of her entire body mark this regression. On the train back to Bologna, Delia's own body turns into Amalia's body, as she wears her mother's old clothes, and even adopts her name, finally relaxing in a long-rejected acceptance of her roots.

While being very different in many ways, Caccioppoli and Delia are two unsettled characters who have a peculiar vision of Naples, a city with which they have a relationship of love and hate, of belonging and exclusion. They both roam the city – Caccioppoli walks as if to escape himself and his unavoidable death; Delia as if looking for herself. The results of their distinct quests could not be more different: Caccioppoli leaves the scene for ever, misunderstood by the majority, Delia becomes reconciled with her city, her mother and herself. Their communal perspective on the city is that of an immersion in it – they do not avoid the corners, the galleries, the small lanes; they seem compelled to go down all its shady alleyways. This immersion can even provoke revulsion or fear in them, but they seek it none the less. Both in *Molested Love* and *Morte di un matematico napoletano* the camera, which is usually submerged in the city streets and alleyways, once lifts to show a bird's-eye view of Naples. The characters do not share this broad perspective. They are so absorbed by the city that they cannot see it from above; they do not dominate the city but are, on the contrary, observed and scrutinized by it.

In both films, the city has a strong metaphorical connotation. For Caccioppoli, Naples becomes a metaphor of his restlessness and his imminent death, and of the decay of a whole generation that has lost its values. For Delia, Naples is a metaphor of the loved and hated maternal body. The successful construction of these metaphors lies paradoxically in the concrete nature of the representation – settings and actors have been carefully chosen and are filmed in a way that communicates a sharp and truthful physicality. In *Molested Love*, the symbolism of the maternal body is constructed primarily by means of a strong identification of Naples with Amalia. The body of Naples is like the body of Amalia – the city and the character share the same generous, carnal sensuality, which expresses itself through the corporeal fulness of the dialect and the gestures, and a simultaneously joyful and sorrowful approach to sexuality and to life. Borrowing Giuliana Bruno's words, which refer to Elvira Notari's Naples, we can say that 'modeled on the body's topography, the social anatomy of the city, transferred onto film, becomes a corporeal geography' (Bruno 1993: 173). The metaphor of the maternal body is also achieved through an insistence on womb-like settings, cavities and underground rooms, in which characters hide, meet, dream, consume sex, abuse and are abused. Such womb-like places are the underground rooms of the sweet shop 'Coloniali'; the Stufe di Nerone at Pozzuoli, the public baths where Antonio and Delia swim; the hall of Amalia's apartment building in Galleria Umberto I; and the lift in the same building, where Delia used to hide when she was a child. These cavities within the city, private spaces within the public spaces, bring to mind Walter Benjamin and Asja Lacis' description of Naples as a porous city. 'As porous as this stone is architecture. Building and action interpenetrate in the courtyards, arcades, and stairway' (Benjamin and Lacis 1992: 169). According to the authors, in Naples the stairs 'erupt fragmentarily from the buildings, make an angular turn, and disappear, only to burst out again' (p. 171). Similarly, private and public life intermingle: 'Just as the living room reappears on the street, with chairs, hearth, and altar, so, only much more loudly, the street migrates into the living room. Even the poorest one is as full of wax candles, biscuit saints, sheaves of photos on the wall, and iron bedsteads, as the street is of carts, people, and lights' (pp. 174–5). Although both of Martone's films accurately avoid the depiction of folkloristic clichés, such as those listed by Benjamin and Lacis, the porous quality of Naples is evident in *Molested Love*, and is linked to the metaphor of the maternal body. This body is in fact a mix of private and public, of youth and decay, of joy and sorrow. Furthermore, the Naples of the 1950s and contemporary Naples are fused together to the extent that the old city re-emerges in the new one with its signs, memories and meanings, accentuating the impression of a porous Naples.

The metaphor of the city as an organism is a modern one: the modern industrial city has often been described as a diseased body that needs to be cured (see Donald 1992: 425–8). Naples in *Molested Love* is not only the maternal, porous body, which is attractive and repulsive at the same time, but also the diseased body endangered by the maladies of modernity: traffic congestion, pollution, overcrowding, long-standing problems such as unemployment and crime – to the extent that it is almost impossible to run a private business such as a shop. All these problems seem to materialize in a blind dissatisfaction exposed by Alessandra Mussolini's campaign in the administrative elections.

Postmodern Naples: *Teatro di guerra*

Teatro di guerra radically differs from *Morte di un matematico napoletano* and *Molested Love* in the style of the cinematography, in the type of narrative, in the communicative strategy and in the city that it constructs.

In *Teatro di guerra*, an avant-garde theatre company plans to stage Aeschylus' *Seven Against Thebes* in Sarajevo, during the Yugoslavian civil war. The film follows the rehearsals of the ancient tragedy on fratricidal war, which take place in an underground theatre in the ramshackle and crime-plagued Neapolitan area Quartieri Spagnoli. The actors, led by their director, Leo, discuss their characters' personalities and motivations, debate different approaches to the text, and prepare themselves physically and psychologically to interpret their roles. This preparation consists of exercises, some of which are improvisations, for instance on the theme of feeling threatened; others are narrative exercises that bring into play the actors' imaginations, such as in the invention of the dreams dreamt by the tragedy's characters during the siege.

The preparatory phase is followed by the actual rehearsals of the show, which are a creative and demanding process for both the director and the actors. Fragments of the rehearsals, which finally culminate in the first performance, intertwine with events in the actors' and in the director's lives, many of which are connected to the show. Among these episodes are Leo's attempts to find funds for his project; the main actress, Luisella, leaves the rehearsals to act in a film in Rome; a new actress, Sara, joins the company, at first sceptically, only to become increasingly involved; Leo receives letters from his friend Jasmin, the director of the theatre in Sarajevo where the show is supposed to be staged; Riccardo looks for stage objects in a hospital storeroom; Adriano records noises of shots and explosions for the show; and the police even arrest members of the company for carrying (fake) weapons in the alleyways around the theatre. Other episodes are less directly connected to the show: Vittorio does voluntary work with children from the Quartieri Spagnoli; one of the young actresses takes an exam in the university; Lucia and Adriano play at a concert; Rosario is arrested for possession of cocaine; and a minor camorra boss of the Quartieri Spagnoli, Silvano, is shot dead in via Toledo.

At the end of the film, following the first performance of their show in Naples, the members of the company and their friends have a party at Sara's place. These sequences are very open and fluid, and in this they recall the scenes of the funeral that conclude *Morte di un matematico napoletano*. The friends chat, drink, discuss politics and various other matters, play and sing. At dawn, Sara and Vittorio join Leo on the big terrace of the house, and sense that their friend is distressed. Leo finally confesses what he had kept secret for a while: Jasmin died two or three weeks before, and the production will never go to Sarajevo.

Although the story is always intelligible, the narrative is unconventional, fragmented and drifting. Unlike the two previous films by Martone, *Teatro di guerra* does not have a main character, but presents us with a set of characters endowed with similar importance; even Leo, the director, is but one of the many bodies traversing this film. This has implications for the representation of the city. In *Teatro di guerra* Naples is not mediated through the eyes of a character, as it was in *Morte di un matematico napoletano* by Caccioppoli, and in *Molested Love* by Delia. It is the camera that directly constructs the city.

Teatro di guerra primarily shows us central Naples, and in particular the area of Quartieri Spagnoli, in which the Teatro Nuovo is located. In the film's screenplay, Martone describes it in the following manner: 'Teatro Nuovo is a rather small and dilapidated theatre. It sits like a fort in the middle of the swarming alleyways of Quartieri Spagnoli, also simply called "i Quartieri", in the historical centre of Naples. Heroin dealing, camorra turf wars, desperate motorcycle races are an integral component of this area's scenery' (Martone 1998: 119; our translation). The company mainly gravitates towards the theatre. Leo, who shares an apartment with one of the actors, Diego, lives not far from it. Luisella and Diego go to a café in via Paladino, next to the university, and later in the film we see them chatting and smoking hashish at night in piazzetta Nilo, which is also near the university. A group of actors eat in an Eritrean restaurant in the Quartieri; later, two of them walk along the sea at *lungomare* Santa Lucia. The camorra boss Silvano lives in a mod-

8.   *Teatro di guerra* (1998), dir. Mario Martone

ernized *basso* in an alleyway of the Quartieri. Vittorio works at the
Associazione Quartieri Spagnoli. During the film, we are shown an
image of the central corso Umberto I with the traffic paralysed by a
protest march against unemployment.

Other areas of Naples appear briefly in the film. Rosario goes to eat
at his parents' house in the suburban area of Scampìa in Secondigliano.
Also known as 'la 167', this area was built as part of the 1965 plan for
working-class, low-cost housing, which was developed in accordance
with law 167 of 1962 for the regulation of urban development. The

area was supposed to be an autonomous, self-sufficient entity, endowed with all services. Most of the buildings are tall, tower-shaped or sail-shaped, with a high-density population, and present problems of ventilation and illumination. Many of the planned services were never realized. Scampìa, in common with other examples of this type of modernist building in Italy and abroad, is separated both physically and culturally from the surrounding historical centres and is a site of alienation and ghettoization. Significantly, we see Rosario walking by a huge hole opened by a house that collapsed due, as we are informed by Martone, to a gas explosion (Martone 1998: 131). Scampìa is a recurrent set in new Neapolitan cinema. It appears also in Salvatore Piscicelli's *Le occasioni di Rosa* (1981); in Antonio Capuano's *Vito e gli altri* (1991); and in Pappi Corsicato's *Libera* (1993).

In an ex-ironworks at Bagnoli a rave party takes place; hundreds of young people dance to the obsessive rhythm of the music. Bagnoli is the extreme western periphery of the conurbation of Naples. Its urbanization was encouraged by the construction of the Cumana railway, which connected the area of Campi Flegrei to Naples, and by a process of industrialization that started in 1904 with the erection of the ILVA ironworks. The settlement grew rapidly around the ironworks and other factories, all of which were dismantled between the end of the 1980s and the beginning of the 1990s. The local administration is currently discussing projects for reclaiming and rezoning this area.

In *Teatro di guerra* central Naples is chaotic, overcrowded and sometimes violent. The uproar that dominates the soundtrack of *Molested Love* is moderated in the portrait of this city, but re-emerges strongly during the rehearsals, thanks to a generator that is used by the company not only to illuminate the stage, but as a source of noise recalling the clamour of war. The streets of the city centre are always congested by traffic, if not by a protest rally. The alleyways of Quartieri Spagnoli swarm with people and motorcycles. Although these elements also characterize contemporary Naples in *Molested Love*, in *Teatro di guerra* Naples looks much more like a city of our times. This is because of the presence of many features characteristic of a postmodern urban environment. Whereas the considerable presence of non-European immigrants in Naples does not register in *Molested Love*, in *Teatro di guerra* we find a city inhabited by various ethnic groups, with their meeting points and clubs. As already mentioned, members of the company eat at an Eritrean restaurant, defined by Martone as a sort of club for *extracomunitari* (non-

EC immigrants) at the Quartieri Spagnoli (Martone 1998: 185). Leo is shown buying hashish from some Tunisians. One rehearsal is interrupted by noise coming from the upper room of the Teatro Nuovo; the actors go upstairs to complain and find the theatre full of Senegalese gathered for a concert.

The Naples in *Teatro di guerra* is not simply more cosmopolitan than the one in *Molested Love*. A further sign of its belonging to a postmodern era is the fact that an ex-industrial complex is now used as a site for concerts. The tendency to renovate ex-industrial spaces, such as factories and warehouses – remnants of the modern urban landscape – and to convert them to other uses is characteristic of a late-capitalist society. Significantly, the ex-ironworks of Bagnoli is in the film the stage for a concert against capitalism, the market economy, totalitarian ideologies, the mass media and violence. The following is a fragment of 'Sarajevo Supermarket', the song by C/P 01 Contropotere that we hear during these sequences: 'Cross – Rapes – Tortures – Video – Video agonies – Video communications – Video raids – Video vampires – Video executions – Hebraic stars – Red stars – Stars and stripes – Blue helmets[2] – Green helmets – Hammer and sickle – Black cross – Hooked cross[3] – Islamic cross – Christian cross – Sarajevo Supermarket – Sarajevo Supermarket.'

As the lyrics of 'Sarajevo Supermarket' emphasize, this Naples is part of a society in which other places, other experiences, other lives are easily available on television, which reduces them to a spectacle within the daily show of mass communication. Martone never shows us fragments of the war on TV, but the presence of Sarajevo is strong, and not only because the subject of the war recurs in the dialogue. In *Teatro di guerra*, Naples itself becomes Sarajevo; the two cities are superimposed and combined throughout the film. In particular, the dilapidated and crime-plagued Quartieri Spagnoli is portrayed as a war front, where people are killed in broad daylight in the middle of a crowded street.

The analogy between Sarajevo and the Quartieri Spagnoli is mediated by the Thebes of the tragedy of fratricidal war staged by the company. Aeschylus' *Seven Against Thebes* is updated by the use of modern costumes, and in particular of uniforms and guns that could well feature in a contemporary war between impoverished factions, such as the conflict in former Yugoslavia.

The conditions in which the actors are forced to rehearse offer the pretext for strengthening the analogy. The company does not have the use of the main stage, but of the underground room of the Teatro Nuovo, which is a rather limited space. More and more frequently during the film the actors enter and exit through the theatre door, in order to make use of the street as a backstage. Injured characters, armed soldiers, dead people spill into the alleyway, bringing the ancient war – and the Yugoslavian conflict – on to the street. These episodes also make the point that avant-garde theatre is a 'theatre of war', war against the establishment, represented in the film by the prosperous company of the Teatro Stabile, which is publicly financed, and is rehearsing Shakespeare's *The Taming of the Shrew*.

The effect of amalgamation of Naples and Sarajevo, of outside and inside, is not only confined to the narrative, but is also achieved through the filmmaking, and in particular through the use of point of view. The incorporation of the street into the theatre and vice versa is not only circumstantial, but is due to an intuition of Riccardo, the set designer. In a dialogue with Leo about the theatre in Sarajevo, he suggests that they use the backstage as a set: 'We can reverse the perspective, make use of the landing, the stairs, the back door; that's a ready-made set.' This is, in fact, the central idea of *Teatro di guerra*. The film's complex space is constructed on the inversion of the point of view, a mechanism applied so incessantly that it constitutes a true signifying strategy. In the theatre, the backstage becomes the real stage, while the street becomes the backstage. Likewise, each closed space in the film is shot from a reversed perspective, which opens that space, incorporating the outside in the inside. Most of the interiors in *Teatro di guerra* seem porous, to use Benjamin and Lacis' terminology. In Leo and Diego's apartment the windows are often wide open, and the glass is not visible. These windows are not a barrier to the outside, but rather incorporate it in the inside, so much so that at times we wonder where the interior ends and the exterior begins. The same effect is reached in the scene in which Leo reads a letter from Jasmin while sitting before a big open window on a landing in his building. Another time, Leo is shot from the outside through a window, while sitting at his desk. When Leo goes to meet Vittorio at the school of the Associazione Quartieri Spagnoli, he enters, closes the building's main door behind him, yet finds himself in an open courtyard framed by columns. Characters are often shown sitting in doorways, as if they lived partly inside and partly outside. Adriano goes to visit his father in a dilapidated hospital, opens a window and, instead of the expected landscape, uncovers a wall. The Neapolitan *bassi* are basement habitations in which the front door opens directly on to the street, so that the barrier between inside and outside almost disappears. The house of Silvano, the boss of the Quartieri, is one such *basso*; in another, full of sacred images and decorative lights, Rosario meets a friend.

The significance of these porous places would probably be lost if the camera did not confirm and multiply their presence by being systematically placed in a way that suggests an inversion of the perspective, that incorporates the outside in the inside and reverses back and front. In *Teatro di guerra* even noise is used to similar effect, to construct a multidimensional, stratified space. Once, for instance, the noise produced by the generator used during the rehearsals provokes a reaction from the inhabitants of the area, who complain that they cannot sleep because of the clamour; in other words, the stage noise spills out into the street, and street noises are conversely heard in the theatre, during the rehearsals. Spaces in *Teatro di guerra* invade one another and re-qualify each other – the street and the theatre; Naples and Sarajevo; public spaces and private spaces. The film itself is porous, since the images of the rehearsals that are interspersed with the rest of the narrative are in fact documentary footage of the rehearsals for the production of *Seven Against Thebes*, which was staged by Martone's company in 1996 – a documentary film and a fiction film thus merge in *Teatro di guerra*.

The resulting portrayal of Naples is that of a porous city full of unexpected cavities and inversions of perspective and meaning; a city in which past and present, public and private, mainstream and avant-garde, foreign and local not only coexist, but are physically interwoven and determine the postmodernity of its urban lifestyle.

Porous Naples

Many elements combine to characterize the Naples shown in *Morte di un matematico napoletano* and *Molested Love* as modern cities. Some of these elements are typical of a modern sensibility, such as the emphasis on metaphors (the maternal body, the womb and the gazing city) and on symbolism (the white raincoat and the skin-tight red dress), and the presence of two protagonists characterized by modern feelings such as disquiet, uneasiness and introspection. The Naples of 1959 in *Morte di un matematico napoletano* is the bohemian city centre inhabited by intellectuals, by homeless people, by prostitutes – a dying world that has produced a modern urban myth, Caccioppoli. In *Molested Love* two Naples are juxtaposed: contemporary Naples, which is severely affected by traffic, pollution and overcrowding, and the Naples of the 1950s with its working-class suburbs and its almost rural aspect. On closer analysis, though, the difference between the two Naples is reduced by the protagonist's perspective: in contemporary Naples Delia looks for the signs of the city of her childhood, and reads the urban text as a site of sedimentation of past meanings. Furthermore, the past city and the present city are porously intertwined, and combine to form the metaphor of the maternal body.

The style of the filmmaking is, in both films, controlled, not invasive, and very experienced, to the extent that it confers an almost classic look to *Morte di un matematico napoletano* and *Molested Love*. The narrative is also controlled, always intelligible, and of an almost literary quality, a characteristic that is partly due to the contribution of writer Fabrizia Remondino to the screenplay of *Morte di un matematico napoletano*, and to the derivation of *Molested Love* from a novel of the same title by Elena Ferrante.

Teatro di guerra is set in contemporary times and in three different areas of Naples: Quartieri Spagnoli and, more transitorily, Secondigliano and Bagnoli. The Quartieri – sometimes referred to as the Neapolitan Bronx – is a central, crime-plagued, dilapidated area that the film fuses with the Sarajevo devastated by civil war. The Quartieri is portrayed by *Teatro di guerra* as chaotic, overcrowded and violent.

The areas of Secondigliano, with its ramshackle working-class housing estates, and Bagnoli, with its dismantled ironworks, represent the failure of modernist urban planning and of industrialization. They are the remains of the modern era and signal that Naples is now part of a different, postindustrial society.

The deeply rooted presence of various ethnic groups is one sign of the city's membership of a global society, and firmly places *Teatro di guerra*'s Naples within postmodernity. The intertextual presence/absence of Sarajevo and of the televised civil war create an image of Naples far from established filmic imagery, tourist routes and well-known clichés. The filmmaking is radically postmodern, first because of its fragmentary and drifting style; second, because it challenges the borders between reality and fiction, as well as between cinema and theatre; third because it experiments methodically with an inversion of the point of view, that once more reveals Naples' porosity.

This attribute of Naples, first identified by Benjamin and Lacis, is permanent and adaptable, as it emerges both in Martone's modern and postmodern portraits of this city. Whereas in *Molested Love* Naples' porosity contributes to the construction of the modern metaphor of the city as maternal body, in *Teatro di guerra* it enhances the postmodernity of the city, by constructing a multidimensional space full of inversions of perspective and meaning. Adaptability and mutability truly seem to be the mark of Naples.

4

Marseilles: Intersection, Fragment, Ruin

Marseilles, the principal port city of France and of the whole Mediterranean area, the second most populous French conurbation after Paris, can be seen as a case in point of the crisis of the European city in postmodern times. Once a rich port (importing petroleum, wine, fruits, olive oil, hides and skins, and exporting wines, liqueurs, processed foods, cement and metal products) and the headquarters of heavy industry (petroleum refining and shipbuilding), Marseilles was catalogued ten years ago by Conti and Spriano (1990) as being among those European cities of maritime tradition that are in negative industrial transition, together with Genoa and Antwerp. Today, trade and industry are still an important component of Marseilles' economy, but the prevalence of its service industry, which employs four out of five members of the workforce, is patent. Aix-Marseilles is significantly the second centre of research in France after Paris. A city that was always characterized by a powerful mix of continental and exotic cultures and atmospheres, so much so that it is sometimes compared for its cosmopolitanism to New York, Marseilles presents a population in constant evolution. It is calculated that one inhabitant out of three has arrived in the city in the course of the last twenty-five years; the most recent wave of immigration comes from Eastern Europe – from Poland, Czechoslovakia, Russia, Romania. After decades of economic decadence and apathy (a consequence of deindustrialization), of organized crime (French connection) and of constant deterioration in living conditions (unemployment is currently very high), Marseilles is today experiencing an urban and cultural renaissance, which does not hide the evident marks of recession. Once a bastion of communist faith, in recent years part of Marseilles' working class has shifted to the far-Right movement of Jean-Marie Le Pen, the Front National, which originates in this region. In Marseilles' recent history it is easy to read the signs of the economic and ideological transformations of the European conurbation in the passage to postmodernism and late capitalism.

Marseilles in the Cinema

The character of cinematic Marseilles was established very early, and any discussion of current films set in this city must take into account its long history of filmic representation. With its picturesque sites and its intense light, which attracted painters such as Cézanne and Georges Braque, Marseilles became a film set at the very beginning of the 1900s – pioneer Victorin Jasset filmed there in 1906 and 1907, and local cinematographic activity is clearly documented since 1914. Among the well-known early directors who worked in Marseilles are avant-garde filmmakers Louis Delluc (*Fièvre*, 1921), Jean Epstein (*Coeur fidèle*, 1923) and Alberto Cavalcanti (*En rade*, 1927), who set there tragic love stories in which the Vieux-Port 'expresses the poetry of far away places, an "inner exoticism", a bridge between two worlds, the East and the West' (Armogathe and Echinard 1995: 50; our translation). In contrast with the stylized quality of the images in these films, as well as with their dream-like, exotic vision of Marseilles as door to the East and port of the Seven Seas, *Marseille-Vieux-Port* (1929) by Hungarian director Laszlo Moholy-Nagy showed the port's cross-border bridge as a constructivist sculpture, and portrayed Marseilles as a city in a critical condition, poverty-stricken, the streets invaded by rubbish.

Silent films made before 1930 largely concentrated on the liveliest areas of the city, and almost completely excluded the periphery and industrial Marseilles. They established patterns and contributed to the creation of stereotypes, such as the busy streets, the gesticulating conversants, the myth of the 'golden idleness', which – with the addition of the typical southern accent and of details of the local lifestyle – crystallized into the 1930s in the so-called 'Marseillais genre'. This introduced 'a particular way of seeing and of representing Marseilles, which played on a light-hearted register the situations of popular melo-drama, based on an infinite number of variations on the same themes, in the same settings, with highly colourful, loud-mouthed characters' (Armogathe and Echinard 1995: 84; our translation). These films' plots frequently told the story of a young couple divided by ambition or by an external factor, such as a femme fatale, who are in the end reunited in Marseilles to lead a healthy and simple married life. Marseilles was therefore represented as the provincial alternative to Paris (epitomizing the allure, but also the danger and falsity, of the big city), and as the cradle of a simple and ordinary life, enriched by pleasures such as local beverages (pastis) and cuisine (aïoli). This vision of a charming, pro-vincial town where life is quiet and truthful was partly modified on the one hand by the presence of the port, which continued to function as a tempting gateway to cosmopolitanism and to exoticism and, on the other hand, by an insistence on the not-so-licit affairs of some of the characters that created the image of a widespread dishonesty, an image that has been long associated with Marseilles. This air of pervasive yet amiable delinquency was transformed into and culminated in the image of a violent, crime-ridden city typical of more recent films. The most prominent representative of the 'Marseillais genre' was Marcel Pagnol (1895–1974), who was responsible for a whole cinematographic industry in Marseilles, and was the author of a trilogy set in the city composed of *Marius* (1931), *Fanny* (1932) and *César* (1936).

> Pagnol's contribution was to give a local inflexion to the populist iconography of working-class and *petit-bourgeois* milieu: cafés and shops, 'ordinary' people in everyday clothes: baggy trousers, cloth caps, aprons, rolled-up sleeves; and of course the accent. These attributes [were] metonimically representative of a 'sub'-culture (Marseilles), and metaphorically of a whole (French) culture. (Vin-cendeau 2000: 18)

Very few films made in the 1930s deviated from the imagery provided by the 'Marseillais genre' – among these are Jean Renoir's *Toni* (1935) and *La Marseillaise* (1938).

After more conventional representations such as those offered by the films of Henri Verneuil (b. 1920) and by a series of postwar gangster movies, the cinematic image of Marseilles was renovated by the indepen-dent and marginal cinema of Paul Carpita. The city in *Le rendez-vous des quais* (1953–55) – a film shot on location with non-professional actors – is the true Marseilles of the hard life of the docks, filmed with a documentary-like spirit and a pacifist inspiration. In contrast with the cliché of 'golden idleness', 'the Marseilles of Carpita is also the space of a cosmopolite society where small, traditional jobs flourish' (Armogathe and Echinard 1995: 84; our translation).

Most films that have been set in Marseilles in the last thirty years do not avoid the usual stereotypes; there are numerous cop thrillers and spy stories, few of which stand out for their originality. In a category apart is the cinema of Marseilles-born René Allio (1924–95), active since the mid-1960s, who offered the nostalgic image of a stylized, photogenic and poetic Marseilles in films such as *La vielle dame indigne* (1965), *Retour à Marseille* (1979) and *Transit* (1990). Among the most recent films Bertrand Blier's *Trop belle pour toi* (1989) and *Un, deux, trois, soleil* (1993) also stand out – Marseilles in them is no longer a recognizable city with its famous landmarks, but becomes 'a sort of "urban non-place", where the shapes are so fragmented and are framed so indirectly that the story could be set anywhere' (p. 168). A similar impression is conveyed by Gérard Pirès' *Taxi* (1998), a film written and produced by Luc Besson, which is set in an even more unrecognizable, postmodern Marseilles; and partly by Philippe Faucon's *Samia* (2000) in which, although the city is more present, characters always talk about living not in Marseilles but in 'France', as opposed to living 'at home', in Algeria.

A contrasting tendency seems to be represented by the films that will be the object of our analysis in this chapter. Karim Dridi, Claire Denis and Robert Guédiguian are the directors of films in which, according to a critic, 'beauty largely resides in the gaze laid on the city'; furthermore, thanks to their films, 'a sort of contemporary body of work on Marseilles is slowly in the process of forming' (Bouquet 1995b: 36; our translation). We will analyse in the following pages Dridi's *Bye-Bye*, Denis' *Nenette et Boni* and Guédiguian's *Marius et Jeannette*, to test the assumption that they do portray Marseilles in a different, novel way.

Bye-Bye: The City-intersection

Bye-Bye (1995) is the second feature directed by Tunisian-born Karim Dridi who also made *Pigalle* (1994) and *Hors Jeu* (1998). Paris-based Dridi made his first short with a Super-8 camera when he was twelve, and developed his expertise in filmmaking directing a series of shorts and documentaries, including *Citizen Ken Loach* (1996). *Bye-Bye* was awarded the Prix de la Jeunesse and the Prix Gervais-Un Certain Regard at Cannes Film Festival in 1995.

After the death of his handicapped brother in a fire, for which he irrationally holds himself responsible, twenty-five-year-old Ismaël leaves Paris with his fourteen-year-old brother Mouloud and reaches Marseilles, where his uncle, his aunt and his three cousins live. Silent and withdrawn Ismaël is found a temporary job by his uncle at the docks, where he befriends Jacky, a white fellow worker. His teenage cousin Rhida introduces Mouloud to dealer Renard's dangerous world of drugs and violence. Mouloud is awaited by his parents in Tunisia, but refuses to go and runs away from home. Ismaël, in the meantime, finds himself irresistibly attracted to Yasmina, Jacky's girlfriend, who quite overtly seduces him. Confronted by Jacky, who had been informed of the betrayal by his brother Ludo and his racist friends, Ismaël decides to leave Marseilles, but not before finding Mouloud and freeing him from Renard's dangerous influence. The film leaves Ismaël and Mouloud heading on foot in an as yet undecided direction.

The screenplay for *Bye-Bye* was written by Dridi in Paris, and initially it was planned to shoot the film in the Parisian quarter of Belleville, but the author could not find suitable locations in an area that was quickly being transformed – this is clearly shown in Daniel Pennac's novels set there: *Au bonheur des ogres* (1985), *La fée carabine* (1987), *La petite marchande de prose* (1989). Also, as Dridi has said in an interview:

> I had the feeling that too many films were made in Paris and too few in the South of France ... To set my film there gave me the possibility of tending towards the other shore, of looking at Africa from the other coast. Marseilles is a city at the intersection, like I am, who am half Arab and half French. It's a very mixed city. (Jousse and Lalanne 1995: 39; our translation)

It is precisely as a city-intersection that Marseilles is represented in the film. First, the town plays the role of a crossroads and of a turning point in the narrative: at the beginning of the film we see Ismaël and Mouloud on the motorway, travelling in their old car, coming from Paris (from Belleville, probably); during the narrative we are often reminded by the characters that Marseilles is only a stage on their trip, and that at the least Mouloud is directed to Tunisia; at the end of the film the two brothers leave the city and head in an unknown direction, possibly towards Spain.

Marseilles is also a city-intersection from the point of view of its visual representation. Whereas in other recent films set here the port hardly figures at all, in *Bye-Bye* the sea is given great importance. This is not only because the water by contrast recalls the fire that devastated Ismaël's life, but also because the sea and the port in general are a symbol of departures and arrivals, and the Mediterranean in particular is the sea that both divides and joins Europe and Africa. As Dimitris Eleftheriotis observes:

> Water is a material and visual manifestation of fluidity and ... fluidity involves first and foremost a renegotiation of identity. This entails a restructuring of the relationship between similarity and difference that supports any identity ... In a geographical sense water seems to reproduce this dynamic relationship between similarity and difference, union and separation: seas and rivers are not only physical frontiers and markers of national borders, but also routes of communication linking and connecting ports, peoples and cultures. (Eleftheriotis 2000: 99–100)

Several episodes in the film are set at the docks, where Ismaël works, or more generally in the port (like the concert during which Ismaël falls in the water), and by the sea (as in the scene of swimming with Yasmina and Jacky). Even more importantly, the sea and the port appear several times in panoramic shots of the city and the coast, shots that, in all cases, show Ismaël looking out, towards the south, towards Africa and Tunisia. Often a ferryboat is included in the frame, confirming the supposition that Ismaël is thinking about his homeland. Similar images can be found in a recent film by Algerian-born director Philippe Faucon, *Samia*, the story of an Algerian family living in northern Marseilles, which is concluded by Samia and her sisters' return by ship to Algeria with their mother.

Marseilles is a crossroads in yet another way, one that is suggested by Dridi himself in the already mentioned interview – this is a city of the *metissage*, in which different ethnic groups cohabit, even if not always peacefully. In this sense, the city-intersection is represented by a specific quarter, the central Panier, or Vieille Ville (old town), surrounding the Vieux-Port and traversed by the artery of La Canebière, first inhabited by Italian immigrants. The choice of the Panier, 'something in-between

Belleville and Barbès, plus sun and sea' (Bouquet 1995a: 38; our translation), was dictated, according to Dridi himself, both by a desire to
avoid the northern areas of Marseilles, often shown on French television
as an example of suburban disquiet, and by the director's shocked
reaction to 'Chirac's reflection on the bad odours in the cities of
immigrants: I wanted to make a film that suggested the opposite' (Jousse
and Lalanne 1995: 38; our translation). The Panier is a popular and
multi-ethnic area, predominantly inhabited by immigrants, but – unlike
the northern *cités*, suburbs whose squalid living conditions are described
by Jean-Claude Izzo in his three noir novels (*Total Khéops*, 1995; *Chourmo*,
1996; *Solea* 1998) – it retains the feel of an old Mediterranean city
centre. Dridi and cinematographer John Mathieson used the space of
the Panier 'as a centripetal force that ensures the coherence of the
ensemble', and filmed this area as enveloped in a warm light, which
makes the quarter live 'physically and almost carnally' (Bouquet 1995a:
38; our translation). The depiction of the Panier, though, is neither
picturesque nor stereotypical. The cinematic image of Pagnol's old town
is revisited and updated: prostitution and drug-dealing are widespread
in the streets, graffiti are visible on the walls, youngsters wear coloured
T-shirts of their favourite groups, rap and traditional North African
music mix and merge, conveying the feel of a postmodern city-intersection where the barriers between different cultures fade. It must be
said that not everything is non-stereotypical in *Bye-Bye*. The figure of
the dealer Renard is, for instance, rather conventional, and Dridi himself
recognizes that he has his models in the characters of films like *Scarface*
(Jousse and Lalanne 1995: 39); but for precisely the reason that he
comes out of an American film, Renard is another sign of the globalization that characterizes postmodern European culture.

Inside the quarter of Panier is the house of Ismaël's uncle, which
reproduces on a smaller scale the figure of the intersection: the uncle
is Algerian, the aunt is Moroccan, the children are Algerian, Ismaël and
Mouloud are Tunisian. The house is also an intersection of different
generations, genders and values – in particular, the uncle represents the
attachment to tradition and patriarchy, as opposed to his son Rhida
who epitomizes the French-born generation trying to find a place in the
local culture burdened with contradictory attitudes of adoption and at
the same time rejection of its values. In the middle is the aunt, a strong
and intelligent woman who mediates between past and present, Africa
and France, tradition and integration. Ismaël's position is unclear – he

9. *Bye Bye* (1995), dir. Karim Dridi

is often seen looking at the sea, probably thinking of Tunisia, but his return home is never envisaged, unlike Mouloud's. He is strongly affected by his guilt for the death of his handicapped brother, which is slowly revealed in a series of flashbacks to have been a true accident. In fact, Ismaël's remorse seems more the materialization of his guilt for not being able to protect his brothers, as his role of eldest son would traditionally require. This feeling is therefore a sign of Ismaël's not unproblematic detachment from traditional values, and in fact his gazing towards Africa looks less like a longing and more like a questioning of fading traditions and responsibilities. Not surprisingly, at the end of the narrative Ismaël will not send his brother to Tunisia, thus challenging his father's will and authority.

Marseilles in *Bye-Bye* is represented as a crossroads of cultures, peoples, migrations and epochs. The old Mediterranean quality of its centre is partly preserved, partly changed by the new lifestyles of the *metissage*, the mix of cultures typical of postmodern Europe. Some characters react rigidly to the change, and adopt extreme positions, like Ludo and his Front National-type friends, but also like Ismaël's father who inflexibly but impotently tries to preserve old traditions. The younger generation looks instead for a place in this society and for a new way of living, but they suffer from a lack of valid models who can show the way. Mouloud tentatively but boldly looks for his own way in life, as shown by his self-written rap in which he sings of his disdain for the title '*beur*' (given to people of Maghrebi descent), as well as by his election of Renard as his model. Ismaël, instead, is paralysed by his feelings of guilt for his detachment from paternal authority and from the past – but he will find at least the courage to say bye-bye to Marseilles, city-intersection, place of passage, and to continue his search elsewhere.

Nenette et Boni: Out of the City, into the Womb

Nenette et Boni (1996) is the fifth fiction feature by Claire Denis, former assistant to Rivette, to Jarmusch and to Wenders, and the director of *Chocolat* (1988), *S'en fout la mort* (1990), *J'ai pas sommeil* (1994) and *Beau travail* (1999). *Nenette et Boni* is better described as a dream-like, sensual flux of images that first enfolds the audience and then draws them inside the film, as if it were under the skin of its protagonist, Boni. This result is achieved through a skilful use of the filmic technique: a close-to-the-skin framing style, characterized by an abundance of close-ups and detail shots, particularly those on Boni's body and face; the adoption of a lightweight hand-held camera, permitting greater mobility and speed; and the systematic avoidance of the standard markers of the distinction between 'real' and 'imaginary' sequences.

Nenette and Boni are a young brother and sister who have lived apart for some time as a consequence of their parents' separation. Fifteen-year-old Nenette has lived with their father Felix, a lampshade salesman who has shady connections with racketeering; she now attends a boarding school. Nineteen-year-old Boni stayed with their mother and, after her recent death, has continued to live in her house. Boni works as a pizza-maker in a van with some friends, and spends most of his time lost in erotic fantasies about the sensual local baker's wife. His routine and isolation from reality are broken only by the arrival of his sister Nenette, who has run away from school and is looking for shelter. At first Boni rejects her and is annoyed by what he perceives as an unwanted intrusion, but when he finds out that his sister is pregnant, he accepts her presence, makes room for her, accompanies her to the gynaecologist. When Nenette is told that it is too late for her to have an abortion, she decides to have the child and then give him away; but after she gives birth Boni breaks into the hospital and kidnaps his nephew, determined to give him a family.

Boni lives in the 14th arrondissement of Marseilles, an area northwest of the city centre, of the Vieux-Port and the Panier. The city is inconspicuous in the film, as almost no landmark is shown, if we exclude a quick view of the port – and in fact we could be almost anywhere else in Europe. The urban fabric and city life described by the film are characterized by an intense fragmentation. The population is a mix of tradition and innovation – on the one hand immigrants from the Philippines and Taiwan, but also from the United States (the American baker); on the other hand, established local figures, straight from a Pagnol film, such as the *boulangère* and *boulanger* (who is once seen dressed like a sailor), or from more recent and violent depictions of Marseilles, such as the three mafia men, who first abuse Felix for not paying his dues, then send two hitmen on a motorbike to shoot him in the head.

The fragmentation is not solely conveyed by the diverse composition of the population. The camera never shows an overview of the city and uncovers only small portions of streets and locales; there is no centre or meeting place for the characters, and this gap is epitomized by Boni's way of working, driving around in his pizza van. The characters' lives lack not only a physical centre, but also permanence. Not even the family functions as a hub – in fact, it only replicates the dispersion and transience that characterize the city. Boni greatly suffers from this situation. At the beginning of the film he is portrayed as strong and at ease when in his house. Here he does as he pleases, and seems to dominate his environment, but his self-confidence is mainly the result of isolation from real life, so much so that Nenette's arrival is experienced as an intrusion that tears apart Boni's poise, but that also ends his detachment from reality. Before her arrival, we see him on the balcony, looking out on the surrounding roofs and confidently exclaiming, 'This is my neighbourhood!' Significantly, though, the film never conveys a sense of 'neighbourhood'. Even the local bakery does not function as a meeting point and does not help to forge a sense of community, partly because the shop is depicted as a series of detached fragments of a place, partly because it is a setting for Boni's erotic fantasies, and therefore it is also an imaginary place. At one stage the *boulangère* laments that they must keep up with the competition, hence the lotto that they organized – in this city there is no sheltered life for a local shop. Boni's house, instead, is a safe haven, which must be protected from the outside and from any intrusion, even by resorting to a rifle with which he scares his unwanted father away. The camerawork constructs the house as an

10.   *Nenette et Boni* (1996), dir. Claire Denis

enclosed, dark, almost damp place, saturated with shades of blue, enveloped around Boni's sensual, often naked body – a body that sharply contrasts with his adolescent face. The young man seems to float in this place, as much as Nenette is shown floating in the water of a swimming pool at the beginning of the film, her long black hair suspended around her face. Of course, these remarks suggest a home-uterus, an idea indirectly confirmed by Denis. When preparing to shoot, the filmmaker was thinking about Marseilles' sea as an amniotic liquid wetting the city (Bouquet 1995b: 37; Bouquet 1996: 55). Whereas this idea was not developed in the film, it has certainly had an influence on the construction of the place in which Boni lives. It is significant that this is the house of Nenette and Boni's mother, and one still strongly marked by her presence/absence, as in the sequence in which Nenette spends some time in her room, left untouched since her death, looking at her mother's picture and smelling her clothes. The reaction against the father's intrusion is even more significant if read from this perspective – as the invasion of a place that the man had already deserted, or from which he had already been expelled. In this safe womb, Boni leads a sensual, gratifying and safe life detached from the outside and from reality; when he has to go out, he does so in his van, which functions as an extension of the mother's uterus – and in fact here the erotic fantasies of fusion with Woman can continue. The one time that we see him in the city without his van, Boni stands for an extended period in the middle of a crowded footpath, staring in front of himself, petrified, lost, almost carried away by the flow of people; the baker's wife, the object of his fantasies, comes up to him and invites him to a café, where he just sits and stares at her for the whole time, incapable of saying even one word.

After Boni realizes that his sister is pregnant, his attention shifts to Nenette and the life growing inside her; she is now the uterus, the link, and the mother. Boni detaches himself from his fantasies, tries to convince his sister not to abort and not to abandon her child. He wants to know who the father is, and Nenette's reticence makes us even suspect that she was the victim of incest – even if the film will never confirm this suspicion. Nenette and Boni's bodies draw closer to each other and experience once again – or for the first time – that siblings' feeling of reciprocal attraction, the sense of belonging, of being one and the same, of having inhabited the same womb. Boni leans over his sister and feels the foetus's movements. When he accompanies her to the doctor, he assumes the role of husband and father. For a while he seems to succumb to his sister's determination, but ultimately he reacts and, after the birth, kidnaps the baby and takes him home. Fantasy or reality, we cannot know – the camerawork in this film has consistently blurred the difference between imagination and truth. It is clear, though, that Boni wants to give Nenette's child the sense of wholeness and unity that he has not been given, and protect him from the fragmentation of the social and urban environment. The last images of the film show him holding the baby in his arms, in close contact with his bare skin.

Marius et Jeannette: Re-enchanting the City in Ruins

Robert Guédiguian's *Marius et Jeannette* (1998) is set in the peripheral and proletarian area of Estaque, north of Marseilles, where the director was born. The film is even defined in the opening titles as 'un conte de l'Estaque', a tale from the Estaque. Here most of the director's films take place. After making *Dieu vomit les tièdes* (1989), in fact, Guédiguian ironically described himself as a 'district filmmaker'; nevertheless, his films are set by his admission in a wider, northern area of Marseilles, and other parts of the city are often shown. Lately Guédiguian has widened his cinematographic horizons: *À la place du coeur* (1998), for instance, is set in other areas of Marseilles, and a section of this film even takes place in bombed Sarajevo. In *Marius et Jeannette*, however, the camera never leaves the Estaque and the rest of Marseilles does not feature at all in this film. Estaque is a small port with 8000 inhabitants; here Marseilles' last remaining shantytown can be found. Immigration, unemployment and delinquency are widespread; an old communist bastion, the Estaque has recently seen a growth in allegiance to the far-Right movement of the Front National.

Jeannette lives with her children Megali and Malek in a house that opens on to a courtyard, as do those of their neighbours – Dédé and Monique, a married couple with three young children; Justin, a retired teacher; and Caroline, who in her youth was sent to a Nazi concentration camp on account of her communist background. Jeannette, who has lost her job at the checkout of a supermarket due to her unrelenting critical spirit, meets Marius, who works as a security man in the local cement works, now in the process of being dismantled. Marius, who confesses to Jeannette that he got the job over an unending queue of unemployed men by pretending he had a limp, begins to visit the courtyard regularly in order to help Jeannette paint her house. In the next few weeks he establishes a relationship not only with her, but also with her children and her neighbours. One day, Marius does not show up. Jeannette refuses to look for him, but Dédé and Justin bring him back to her after hearing from a drunken Marius the secret that had kept him away: one night he lost his wife and two children in a car accident.

The Estaque in *Marius et Jeannette* is represented as a city in ruins – most of the environments shown point to a better past and signify decay. The film is set mainly in two places: the abandoned cement works and the courtyard of Jeannette's house. Little else of the city is seen – the supermarket where Jeannette used to work; a restaurant in the park where Marius and Jeannette dine; a street market where the ingredients for a communal aïoli are bought; a sunny beach; and the port, which is seen at the beginning of the film, in a metaphorical sequence in which a globe floats towards the shore accompanied by a traditional song ('Il pleut sur Marseille'), and twice afterwards, first when Jeannette joins a long queue of unemployed women applying for a job, then when Marius, Dédé and Justin sober up after a fight in a bar.

The cement works is a key location in the film. It is the setting of Jeannette and Marius's meeting. Jeannette's father used to work there, and there he died because of an exploding steam-pipe when he was only thirty-six. Not only Jeannette, but other characters as well are saddened and even offended by the dismantling of the cement works, which is regarded by them as a part of their life and as a symbol of their town and their social class. 'Why is this cement works being demolished? They must have a reason for doing it, but we will never find out. Who has made the decision, and when, to destroy the place where my father died? By what right? People still use cement, don't they?' Jeannette's reaction should not be read only at a personal level, but also stands for the people's frustration at decisions taken over their heads, for no apparent reason. The transformation of the urban landscape in postmodern times includes the dismantling and sometimes relocation of factories, which are seen by planners as unsightly and useless remnants of modern society. A consequence of changes in the local economy, often dictated by global capitalism, these events should not just be seen as part of that constitutive element of postmodern planning, the 'beautification' of the urban landscape, but also as the effacement of places that have been the symbol of employment and perhaps of the dream of social progress for whole generations of citizens, as well as the locus of the development of feelings of belonging to a place and to a social class. The erasure of such sites thus can provoke a widespread experience of displacement and loss of identity.

The characters in Guédiguian's film, though, have not given up the struggle. The women in particular display a belligerent spirit, softened only by their acute sense of humour – Jeannette is not scared of being fired and continues to complain about the working conditions in the supermarket; Caroline is the political conscience of the group, reads *L'Humanité*, and protests against Castro's openness to capitalism and the Church's attitude to family planning; Monique urges her husband to go on strike and keeps making fun of him because he once voted for the Front National. Even Jeannette's young daughter decides to move to Paris to become a journalist and, as we are told by the voice-over that accompanies the film's last sequence, one day she will write: 'The walls of the poor of the Estaque are painted by Cézanne on canvas that will fatally end up on the walls of the rich.' The three main male characters of the film seem to be more drained by life. Taciturn Marius is still conditioned by the shocking memory of the loss of his family, and finds it difficult to begin a new relationship and expose himself to the risks of life once again. Naive Dédé, whose faith in communist ideals is vacillating, no longer sees the point in striking, and has been tempted by the different solutions offered by the far-Right movement – a change of political position that lured many French proletarians, and that was also described in depth by Guédiguian in *La ville est tranquille* [The Town is Quiet, 2000]. Justin is the philosopher of the group, and twice during the film we see him discussing religion and integration with his friends' children.

Confronted with a current socio-economic situation that marginalizes them, the characters react by forming a community, based on their belonging to the proletariat in general and to the Estaque proletariat in particular. Guédiguian's narrative invention of such a compact working-class society, strongly based on love and friendship, but also on the sharing of communal roots and values, has been seen by some critics as too idealistic – but the irony and sometimes cynicism that accompany the characters' general attitude testifies to an awareness of their belonging to a postmodern, post-ideological era.

The most important action taken by the community is the requisition of spaces and their subsequent transformation into liveable, even enchanted places. The dismantled cement factory, whose demolition continues during the film, is not only the place where Marius works or the cradle of personal memories, the characters use its space in many significant ways. Jeannette and Marius first meet and later have important conversations here, such as the one about Jeannette's past love life. Jeannette, following her father's death, has developed the habit of coming here on her own to think – thus the place is invested with a specific function in her life. Later in the film all the main characters and their children meet at the cement works to prepare and then share an aïoli. During the lunch, eaten on an improvised table in the open air, Caroline informs her friends that the palace of the Pope in Avignon has been declared a world heritage site and complains that only places where the rich, the popes and the kings have lived can aspire to such a status, whereas a place like this cement works never will, despite its beauty. 'Why don't they declare this cement works a world heritage site? It is beautiful, it is magnificent, this cement works!' After lunch, the open courtyard of the factory even becomes a dancing platform for the characters.

The cement works is not the only site in ruins to be appropriated and transformed by the characters. Jeannette's house is literally falling to pieces at the beginning of the film, so much so that she tries to steal some paint from the factory. Marius stops her, but later brings her the paint and even helps her to redecorate. This act of redecoration brings Marius and Jeannette close to each other, and brings them happiness – while painting Marius whistles 'O sole mio', the famous popular song expressing joy in the simple things of everyday life. Once the house has been redecorated, we see Jeannette hanging a painting on a wall and taking pleasure in admiring it. The redecorated house becomes the home of a new family, that formed by Marius, Jeannette and her two children.

Whereas we never see the interiors of the other characters' houses, we are frequently shown the courtyard, with windows and balconies opening on to it. The courtyard, the locus of the communal life of the neighbours, also shows signs of decay, but the act of using it as a shared home transforms it into a beautiful and cheerful place. Children are often seen playing outside; the whole group watches a football match on television in the courtyard one evening; Caroline and Justin, who are occasionally lovers but never got married, share a romantic dinner on Caroline's balcony. The way in which its inhabitants use the courtyard transforms it into a sort of Brechtian but charming theatre, in which opinions are exchanged, advice is given, cheerful and sad moments are shared.

As well as the cement works and the characters' houses, the third place to be requisitioned by Guédiguian's characters is an abandoned house in ruins, with its stone walls half-crumbled and invaded by vegetation. Marius and Jeannette at the beginning of their relationship use it as a bedroom to make love. A well-known symbol of Romanticism, the house in ruins could signify melancholy and refer to a better past, but once again the characters occupy it and bring it to life with their presence and imagination.

'Re-enchantment' and 'beautification' are key words in the postmodern conception of urban living. In *Marius et Jeannette*, these concepts are borrowed and then redefined as in a proletarian fairytale, partly reminiscent of *Miracolo a Milano* [Miracle in Milan, 1951]. In De Sica's film, a group of homeless people, led by naive and generous Totò, build a shantytown in a deserted and frozen land on the outskirts of Milan. This poor and desolate place is transformed by the characters' will and imagination into a true community, with streets, squares and a village fair. Whereas *Miracle in Milan* ultimately denies its destitute characters a place to live on this earth, and sends them flying away on brooms towards an unspecified 'better land', *Marius et Jeannette* grants its prolet-

11.   *Marius et Jeanette* (1998), dir. Robert Guédiguian

arian community a decent future of love and friendship, confirmed by the voice-over that, at the end of the film, describes the events awaiting the characters.

Conclusions

Whereas in many recent films set in Marseilles the city is either not obviously present or is shown as a stereotypical postmodern 'any-town', Dridi's *Bye-Bye* and Guédiguian's *Marius et Jeannette* are strongly connected to and amply describe the urban areas in which they are set – the central, old quarter of Panier and the northern periphery of the Estaque respectively. In Denis' *Nenette et Boni*, instead, the relationship between the film and the city is more loose, and Marseilles is shown as a worryingly fragmented environment that pushes the young characters towards withdrawal and seclusion. Each of the three films offers a particular vision of Marseilles. Dridi's *Bye-Bye* chooses to look at a cosmopolitan, multi-ethnic and Mediterranean Marseilles, a port, a city-intersection where cultures and old and new lifestyles clash and are not reconciled – to the extent that the protagonists precipitously leave the city at the end of the film, heading in an unknown direction. Denis' *Nenette et Boni* privileges a more 'continental' Marseilles and presents it as an unknowable, fragmented city that could be found almost anywhere else in Europe. Guédiguian's *Marius et Jeannette* concentrates on an area of the city that is almost a town of its own, and on a close-knit proletarian community within this area. *Marius et Jeannette*'s city is epitomized by a neighbourhood showing evident Mediterranean and local traditions, which is confronted by the changes brought about by globalization and late capitalism. Together, the three films present the image of a strongly postmodern city, in the process of evolving towards new forms of urban and social life.

II

Postcommunist Europe

Cities and Cinemas after Socialism

Central and Eastern Europe have experienced a dramatic transformation in the last decade: the shift from communism to postcommunism. The main cause of this upheaval was the same in all the countries involved: an acute crisis in the socialist political and economic system. The forces that produced these changes were predominantly urban, even metropolitan; the destruction of the Berlin Wall in East Germany, the Velvet Revolution in Czechoslovakia, the overcoming of the Russian military coup and, more recently, the rejection of President Milosevic's rule in Serbia all took place in the respective capital cities. As Michael Harloe notes, 'the Soviet system, which was born as an immediate consequence of an urban-based struggle for dominance, between 1989 and 1991 died in similar locations' (Harloe 1996: 1).

After the collapse of communism, urban and metropolitan life experienced greater changes than life in provincial towns or in the country. For example, East Berlin, united with West Berlin, became the capital of the most populated country in Europe, while Prague lost its status as the capital of the whole of Czechoslovakia. Moreover, many capitals and large postcommunist cities quickly acquired a 'capitalist' veneer and nowadays look not unlike their Western counterparts. The old Soviet bloc was by no means homogeneous in terms of politics, economy and culture. Similarly, there were great variations between socialist cities.

The break-up of the European socialist world exposed and increased some of the old differences and brought about new ones. For example, some of the cities became arenas of acute ethnic and political conflicts. This applies particularly to cities of the former Yugoslavia, such as Sarajevo, but also to a large extent to Moscow and Berlin, which became the centres of extreme-Right movements.

There were also significant, if less dramatic, changes in the cinematographies of the old Soviet bloc countries. Although in most postcommunist countries the state still plays an important role in supporting the national cinema, it no longer is the sole source of funds for film production, as more and more films have access to private resources. As a result of this, as well as abandoning the traditional political censorship, the state became less powerful in imposing on filmmakers a particular subject, ideology or style. On the other hand, filmmakers from Central and Eastern Europe experienced new constraints and challenges, resulting from the requirement to compete with increasing numbers of foreign films, particularly American, and to repay the costs of production. The strategies of competition vary from one country to another and even from one filmmaker to the next. For example, one of the most distinctive cinematic phenomena after the collapse of communism in Poland is that of criminal films and of comedies that emulate the style of Hollywood films, and of heritage cinema based on nineteenth-century literary masterpieces. However, a substantial proportion of postcommunist films, particularly those enjoying recognition in their native countries and abroad, are urban, even metropolitan, both in their setting and in showing specific problems, as well as advantages, that result from living in a large city. Through the analysis of a number of films set in three cities, Warsaw, Moscow and Berlin, an analysis conducted in a broad historical and cultural context, we aim to show the relationship between these films' content and form and some of the changes that have taken place in Central and Eastern Europe since the collapse of communism. Claiming that such a relationship exists does not imply that the films reflect these changes in any simple sense. However, our argument is that they do respond to them somehow and that the manner of this response helps to create the cultural perspective through which the viewers perceive the environment in which they live.

5

Any Town? Warsaw in *Girl Guide* and *Kiler* by Juliusz Machulski

Among the postcommunist countries, Poland is regarded as the one that made the greatest progress towards assimilation with the Western world. The return to democracy and the introduction of a capitalist economy, including privatization of state-owned enterprises, moved faster and the living standards of its citizens increased on average more than in the neighbouring ex-communist countries. Among the states of the old Soviet bloc, Poland is also in the vanguard of those seeking early membership of Western economic and political structures, such as the European Union and NATO. Being relatively homogeneous in terms of ethnic composition, religion and regional constitution, Poland also managed to avoid many of the problems and conflicts experienced by countries such as Yugoslavia, Slovakia, East Germany or the old Soviet Union.

Along with satisfaction and pride in economic progress and political stability, there is also a loud lament for the country's apparent loss of its distinctive national identity, and a backlash against Poland's rapid westernization is discernible. Cinema, particularly films about contemporary times, as well as film criticism, played a significant role in the debate about the new Polish cultural identity. The most common criticism voiced with reference to films made after the collapse of communism was their indifference towards Poland's uniqueness. In an article written in 1997, the critic Andrzej Kolodynski argues that in the bulk of Polish films made in the 1990s – such as *Nocne graffiti* [Night Graffiti, 1996] by Maciej Dutkiewicz, *Tato* [Dad, 1995] and *Sara* (1997) by Maciej Slesicki, *Szamanka* [Shaman, 1996] by Andrzej Zulawski, *Pulapka* [Trap, 1997] by Adek Drabinski and *Sztos* [The Sting, 1997] by Olaf Lubaszenko – most of which are set in Warsaw, it is hardly possible to recognize the town or even the country where the story was set. It could be, as he put it, 'any place, any town' (Kolodynski 1997: 33). This, as Kolodynski suggests, applies not only to the appearance of the streets, which are stripped of any recognizable Polish features, but also to the characters' lifestyles. This unwillingness to reveal details of contemporary Polish culture results from a desire on the part of the young directors (and some older ones) both to avoid any accusation of parochialism and to produce films that are able, at least in the Polish market, to compete with American mainstream movies. The results of these attempts are in most cases contrary to what was intended: the films look like second-rate imitations of American productions. Against the background of contemporary mainstream movies, *Girl Guide* (1995) and *Kiler* (1997), two films made by Juliusz Machulski (b. 1955), commercially the most successful Polish director in the whole postwar era, look somewhat different. They are lauded by the critics as more professional than the productions of his colleagues and less naive in their desire to emulate the style of Tarantino. However, Machulski is also accused of insufficient use of the local culture, of unwillingness to show Warsaw and Poland as they really are (Kolodynski 1997: 33; Berent 1996: 74).

Like a Phoenix from the Ashes – Warsaw after the Second World War

Since the end of the Second World War, Warsaw had served not only as a film location, but also as an important element of the narrative, almost a character in its own right.[1] The elevation of Warsaw in Polish cinema to this high position (matched by its prominent presence in poetry and fine arts of the postwar period) stemmed from its tragic fate during the last stages of the war, particularly in the Warsaw Uprising of 1944, when it was completely destroyed. By 1945 over 90 per cent of the buildings were razed to the ground and fewer than 20,000 inhabitants remained. After the war Warsaw 'rose like a phoenix from the ashes'; an extensive programme of rebuilding was introduced, leading to the

reconstruction of the Renaissance Old City and almost all other monumental buildings and later still Warsaw became the largest city in Poland,
reaching a population of over 1.6 million by 2000.

Between 1945 and the early 1960s Warsaw featured in over forty
films. These can be divided into three main types. The first celebrated
the city's resurrection after the war's devastation, the most famous being
Skarb [Treasure, 1948] and *Przygoda na Mariensztacie* [Adventure on
Mariensztat, 1953], both directed by Leonard Buczkowski. *Treasure*, which
is regarded as the most successful Polish film made before the advent
of the Polish School, showed the tragicomical trials and tribulations of
a young couple after the Second World War trying to find a place to
live. The end of their story was marked by receiving the keys to their
own apartment in a new council block. Directors of the Polish School,
such as Andrzej Wajda in *Pokolenie* [Generation, 1954] and *Kanal* [Canal,
1956] or Andrzej Munk in *Eroica* (1957), concentrated, on the other
hand, not on the communal efforts to rebuild the capital, but on the
grievous situation of Warsaw during the war. The films of Andrzej
Wajda, whose visual style was described by Raymond Durgnat as 'tormented baroque' (Durgnat 1967: 114) – in Poland his style was compared
to Expressionism – are particularly important, because they contributed
in a major way to the myth of Warsaw as the ultimate martyr, sacrificed
for the life and freedom of the whole country. A notable exception to
this rule was Wajda's *Niewinni czarodzieje* [Innocent Sorcerers, 1960], which
centres on young, hedonistic Warsawians, who seem to forget the horrors
of the war and enjoy the pleasures of cafés, jazz clubs and strolling in
the Old City. Piotr Lis describes *Innocent Sorcerers* as a film that captures
its *genus loci*, being an almost perfect portrayal of Warsaw (Lis 1989:
275). There was also a handful of films that referred to Warsaw's more
distant past, such as *Warszawska premiera* [Warsaw's Premiere, 1950] by
Jan Rybkowski, set in the middle of the nineteenth century, or Tadeusz
Makarczynski's *Warszawska syrenka* [Warsaw Mermaid, 1955] about Warsaw's mythical beginnings. They served a similar function to *Treasure* or
Adventure on Mariensztat – boosting the morale of those who lived in
Warsaw under difficult postwar conditions.

After the end of the Polish School the presence of Warsaw in Polish
films gradually diminished. If it was represented at all, it rarely played an
important narrative function. The exception were comedies, particularly
Stanislaw Bareja's *Nie ma rozy bez ognia* [Every Rose Has Thorns, 1974],
concerned with the shortage of flats in Warsaw and the bureaucracy that

had to be overcome in order to register as living in Warsaw. Interestingly, the majority of films from the most distinctive paradigm in the Polish cinema after the Polish School, the Cinema of Moral Concern, such as Krzysztof Kieslowski's *Amator* [Camera Buff, 1979], Agnieszka Holland's *Aktorzy prowincjonalni* [Provincial Actors, 1978], Andrzej Wajda's *Dyrygent* [Conductor, 1979] or Feliks Falk's *Wodzirej* [Top Dog, 1977], were all set in provincial Poland. The reason for this was the desire to show a particularly grey, grim, depressing and corrupt Poland. However, even in these films Warsaw was somehow present, because their provincial protagonists, as Piotr Lis observes (Lis 1989: 267), typically equated career with emigration to the capital.

In the 1980s the most interesting portrayal of Warsaw was provided by two television series: *Dekalog* (1988) by Krzysztof Kieslowski and *Alternatywy 4* [4 Alternatywy Street, 1981], a satirical comedy by Stanislaw Bareja, director of *Every Rose Has Thorns*. Both were set on housing estates, far from the city centre, Ursynow in *Dekalog* and Natolin in *4 Alternatywy Street*. Both estates consisted of ugly, poor-quality blocks with no cultural or community centres such as cinemas, pubs or restaurants. Even the roads were hardly passable with potholes and puddles of water. Moreover, in Bareja's film the newly built housing estate, complete with an image of a cow grazing on the grass a few yards from the blocks and some residents keeping pigeons in a nearby shed, looks more rural than metropolitan. In spite of the many similarities between the urban design, Kieslowski and Bareja give a very different view of life in an apartment block. Kieslowski's characters live in almost complete anonymity, shut in their flats, unable and unwilling to talk to their neighbours. In Bareja's comedy, on the other hand, they create a tightly-knit community. This is partly due to the caretaker, who introduces an almost Stalinist regime to the block for which he is responsible. He forces the inhabitants to take part in many communal activities, such as cleaning the block's surroundings or organizing festivals. Eventually, they forge an informal coalition and overthrow him. The 1980s were the last decade when Polish filmmakers ridiculed the communal and regimented lives of inhabitants of co-operatively owned tenement blocks. Ten years after the collapse of communism the vast majority of urban Poles still live in the blocks, but nobody in authority forces them to live like a community or to adhere to any particular set of values.

Girl Guide – Graffiti Warsaw

Girl Guide reflects this new, more individualistic spirit of life in Warsaw. The narrative revolves around a mysterious suitcase belonging to the American Gary Wise, who supposedly comes to Poland in order to marry his Polish girlfriend, Kinga. In reality, however, the purpose of his visit is to sell the contents of the suitcase – a computer able to launch missiles, called 'Girl Guide' – to the Arabs who plan to use it in war. Soon after arriving, Gary disappears and Kinga sets out to find him. She does this with the help of her English teacher, Jozek, who is secretly in love with her. After a series of tragicomic incidents the suitcase is destroyed, gangsters belonging to various groups shoot each other and Kinga and Jozek end up with half a million dollars. Moreover, after learning about Gary's true identity and Jozek's intelligence and bravery, Kinga gives up her rogue fiancé and returns Jozek's love with equal affection.

Jozek is the main character and the narrator of the film. He is a graduate in English philology who has come to Warsaw from a small village in the mountains. In Warsaw he does not look for a regular job, but tries to make his living by giving private English lessons, promising 'to teach English in six weeks'. Although on several occasions he describes himself as an unsettled person who does not have much to be proud of, his material surroundings and social milieu suggest otherwise. Perhaps he is not rich, but his standard of living is well above the average for Poland. The apartment that he rents is not the usual cramped 'bachelor flat' sought by those who come to Warsaw from the provinces in pursuit of work, but several spacious rooms filled with hundreds of books, modernist pictures hanging on the walls and an old-fashioned stove. Moreover, it is not located in any of the anonymous, suburban housing estates where the majority of Warsawians live, but in the Old City, the most elegant and expensive part of Warsaw, associated with the prewar intelligentsia. From his wrought-iron balcony, Jozek enjoys a pleasant view of trees and the Palace of Culture. There is no noise as cars are excluded from this part of Warsaw.

Jozek's choice of friends matches his choice of accommodation. His spiritual mentor is Mr Michalak, a blind musician who discusses with Jozek the subtleties of Glenn Gould's interpretation of Bach. Mr Michalak also lives in an old flat, presumably in the Old City, having an old piano and plenty of vinyl discs. Another Warsaw flat shown in *Girl*

Guide belongs to Kinga. It is a typically feminine place, full of flowers and warm, soft furnishings. Each flat has its own, distinctive style, contrasting with the uniformity typical of earlier, communist times. The route between these three flats is never shown. When Jozek leaves his flat, the cut is made directly to the apartment of Kinga or Mr Michalak. This creates the impression that all the characters live within walking distance of each other. Similarly, there are no bus or tram journeys, which filled much of the time in *4 Alternatywy Street*. When the characters meet in the city, they are always walking to their destinations. There are only a handful of scenes actually shot on the streets of Warsaw (which is partly the result of the film's relatively small budget). In contrast to Kieslowski, who concentrated on anonymous, grey suburbs, filled with archetypal communist blocks, Machulski limits himself to showing only the centre of Warsaw, such as the Old City and Aleje Jerozolimskie, the street where the most important buildings are placed. The bulk of them were erected before the war and during the period of communism. The only building shown by Machulski in all its glory is the shiny skyscraper housing the Marriott Hotel, the Polish National Airlines offices, casinos and some expensive shops. This building, known simply as 'Marriott', which was started in the 1970s and was finished after the collapse of communism thanks to foreign investment, epitomizes the new, post-communist Warsaw. The colours are bright and warm, with plenty of red. On the whole, Warsaw seems to be pleasant, compact and accessible, a perfect place for contemporary *flâneurs*.

The first scene in *Girl Guide* is one of the most meaningful. It opens with fast edited shots of a long wall covered in graffiti. Suddenly a part of the mural comes to life and takes the shape of a young man, one side of whose face and body is painted. He turns to show the other, unpainted side. This man is Jozek, the main character of the story. Wherever Jozek goes, graffiti accompany him. First, he and Kinga play on a seesaw against the background of a wall covered with graffiti. After Kinga visits him with Gary, he covers the walls and doors of his rented flat with colourful shapes, recollecting the styles of Picasso and Matisse. Later he approaches his musician friend who allows him to stay in a small room behind a garage, where his rock band rehearses. Again, the garage is covered with murals. The set recollects the garage-loft where Jules, the main character of *Diva* (1981) by Jean-Jacques Beineix, lives. In both places one finds gigantic murals, masses of sound equipment and strange *objects d'art*, such as pieces of armour. Even their

12. *Girl Guide* (1995), dir. Juliusz Machulski

narrative functions are similar, as both are invaded by gangsters. Yet, there are also differences – the garage where Jozek lives is smaller, more modest than Jules's loft. The murals are also different – the French one is a photorealistic image of cars and women, bearing associations with David Hockney's pictures and television advertisements, while the Polish is less elaborate and neat, more abstract, rough and wild.

Graffiti are highly controversial. Suzi Gablik, commenting mainly on graffiti in New York, states:

> To many people, the presence of graffiti in the environment has come to symbolize violation, social anarchy, and moral breakdown. They see it as vandalism, pure and simple – a crime signifying that we no longer take orderly society, its laws and arrangements, for granted … There are others, however, who believe graffiti art represents a genuine aesthetic, the personal expression of an oppressed and disenfranchised people … Norman Mailer, an early and sworn supporter, wrote in his 1974 book *The Faith of Graffiti* that the phenomenon was a tribal rebellion against an evil industrial civilization, and 'the beginning of another millennium of vision'. More recently Diego Cortez, who has curated a number of influential exhibitions of work by graffiti artists, stated in *Flash Art* that 'graffiti should be looked at as a highly sophisticated art

form which is the image of New York, and is definitely the soul
of the underground scene at the moment'. (Gablik 1984: 103–4)

Graffiti also played an important part in the youth culture of Russia
and Eastern European countries during the late period of communist
rule, although, obviously, the enemy of graffiti artists in Warsaw, East
Berlin or Moscow was different from that of their counterparts in New
York. It was not 'evil industrial civilization', but collectivism, lack of
personal freedom and the uniformity of communism. Even after the
victory of the Solidarity movement graffiti remained popular among
Polish youngsters, this time often in the form of inscriptions denouncing
the power and hypocrisy of the Catholic Church. It also found its place
in official culture, particularly in Warsaw. For example, in the last years
there were several competitions for graffiti artists, sponsored by the
police. One organized in September 1998 and entitled 'Colour Against
Violence' gathered almost 1000 painters from Warsaw and other parts
of Poland. The artists were asked to cover a wall 300 metres long with
pictures and inscriptions promoting safety on the city streets. The very
popularity of graffiti in the postcommunist world can be regarded as a
part of the wider phenomenon of the shift from high/literary to low/
visual culture (see Condee and Padunov 1995).[2]

In the Polish movies made in the 1990s graffiti feature prominently.
The majority of films previously mentioned, particularly *Shaman* and
Night Graffiti (the title speaks for itself), include images of graffiti. In
terms of iconography, graffiti are the chief common denominator of
films made in Poland in the first decade after the collapse of communism. They are also a 'visual link' between new Polish cinema and its
foreign counterparts. Apart from the previously mentioned *Diva*, one
can find images of graffiti in such films as *Raining Stones* (1993) by
British director Ken Loach, *Slacker* (1991) by American Richard Linklater,
Caricies [Caresses, 1998] by Basque director Ventura Pons, *IP5: L'île aux
pachydermes* [IP5: The Island of Pachyderms, 1992] by Jean-Jacques
Beineix, as well as films discussed in this book, such as the Russian *Taxi
Blues* (1993) by Pavel Lungin, the Spanish *La flor de mi secreto* [The Flower
of My Secret, 1995] by Pedro Almodóvar, the French *Bye-Bye* (1995) by
Karim Dridi, and German *Nachtgestalten* [Night Shapes, 1998] by Andreas
Dresen.

A careful viewing of *Girl Guide* shows a variety of images and
messages painted on the walls, as well as techniques used by the artists.

There are pictures of children and flowers, abstract shapes, symbols, such as the swastika and the hammer and sickle, as well as single words and whole sentences, private messages, such as 'I love Kinga', and political statements. Moreover, there are no separate walls for fascists, communists, rastafarians and those who are simply in love. Similarly, there are common walls for true artists, using sophisticated techniques, and the untidy scribblers. All the signs coexist in apparent harmony, forming a living collage. Often there are many layers of paintings, produced by different artists, for example realistic shapes superimposed on abstract signs. By saturating his film with images of murals, Machulski gives the impression of Warsaw as a young and tolerant city, where people are free and willing to express themselves and where public space is devoted to private messages. Moreover, it is a place of pluralism and heterogeneity of discourses and lifestyles. In 'graffiti Warsaw' the language of ideology no longer matters, as all ideas and opinions are permitted – as long as they do not attempt to impose themselves upon other ideas and opinions. Warsaw in *Girl Guide* is also a city in transition, remembering its past, particularly its pre-communist history, but also looking into the future. Needless to say, this 'graffiti Warsaw' could not exist (even less be represented in official art) in communist Poland. Communism had found it necessary to introduce a hierarchy of ideas and prevent heterogeneity and dissent.

David Harvey points out that collage is the primary means of post-modern discourse:

> The inherent heterogeneity of that (be it in painting, writing, architecture) stimulates us, the receivers of the text or image, to 'produce a signification which could be neither univocal nor stable'. Both producers and consumers of 'texts' (cultural artefacts) participate in the production of significations and meanings ... Minimising the authority of the cultural producer creates the opportunity for popular participation and democratic determinations of cultural values, but at the price of a certain incoherence or, more problematic, vulnerability to mass-market manipulation. (Harvey 1990: 130–72)

Accordingly, the Warsaw of *Girl Guide* is a quintessentially postmodern place. We will also argue that Machulski looks at the brighter side of postmodernism. A 'certain incoherence' seems to be a price worth paying for the 'opportunity for popular participation and democratic determinations of cultural values'; in particular, to paint one's own piece of the wall. Moreover, there are no signs of 'vulnerability to mass-market manipulation'. *Girl Guide* is almost free of the symbols of consumerism, such as fast food restaurants or billboards on the streets. It is also worth adding that graffiti in *Girl Guide* have different connotations than in Zulawski's *Shaman* and Dutkiewicz's *Night Graffiti*. Whereas in Machulski's film graffiti are somehow tamed, domesticated, even legitimized, in the latter films they are still the language of the underworld – their spray-can acrylic pictures convey mainly violent messages and the painted walls serve as a background for vicious, criminal acts, performed mainly at night. The diversity of techniques used by the graffiti artists corresponds to the variety of languages used in the film – apart from English, used by Gary, there are three versions of Polish: a correct one, used by Kinga and Jozek when in Warsaw, mountain dialect, used by Jozek at his mountain home, and broken Polish, used by foreigners.

The omnipresence of murals in Machulski's film significantly reduces the depth of space. One never learns what is behind the colourful surfaces, but some of the Polish viewers probably assume it is something ugly, as it was a Polish speciality in communist times to erect walls in order to conceal decayed or unfinished buildings. This flatness of images also places Machulski close to many other postmodern filmmakers who indulge in the 'aesthetics of surface', such as Pedro Almodóvar, Wong Kar-Wai or Jean-Jacques Beineix.

Jozek's affinity with graffiti is in tune with his multifaceted character and Renaissance or, perhaps, Generation X interests. He can speak as well in 'high' Polish, as in his local mountain dialect. He knows Shakespeare by heart, as well as a smattering of Romanian. His flat is full of books, mainly poetry that was forbidden by the communists. We also learn that he used to play in a rock band and we listen to him joining a group led by his friend and singing '*Chodz tu mila, bedziesz ze mna wino pila*' (Come here, my dear, we will drink wine together). In reality the song is sung by Piersi, a band that uses a postmodern form – mixing rock with folk music – to convey postcommunist messages: promoting hedonism and ridiculing the anti-liberal stance of the Catholic Church. The leader of Piersi, Pawel Kukiz, plays Jozek's part. This reaffirms his character as a postmodern man who is at ease with various traditions, but who does not commit himself to any particular culture or ideology.

The ease with which Jozek changes places, moving from flat to flat, from Warsaw to Cracow, from the city to the country, might have concerned E. M. Forster, who in *Howards End*, written at the beginning of the twentieth century, contrasted Mrs Wilcox's attachment to her family home with the hectic lifestyles of her husband and children, constantly travelling to and from London, but, almost a hundred years later, it looks completely natural. However, in Poland and, accordingly, in its cinematic representations, this mobility is a new thing. Even in the films made in the 1980s, Poles, including Warsawians, were still shown as a static nation. Their homes, however humble, were their castles, where they spent most of their lives. For example, a significant part of the narratives of *4 Alternatywy Street* revolved around characters renovating, enlarging, refurbishing flats or quarrelling with noisy neighbours. They cherished their standardized apartments, knowing that they probably would not be able to afford anything better. The attachment to one's home results also from Polish history, particularly the period of Partitions, when Poland did not exist as a separate state. At the time home stood for the homeland, its walls separated its inhabitants from the enemies. Bachelard's definition of a certain type of house as 'an instrument with which to confront the cosmos' (Bachelard 1969: 46) is an accurate description of the role the house used to play in Polish culture. Jozek's mobility shows not only the transformation of the Polish house, but also the changing role of the 'cosmos' – in the 1990s it is much less strange and terrifying than it used to be in previous epochs.

Not all of *Girl Guide* is set in Warsaw. During the middle part of the film the action shifts to Pisarka,[3] Jozek's home village. The house where his family lives, typical for this region of Poland, is a wooden cottage. However, contrary to expectations, Jozek's family is not a bastion of Polish tradition. The scene that he encounters at home is even more postmodern than anything that was going on in Warsaw – he finds his whole family making music with a group of rastafarians. The song is a mixture of mountain folk music and Jamaican rhythms, sung in English and Polish. Jozek's family is played by the members of the folk group Trebunie-Tutki, well known for performing with the Jamaican reggae group Twinkle Brothers. Still, for Jozek his home and family are too conservative – he mocks his father's traditional hat with feather and the naive pictures hanging on the wall. Ultimately, when his business is completed, he returns to Warsaw, which better suits his cosmopolitan taste.

Kiler – Warsaw of the Nouveaux Riches

The point that Warsaw is no longer the capital of a communist country, but a city enjoying a capitalist economy, is strongly emphasized in *Kiler*. Not only are its inhabitants allowed to buy and sell goods freely, but practically nothing is sacred when it comes to the power of money. Testimony to this is the deal at the centre of the narrative – the selling of the Palace of Culture to a group of foreigners. In order to understand the meaning of the transaction, it is useful to know something about the building itself. Erected by the Russians in 1952–55 as a gift to the Polish nation and surrounded by a large square, it was and still is the most imposing building in Warsaw, effectively marking the centre of the city. It is important to remember that the city centre, as Hartmut Haussermann notes, had a special significance for the planners and builders of socialist cities. Its importance was emphasized by locating a skyscraper there, to underline the 'size and dimension of socialism's victory and … [to] be a symbolic competitor to cathedral-building in the pre-industrial city' (Haussermann 1996: 216). The special significance of the centre was outlined in the *Sixteen Principles of Urban Development* established by the government of East Germany in 1950, and applied in many other countries under the Soviet system:

> The centre is the heart of the city, it is the political centre for its citizens. The most important political, administrative and cultural establishments are in the city centre. On the central squares, political demonstrations, parades and festivals on public holidays take place. The city centre with squares, main avenues and voluptuous buildings (skyscrapers in the big cities) determines the architectural silhouette of the city. Squares are the structural basis for urban development. (Haussermann 1996: 216)

The Palace of Culture not only signified the victory of socialism; the fact that it was named after Josef Stalin and that, when it was erected, several similar buildings already existed in Moscow, drew attention to Polish and Soviet ties, but also suggested Poland's inferiority. Today the connotations of the Palace of Culture are varied and often contradictory. For some, mainly older citizens, it symbolizes Polish oppression at the hands of the Russians during communist rule. After 1989 some even suggested destroying it.[4] The younger generation of Warsawians is usually better disposed towards Poland's tallest skyscraper. They point out that the Palace of Culture stands for Warsaw, in the same way that the Eiffel Tower epitomizes Paris, and that without it Warsaw will lose its identity. Moreover, as time passes, the communist period is gradually losing its sinister taste and the new order is showing its less appealing features, the Palace of Culture awakens nostalgia. Some Poles even discover in this oversized building, surrounded by huge, social-realistic sculptures of athletic men and women, a quality of camp. In his film Machulski appeals to this sensitivity. In an interview given around the time of the film, he admits that he finds the Palace of Culture a very amusing place (Sadowska 1997: 24). It is worth adding that Machulski was not always so 'Palace-friendly' – in one of his earlier films, *Kingsajz* (1987), which can be interpreted as an allegory of the Polish situation during communist times, the building has more ominous connotations. The gnomes, who are the main characters of this film, try to escape from their grim lives in the dusty drawers and eventually come to believe that they have fulfilled their dream and have become 'king-sized' – only to realize that they are still minute. The symbol of their ultimate inability to overcome their predicament is the huge Palace of Culture, which they approach in a miniature train at the end of the film.

At the beginning of the narrative of *Kiler* the Palace of Culture is officially in the hands of a Polish politician and millionaire, businessman Ferdynard Lipski. In reality, he has an informal partner, Siara, who is a powerful gangster. They decide to sell this 'monument of camp' to some Colombians who want to use the deal to launder money. Their plan is to transform the Palace into Europe's largest casino. This idea symbolizes the change of cultural attitudes and realities in Poland – in communist times the Palace of Culture belonged to the state and served only noble purposes, providing a home to three theatres, the Polish Academy of Science and several departments of Warsaw University and hosting the International Book Exhibition. In Machulski's market-economy Poland the Palace will no longer be accessible to the general public and cease serving Culture with a capital 'C'. From a commercial point of view the plans of the Colombians are very ambitious: after finishing their business in Warsaw, they want to go to Moscow to buy the remaining social-realist palaces. When they show Lipski and Siara the photographs of all the buildings, the Poles sigh with admiration and envy – their own affairs, they feel, are very provincial.

The main character of the story is Jerzy Kiler, a taxi driver whose identity is mistaken for 'Kiler', a hitman responsible for killing over forty people, mainly gangsters, in Eastern and Western Europe. Sent to jail and unable to convince anybody of his innocence, he decides to accept his false identity. This gives him a superior status within the prison. Soon Siara organizes his escape and Kiler finds himself the most wanted man in Poland. On the one hand the police offer a large reward for his arrest, on the other many want to hire him for contract killings. Siara wants him to kill Lipski, Lipski wants him to kill Siara, and even Kiler's neighbours organize a collection of money to bribe him to get rid of a man on their street who is a nuisance. Paradoxically, Jerzy is the only man who shows respect for human life. Not only does he not kill anybody, but he also helps the police to catch all the gangsters and the true 'Kiler'.

Machulski creates in his film a caricature of the Polish nouveaux riches, the benefactors of 'crony' capitalism, where businessmen, politicians, gangsters and even policemen support each other in order to achieve their mutual profit. An example is Siara, who has a lavish house somewhere near Warsaw, hidden among trees and bushes and protected by bodyguards. It has many rooms with expensive furnishings, mirrors in silver frames and even swimming pools, but no books or old photographs. Everything here is bought, nothing is inherited. Siara also possesses a flat in the centre of Warsaw, which he offers to Jerzy as a base from which to organize his assassinations. This has a different style, with minimalist, ultra-modern furniture in bright colours and a kitch candlestick in the form of a small deer. Siara's wife, Rysia, tells Jurek with pride that she brought in the best Italian interior designers to give the flat an elegant look. Siara, typically for a modern businessman, enjoys life far from the 'madding crowd' of the city and comes to Warsaw only when he has to arrange deals or – as his wife claims – to have affairs with teenagers from the nearby school.

The attitude of Siara and Rysia to their houses is in deep contrast to the traditional Polish approach to home. For them the house is a symbol of wealth and prestige, not a mythical link with one's past. Similarly, it is no longer the centre of their universe, as that which Yi Fu Tuan calls 'mythical space' (see Tuan 1977) is hugely fragmented – they might be in one home or another, stay in Poland or go abroad, go to the bank in Warsaw or use their Swiss account. They belong everywhere and nowhere. In spite of his lavish surroundings and desire to absorb a Western lifestyle, Siara is a 'homeboy', enjoying simple, Polish pleasures and showing his taste for kitsch. At home he wears a kind of tracksuit decorated in silver and gold, reminiscent of the cheap, Turkish clothing popular in Poland in the 1980s. In his swimming pool he drinks alternately champagne and Polish vodka. His silver crockery is used to serve white sausage, which is a rustic Polish speciality and, when drunk, he sings Polish pop songs from the early 1980s. Moreover, his language, with its use of certain expressions, accents and intonations, betrays a long career as a '*cinkciarz*' – a man illegally changing currencies, a job that practically disappeared with the introduction of the free market economy. Siara's attitude to time can be described as schizophrenic, in the sense assigned to it by Fredric Jameson (1985). He tries to accommodate his communist taste and habits to contemporary times, unaware of the ridiculous effect it produces. Rather than being an individual, Siara epitomizes the whole caste of the Polish nouveaux riches, desperately striving to make up for time lost when Poland was communist and backward. The same can be said of his wife, who also likes shiny clothes and prefers Polish vodka to foreign alcohol.

Another interior shown in the film is in the flat belonging to Ewa, an investigative TV journalist, who first meets Kiler professionally, and then helps him to trap Siara and Lipski. She lives in a loft, with tasteful furniture and a stylish fireplace. After businessmen, gangsters and politicians, she represents the next group of Polish postcommunist 'bourgeoisie' – those working in the media. In the director's own words, the majority of interiors and exteriors featured in his film were not built in the studio, but belonged to actual Warsaw millionaires (Sadowska 1997: 24). This only reaffirms the point that *Kiler* gives exaggerated, albeit true, versions of the lives of rich Warsawians.

Similarly to *Girl Guide*, there are few images of streets and houses in *Kiler* and, once again, this is partly for financial reasons. Machulski, who was also the producer of *Kiler*, admitted that temporal and financial constraints forced him to avoid certain camera movements and more complicated camera positions (Sadowska 1997: 23). The rare camera glimpses into 'real Warsaw' show Poland's capital as industrious and alive, with corner shops and stalls selling fresh fruit and vegetables. There are also images of billboards with gigantic advertisements for mobile phones and rather anaemic graffiti on one of the Vistula bridges, suggesting that the anarchistic 'ecstasy of communication' is giving way to a more ordered and costly way of speaking. Typically for Machulski, long shots and long takes are avoided, preventing the viewer from catching any unexpected glimpses of the ugly parts of the city. In

13. Kiler assumes the look of Travis in *Kiler* (1997), dir. Juliusz
Machulski

contrast, the interiors are shot with thoroughness and attention to detail,
allowing the audience to contemplate the affluence of their inhabitants.
Apart from the Palace of Culture and Marriott Hotel, another location
prominently featured in Machulski's film is the airport, Okecie. Here
the container with the cash laundered by the Colombians arrives, the
shooting between Siara's and Lipski's people takes place and, eventually,
the true Kiler is caught by the police. As with the Marriott, the airport
is a part of rich people's lives. The stream of Polish celebrities who
pass by during the confrontation between Lipski and Siara strengthens
this symbolism of Okecie.

Warsaw as depicted in *Kiler* is no longer a city of *flâneurs*. All characters,
including the policemen, have foreign cars; the only exception is Jerzy,
whose taxi is a Polish Polonez. However, after associating with Siara, he
also acquires an expensive sports car. Access to big money is mirrored
in his appearance. While a taxi driver, he wore a tracksuit and anorak,
which gave him a rather provincial look; as 'Kiler' he enjoys well-tailored
suits, elegant shoes and dark glasses. It must be emphasized that the
transformation is not all spontaneous. Before Jerzy decides to play his
role of 'Kiler', his homework includes a pile of video films featuring

hitmen and serial killers, among them *Léon* by Luc Besson, *Taxi Driver* by Martin Scorsese, *Reservoir Dogs* by Quentin Tarantino and the Polish *Psy 2* [Dogs 2, 1994] by Wladyslaw Pasikowski. He tries various styles, eventually deciding to assume the look of a Tarantino character. At the same time as Kiler assumes his new identity, the chief of police asks his subordinate, who is responsible for catching Kiler, to emulate the style of Tommy Lee Jones in *The Fugitive*.

'Look', 'surface', as opposed to 'reality' and 'interior', is a constant motif of the film. The underlying assumption is that look deserves a lot of attention because exterior, not interior, is what people and things are judged upon. For example, the Colombians decide to buy the Palace of Culture not because of what is inside the building, but because of its impression from the outside. Similarly, Jerzy is regarded as a super-successful hitman not because he kills anybody, but because by using cameras, videotapes and television make-up artists he is able to demonstrate that his victims are dead. The case of Jerzy shows that look, image or style do not need to be natural or firm. On the contrary, they can be manufactured and modified when circumstances require it. However, a proper image needs adequate investment, as is observed by Rysia who complains to Jerzy that her husband does not give her enough money to look good. 'I do not have money for massages, I do not have money for cosmetics,' she moans and when Kiler offers her 300 dollars to buy what she needs to improve her look, she gasps: 'What can I buy with this? A packet of cottonwool?' This humorous scene shows both the growing recognition of an attractive appearance and the high living standard of the Polish nouveaux riches. A measure of how rapidly conditions of life and material expectations changed for some Poles is the fortune of Rysia who, as her husband claims, not long ago was a dish-washer in a bar.

Belief in the power of appearances over reality is best represented in several scenes with a television crew shooting and later editing the footage. One can see that in the process of editing actual, documentary images of Warsaw are replaced by different ones, arranged and shot in studio. Similarly, shots of different places are juxtaposed, pretending that they belong to the same space. This can be interpreted as the director's acknowledgement that in cinema space does not exist as such, but is always tainted by those who prepare it for the audience. Accordingly, this can be treated as a warning not to mistake his film for a piece of objective reality. The power of the media is also manifested in the

14. *Kiler* (1997), dir. Juliusz Machulski

fact that the very popularity of Kiler results from media hype. At the beginning of the film, the police inspector says during a television interview: 'Kiler does not exist. It is you, the journalists, who invented him.' This, to some extent, is true, as Kiler's 'achievements' are continuously discussed on television, on the radio and in the press. His public personality is also used to sell things, as shown when Kiler visits Lipski with an eponymous 'Kiler Pizza'.

In the final scene Ewa and Jerzy collect from the airport the huge container of dollars that was meant to be payment for the Palace of Culture. When their figures gradually recede from the screen, a subtitle informs us that they presented all the money to the Polish film industry. This means that no effort was made to recover the palace from its foreigner purchasers and to stop its transformation into a casino. In the light of Ewa and Jerzy's interests and values it seems to be a logical conclusion – they belong to the new generation of Warsawians who, like many Westerners, believe more in the power of images than in solid, concrete things. They might be nostalgic about the old Palace, but only as a visual phenomenon, as a monument to camp, not as the site of the Polish Academy of Science or other old-fashioned, serious institutions.

In reality, the fate of the Palace of Culture was more complex than was suggested in Machulski's film. First, it was not privatized but still belongs to the state. Second, it continues to fulfil most of the cultural functions it did during communist times: providing space for theatres and book exhibitions and accommodating the Polish Academy of Science. In the 1990s this function was even reinforced with the re-opening of a 'Knowledge' cinema which had been closed for over ten years. This is now renowned mainly for showing Polish films and it was precisely in this cinema that *Kiler* was shown for several weeks. On the other hand, the Palace did not avoid the influence of capitalism. Most importantly, a significant part of its floor space is nowadays occupied by a supermarket, BAS, specializing in luxurious Western goods, and many of its rooms are often rented out for commercial events. Its surroundings have also changed, being covered now with gigantic adverts for such products as private pensions. The replacement of high culture with low, consumerist, 'image-based' culture, a phenomenon that we see in *Kiler* and that, to a certain extent, defines the cultural life of con-temporary Warsaw, is by no means uniquely Polish. The same trend can be observed in other postcommunist countries, particularly Russia. The rule seems to be that the more a society was 'oppressed' by high/literary culture in the past, the more eager it is to express itself by participation in low/visual culture.

Both *Girl Guide* and *Kiler* extensively use postmodern aesthetics.[5] They present loose, fragmented structures with numerous threads hindering the development of the main narrative. For example, musical scenes look like ready-made videoclips, shot from unusual angles and fast edited. They seem to be inserted to 'sell' the film to young audiences. It goes without saying that the songs used by Machulski are performed by well-known Polish pop groups. Another postmodern device is the com-bination of animation with live-action, as in the scene in *Girl Guide*, reminiscent of Monty Python, where President Clinton rewards Jozek's cousin for catching Gary Wise. All these devices give the impression that the films do not provide a coherent reality, but create a heterotopia where different realities are juxtaposed.

Conclusions

In *Girl Guide* and *Kiler* Juliusz Machulski depicts a Warsaw in a state of transition, where the old dogma of communism has been replaced first by a plurality of ideas and discourses (as in *Girl Guide*), then by a belief in the power of money (as in *Kiler*). This change has a number of implications, such as, on the one hand, opening up the Polish capital to the outside world, a greater individualism, affluence and freedom of speech and movement for the inhabitants; on the other, widespread corruption and the proliferation of gangsters. By choosing certain sites, such as the Marriott Hotel, the Old City and the Palace of Culture, and certain types of characters, such as businessmen and journalists, the director creates a polished version of Warsaw, comparable to that which is offered to tourists in a travel agency's brochure. Nevertheless, Warsaw in *Girl Guide* and *Kiler* is not 'any town', as it has sufficient individuality not to be mistaken for Paris, Barcelona or Moscow. To a certain extent this is because, as the director shows, the old face of Warsaw shines through the new, westernized veneer – communism is rejected, but not yet uprooted. The genuineness of Warsaw and its attachment to old habits, as depicted by Machulski, is particularly visible when compared to cinematic portrayals of the capital of Poland's western neighbour – Berlin.

6

Berlin, a Coreless City

Berlin – City and Symbol

In terms of sheer stability, the cold war possessed an austere
elegance unlikely to be matched by any subsequent arrangements.

New Republic, 12 April 1989

I should say I'm no Berliner. Who is nowadays?

Wim Wenders, *The Logic of Images*

In the twentieth century few cities in the world gained such a distinctive identity as Berlin. Martin Jesinghausen explains this fact by its historical belatedness.

> No other European city is so inextricably linked up with its recent history. Berlin became what it is today in the course of little more than a hundred years. Whereas Paris was fully developed as a metropolis by the end of the 19th century, Berlin's growth only took off after Paris had arrived ... Paradoxically, Berlin's historical belatedness is also the reason for an acceleration of the speed of its historical development. Within decades rather than centuries, Berlin developed from being a provincial German town into a major centre of German nationalism and a cosmopolitan metropolis. (Jesinghausen 2000: 88–9)

Anton Kaes adds:

> By the 1920s Berlin had become the imaginary center of urban culture, drawing artists, intellectuals, tourists, migrants and im-

migrants into its orbit like a magnet. The city had grown from one million inhabitants in 1877 to two million in 1905 and, after swallowing up the outlying areas, to nearly four million in 1920. Not surprisingly, a city of this size inspired paeans and tirades; it engendered feelings of exaltation and repulsion and led to euphoria and depression. The city became the primordial site of modernity to which painters, poets, and filmmakers returned obsessively. Encapsulating both the beauty and the ugliness, the exuberance and the gridlock, of urban life, Berlin always posed a challenge to representation. Its proliferation of signs, its chaotic diversity, and its kineticism pushed practitioners in various media to explore their limits. (Kaes 1996: 27)

The connection between the real Berlin and its cinematic image was rarely one of simple imitation. Following the arrival of Expressionism in the 1920s, filmmakers tried to enhance Berlin's common-sense experience, achieve a deeper insight into its life, represent Berlin as a model of a rational, perfectly organized modern city or even defamiliarize it. This was the reason why many early films set in Berlin were actually shot in the studio, as it was easier to construct its synthetic or exaggerated vision in an artificial environment than on location. An example is *Die Straße* [The Street, 1923], directed by Karl Grune, for which a full-scale avenue with shop windows, cafés, bars, a dance hall and a police station were built in the studio. This film, as Kaes argues, captured the contradictory reactions to the modern urban experience, 'running the gamut from idolization to condemnation, from intoxication and elation to feelings of anxiety and apocalypse' (Kaes 1996: 26). Another example of this 'universalizing' attitude to Berlin is *Der letzte Mann* [The Last Man, 1924] by Friedrich Wilhelm Murnau, in which skyscrapers 'served as icons of the metropolis in general, presented as a fast-paced, heartless place' (Neumann 1996: 33). *Metropolis* (1927), directed by Fritz Lang, perhaps the most famous 'city film' ever made by a German director on German soil (albeit shot exclusively in a studio), is hardly regarded as a film about Berlin or any other real city, but, as its title suggests, a synthetic, universal metropolis (Neumann 1996: 33–5; Kreimeier 1987: 101–3).

Berlin is also the hero of one of the first ever 'city symphonies' and the model of this genre whose main purpose is to represent the city as a whole (rather than some of its fragments or the lives of some of its inhabitants) and to render its rhythm. This film was *Berlin, die Sinfonie einer Großstadt* [Berlin, Symphony of a Big City, 1927], directed by Walter Ruttmann. Ruttmann, who wanted to honour Berlin as the quintessentially modern European metropolis, used the structure of the symphony and the symphony orchestra as an analogy for the structure of city life.

> In an orchestra, dozens of musicians play instruments that have evolved over history to produce a multipartite, but unified and coherent performance within which the individualities of the contributing musicians are subsumed: in the city, the individual contributions of millions of people (working with technologies that have developed over centuries) are subsumed within the metropolis's mega-partite movement through the day, a movement that reveals several predictable highs and lows. At the end of *Berlin, Symphony of a Big City*, symphonic fireworks celebrate the conclusion of the metropolis's productive daily/weekly cycle and of a visual masterwork of independent cinema. (MacDonald 1997–98: 4)

In representing human beings merely as elements of a larger structure, as design elements, some critics argue that *Berlin, Symphony of a Big City* conveys a hunger for and a commitment to a unified, thoroughly organized and controlled society, which was also the Nazi ideal. In this sense Ruttmann's film foreshadows another pre-Second World War German masterpiece, *Triumph des Willens* [Triumph of the Will, 1935] by Leni Riefenstahl (see MacDonald: 1997–98).

After the Second World War Berlin became a divided city, following the partition of Germany into West Germany, occupied by the Western Allies, America, Britain and France, and East Germany, under Soviet control. In August 1961 a concrete wall, up to six feet high, topped with barbed wire, was erected to prevent inhabitants of the Soviet-controlled zone from fleeing to West Berlin. As J. Hoberman observes, the Wall transsected or destroyed many buildings symbolizing the Nazi rule, such as the Chancellery, the Gestapo headquarters, the Ministry of Aviation, the remains of Hitler's bunker and the back of the Reichstag. Consequently, to a large extent it erased Berlin's Third Reich identity (Hoberman 1998: 7). In the following years, probably against the wishes of its originators, the Wall became a symbol of Berlin, the most distinctive piece of 'political architecture' in the whole of Eastern Europe, and the city's greatest tourist attraction. As Alexandra Richie observes: 'When visitors came they did not search out the monuments or the museums or the shops. To Berliners' chagrin they came to see one thing: the Wall' (Richie 1998: 802). The Wall's connotations were manifold. J. Hoberman writes:

> The Wall embodied the cold war ... [It] saturated the landscape with ideology and reified the yearning for freedom. Truly, the antifascist rampant was a magical Mobius strip allowing Berliners on both sides to feel themselves on the outside looking in. Half fortress, half prison, surrounded by rubble and lit up like a Christmas tree, cold war Berlin was as stylized an urban environment as Venice or Manhattan – and what's more, conceptually so. (Hoberman 1998: 6)

The importance of the partition of Berlin into socialist and capitalist parts, and later of the Wall as a dividing line, was also rendered in the cinema, particularly in the films made from a Western perspective. This applies both to German directors' films and even more so to those made by foreign directors, of which there were many, as the Berlin theme was particularly suitable as a vehicle for cold war propaganda. Berlin and the Wall also became metonymies of wider divisions of a similar sort: the partition of the German nation and the gulf between the whole of West and East Europe. Berlin is depicted in this way in, for instance, *The Man Between* (1953), directed by Carol Reed, *The Spy Who Came in from the Cold* (1965), directed by Martin Ritt, *Funeral in Berlin* (1966), directed by Guy Hamilton, and *Torn Curtain* (1966), directed by Alfred Hitchcock. The narratives of these films are built around people trying, usually unsuccessfully, to flee from East to West Berlin and unscrupulous double agents who prey on their desire for freedom and a better life.

Postwar Berlin was also conducive to horror stories. In *Possession* (1981), made by the self-exiled Polish director Andrzej Zulawski, the Wall and the whole oppressive character of Berlin play a major part in transforming an ordinary housewife into a violent schizophrenic who attacks her husband with a knife and has an affair with a tentacular monster. Moreover, in Zulawski's film every character has a split personality and is also represented by its double, who is physically similar but with a very different mentality to the original, in the same way as Berlin was divided into two separate parts. Thus, the housewife's double is a gentle teacher and her husband's double is a monster. Zulawski was not the only filmmaker to use the Wall as a symbol of different kinds of division. For example, in *Redupers* (1985) by Helke Sander the Wall stands for sexual difference, as argued by some feminist critics (de Lauretis 1987: 133), or for the divisions of the female self (Elseasser 1989: 191). In *Berlin Report* (1991), directed by South Korean director Park Kwang-Su, the Wall stands for the barriers between South and North Korea.

As Ronald Taylor notes, East German directors rarely discussed present-day Berlin: 'The Wall itself gave rise to a handful of misconceived films readily forgotten. The physical and psychological tragedies for which it was responsible were not permitted material for the filmmakers of the East' (Taylor 1997: 349). There were, however, some exceptions, among them two films by Konrad Wolf, East Germany's most accomplished director: *Der geteilte Himmel* [The Divided Sky, 1964], based on the novel by Christa Wolf, and *Solo Sunny* (1979). The first film provides a relatively unpolished vision of the lives of ordinary East Berliners and touches on the taboo subject of illegal crossing of the border. In *Solo Sunny*, Wolf portrays the life of a rather unsuccessful pop singer who dreams about love, career and acceptance in her own right. *Solo Sunny* can be interpreted as a protest against the uniform, impersonal lives of the citizens of East Berlin, and by extension in the whole of East Germany. As Ronald Taylor observes, Sunny's world is 'a sub-culture of individuals seeking self-fulfilment, not a regimented socialist youth club. Sunny may not contribute much to the well-being of society but there is more to life, say Sunny and Wolf, than working on the production line or operating a check-out at a supermarket' (Taylor 1997: 350). Other East Berlin films that deviated from the syrupy image of life under socialism were the so-called 'Berlin-Filme' by Gerhard Klein and Wolfgang Kohlhaase. They included *Berliner Romanze* [A Berlin Romance, 1956], *Berlin–Ecke Schönhäuser* (1957) and *Berlin um die Ecke* [Round the Corner in Berlin, 1965]. Many of them concentrated on the political frustration and anti-social behaviour of young Berliners. What differentiates these films from their Western counterparts and from many less accomplished DEFA films set in East Berlin is their perception of Berlin not so much as a symbol, but as a concrete, material environment: an estate or a street. As Horst Claus observes, when discussing *A Berlin Romance*:

The dominance of wide-angle lenses, the use of high-speed film stock and extensive location work convey a sense of authenticity.

> Even the smell of Berlin seems to have been captured in scenes
> such as those of the fair or the visit to the cinema ... This is a
> lovingly designed, carefully reconstructed representation of work-
> ing class life in Berlin based on in-depth knowledge, extensive
> research and thorough familiarity with the milieu and its people.
> (Claus 1999: 101)

The closer to the date of the destruction of the Wall in 1989, the
more complex the portrayal of the divided city. Instead of concentrating
on the political causes and effects of Berlin's partition, the films made
by West Germans foreground its psychological and existential consequences. Similarly, the image of a 'good' West Berlin and a 'bad' East
Berlin was replaced by a more subtle and balanced picture. One such
film is *Der Mann auf der Mauer* [Man on the Wall, 1982], directed by
Reinhard Hauff. The title character is a man from East Berlin who
dreams of crossing the border and moving to West Germany. Once he
achieves his dream, however, he discovers that he is not happy and
misses his old country very much. In the end, he crosses the Wall again
and returns to East Berlin. Another film that suggested the new attitude
is *Meier* (1982), a satirical comedy directed by East German émigré Peter
Timm. The film is set in East Berlin and draws substantially on the
director's experience. The eponymous main character, an East Berliner,
acquires a Western passport that he uses to cross the border on a daily
basis to buy high-quality Western wallpaper, which his building team
uses to decorate the flats of East Berliners. He even becomes a national
hero, rewarded by Erich Honecker himself. Although Timm's film
contains a fair amount of criticism of the absurdity, ineffectiveness and
injustice of the communist system, it avoids demonizing the Wall. For
example, although Meier is eventually caught trying to cross the border
without the appropriate documents and is brought in front of the Stasi,
his only punishment is to carry on his work without telling anybody
about the true source of his excellent materials. No one in this film is
shot trying to cross the Wall illegally; the only fatal incidents are shown
on the screen of a slot machine in a West Berlin club. The East German
films made in the last days of the country's existence also reveal facets
of the city which previously were deeply hidden. We refer particularly
to *Coming Out* (1989), directed by Heiner Carow, which depicts the lives
of East Berlin homosexuals. Probably the best-known film about Berlin
made shortly before the fall of the Wall was Wim Wenders' *Der Himmel*

über Berlin [Wings of Desire, 1987]. Although the film is set mainly in West Berlin, its German title is reminiscent of the previously mentioned East German film by Konrad Wolf. Moreover, as J. Hoberman argues, it captures the spirit of the whole of the city: 'its stoic melancholy, its somnolence, its self-absorption ... the deep sense of loneliness and desertion that was sometimes called *Mauerkrankheit* (wall sickness) or *Insul Gefühl*' (Hoberman 1998: 7).

Coreless City

The unification of Germany in 1990 resulted in an upsurge of interest in Berlin by filmmakers. The new, post-Wall films on Berlin present a larger thematic, stylistic and ideological variety than those in any previous period. One way of approaching the new situation can be described as 'longitudinal' – discussing the history of Berlin through the examination of the fate of its inhabitants over a prolonged period. Often the characters experienced life on both sides of the Wall. This examination was taken up by veterans of the New German Cinema, Margarethe von Trotta in *Das Versprechen* [The Promise, 1994] and, to a lesser extent, Wim Wenders in *In weiter Ferne, so nah!* [Far Away, So Close, 1993]. Von Trotta's film tells the story of two East Germans, Konrad and Sophie, from the building of the Wall in 1961 to its fall in 1989. Sophie fled to the West immediately after the Wall was erected, while Konrad remained in the East. They meet again in Prague, during the famous Czech Spring of 1968, but the Soviet intervention separates them again. They continue to see each other over the years and have a son who is the fruit of their brief encounter in Prague. At the same time, they develop separate careers: Konrad becomes a famous scientist, Sophie a tourist guide. They set up separate families and gradually grow apart, without ceasing to love each other. The ending of *The Promise* is open – the Wall falls, but the director does not reveal whether Konrad and Sophie are reunited. This can be regarded as symbolic of the doubts that some West and East German intellectuals had in 1989 concerning Germany's speedy unification. Some of them, most notably Günter Grass, suggested 'cohabitation' first (see Taylor 1997: 387).

Far Away, So Close does not make direct references to the period before the unification. However, by being a sequel to Wenders' *Wings of Desire* and by including many of the characters from the previous film, it forces us to think about both periods of Berlin's history. In this group could also be included *Sonnennallee* [Sun Alley, 1999], directed by Leander Haussman, which concentrates on the lives of young East Berliners during the 1970s. The title of the film refers to the street that runs through both East and West Berlin and that was divided by the Wall. Haussman shows that his characters felt deeply inferior to their contemporaries on the other side of the Wall. They knew that West Berliners disrespected them and believed that their contempt was justified, as they had access to clothes, books, records and drugs about which the 'Ossiech' could only dream. Despite that, Haussman refuses to condemn the communist times and demonize the Wall. On the contrary, the period is treated with sympathy, even nostalgia. As in the previously mentioned *Meier*, nobody is killed trying to cross the Wall illegally and the only object shot on the border is a gramophone record. The director himself promoted his film by saying: 'Let's follow the wish of many citizens of this country and reconstruct the Wall for ninety minutes' (Haussman 1999: 15).

Thomas Elseasser notes that 'it is ... to television that one has to turn if one wants to know what has happened to the ex-GDR and its cinema. At first glance it looks as if it has disappeared without much of a trace, since, so far, no formerly prominent East German director has made a name for him/herself in the West' (Elseasser 1999: 14). Indeed, the majority of films about Berlin made after unification make little reference to the time when Berlin was a divided city, but concentrate on Berlin's present day – examples are *Das Leben ist eine Baustelle* [Life is a Building Site, 1997], directed by Wolfgang Becker; *Lola, Rennt* [Run, Lola, Run, 1998] by Tom Tykwer; *Nachtgestalten* [Night Shapes, 1998] and *Die Polizistin* [The Policewoman, 1999] both by Andreas Dresen; *Plus-Minus Null* (1998) by Eoin Moore; *Geschwister* [Siblings, 1996] and *Dealer* (1998), both by Thomas Arslan; *Engelchen* [Little Angel, 1996] by Helke Misselwitz; *Silvester Countdown* (1997) by Oskar Roehler; and *Sara Amerika* (1998) by Roland Suso Richter. The bulk of them are by filmmakers of a younger generation; Tom Tykwer was born in 1965, Andreas Dresen in 1963, Thomas Arslan in 1962, Roland Suso Richter in 1961. In common with the modernist city symphonies, their films often betray an ambition to convey or construct a synthetic vision of Berlin. This, however, is done not by representing Berliners as anonymous elements of a larger structure, but by detailed examination of the lives of various people, who are treated both as unique individuals and as a cross-section of Berlin society. The most complex and inventive way of combining the structure of a city symphony with a feature film is included in the beginning of *Run, Lola, Run*. It shows a monochromatic crowd of people, whose faces are barely recognizable in fast motion. Gradually, a number of individuals emerge from the crowd – they will be the characters in Tykwer's story. They are part of the crowd but at the same time stand out from it, as they are shot in colour and are static. The apparently amorphous and chaotic crowd, when shot from a very high angle, moves in a way that creates the sign 'Lola, Rennt' (Lola, Run), which is the film's title. Afterwards, instead of a traditional credit sequence their faces are shown in a manner reminiscent of police photos and their names and the names of the actors appear on screen. Again, the police photos suggest that they belong to a larger society, as well as being unique human beings. Later, we see a bird's-eye view of Berlin and then the camera zooms into a street and eventually into Lola's house, demonstrating that Lola and her surroundings are part of a larger structure – Berlin.

What is characteristic of the reality portrayed in these films is the impression of temporariness, of moving, changing and becoming, rather than being. The lack of stability applies both to Berlin's urban design and architecture and to people's lives. Hence, the title of Wolfgang Becker's movie *Life is a Building Site* is symbolic of post-Wall cinematic Berlin. The films are full of images of destruction and building, often on a grand scale, when skyscrapers are built using gigantic cranes. For example, *Plus-Minus Null* depicts the redevelopment of Potsdamer Platz and its surroundings (which in *Wings of Desire* was an unnamed wasteland), *Life is a Building Site* shows changes taking place near Alexander Platz, as well as the regeneration of some old East Berlin housing estates, while *Run, Lola, Run* includes images of the building works in the neighbourhood of the Brandenburg Gate and the Wall – the part of Berlin which has changed the most in recent years and will continue to be transformed. Other films, such as *Siblings* and *Dealer*, show redevelopment taking place in the neighbourhood of Schöneberg and Kreuzberg, where many squatters and immigrants, particularly from Turkey, used to live. We also see many people reorganizing and redecorating their houses, or emptying and leaving them, typically unwillingly. Even in the flats and houses of those who have no intention of leaving in the near future, there is abundant evidence of change: boxes, bags and suitcases. One of the most amusing scenes symbolic of the constant change is included in *Life is a Building Site*: two groups of people try to

15. *Night Shapes* (1998), dir. Andreas Dresen

pass each other on the narrow stairs, one carrying a coffin, the other a new wardrobe.

The well-known quarters, streets and squares, as well as the old buildings and monuments, such as Unter den Linden, the Tiergarten, the Victory Column, Charlottenburg Castle, Nikolaikirche or Marienkirche are excluded, or shown in such an inconspicuous way that they pass unnoticed. The centre of the city with the Brandenburg Gate rarely features in these films; most of the narratives take place somewhere in between: on nondescript streets and squares, inside or outside supermarkets and cinemas, on building sites or on run-down estates of high tenement blocks, awaiting redevelopment. When the historic centre of Berlin, which was neglected by the East German authorities and still awaits regeneration, is shown, it looks like a grim area of dark streets of old tenements with crumbling walls. This is also the part of the city where crime flourishes – both in real Berlin and in contemporary Berlin films. Apart from the building sites, the most common architectural features of the films are underground passages, railway stations and metro trains. The characters very often meet or miss each other at the stations or on the trains. The lack of any core and of distinctive architectural features is particularly striking in numerous scenes when the characters view Berlin from an elevated vantage point, typically from a newly-built skyscraper or from their windows in a high tenement block, and see only a vast surface covered with identical-looking skyscrapers (reminiscent of Berlin in Ruttmann's film). Examples are scenes in *Plus-Minus Null*, *Little Angels* and *Dealer*. One wonders if this is a real city or some kind of abstraction. As Wilhelm Roth observes in reference to *Dealer*, the impression is one of anonymity and claustrophobia (Roth 1999: 14) – what the character sees makes him feel as if he were living in a prison cell. The new, unified Berlin does not have any official divisions and borders, but there are many invisible boundaries and forbidden territories, which are a consequence of Berlin's changing social landscape. Hence, the authorities and new, private owners of lucrative areas of Berlin try to clear the centre and other prestigious quarters of the city of squatters, beggars, prostitutes and homeless people, who are regarded as 'pollution' and an obstacle in fulfilling the programme of Berlin's 'beautification'. It is no surprise that these people lead particularly unstable lives and can be spotted most often in places of transition: on the metro trains, in railway stations and in underground passages. Some quarters of the city are left to decay, as affluent people are afraid to visit the areas of highest deprivation and crime. These invisible barriers, which to a certain extent replaced the old Berlin Wall, feature prominently in *Night Shapes*, *Plus-Minus Null* and *Dealer*.

Some of the films here discussed are set mainly inside the borders of the old East Berlin (*Plus-Minus Null*, *Life is a Building Site*, *Little Angel*), some in both parts (*Run, Lola, Run*, *Night Shapes*), some in West Berlin (*Siblings*, *Dealer*). In most cases, however, the appearance of streets, houses, shops or interiors is insufficient to establish in which part of Berlin the story is set. Furthermore, no genuine German products are advertised on the billboards or on television; instead, we see adverts for Calvin Klein or Wonderbra. Neither are the types of cars helpful in establishing Berlin's cinematic geography, as most of the vehicles on the streets are Western (but not only German), while Trabants, the most common cars in East Germany, have become a rarity and an object of camp, rather than a symbol of any real social status. The general impression is that all of Berlin now looks like pre-unification West Berlin, which used to be regarded as the most cosmopolitan and un-German of all West German cities; the old East Berlin identity has been completely erased.

The emphasis on change, destruction and building in the films of the 1990s has much in common with Berlin's reality of the last decade. Not

16. *Life is a Building Site* (1997), dir. Wolfgang Becker (copyright ©
1997 by X Filme)

only was the Berlin Wall demolished, but many buildings were destroyed
and many new ones constructed – in this respect Berlin changed more
than any other postcommunist large city with the exception of Yugoslavian towns. In addition, old urban structures and types of ownership
gradually disappeared and new structures grew up in their place. While
in the old GDR almost all the land in the cities and a large proportion
of the buildings belonged to the state, after unification the land and
many properties were sold for redevelopment or returned to their
previous owners, often Jews dispossessed by the Nazi regime – this being
the result of the programme of restitution (see Haussermann 1996: 222–
7). The old owners of private houses and other properties usually did not
move in, but exchanged their inheritance for cash. Numerous new
buildings have been constructed both in the city centre and on the
outskirts, although of different type. In the centre, most new buildings
are large office blocks for the service industry that typically belong to
anonymous real-estate funds, multinational real-estate companies and
speculators of all kinds. In the suburbs, on the other hand, there is
evidence of a huge increase in privately owned properties. Here the
newly-born Berlin middle class live, a substantial part of whom moved
to the city outskirts from old apartment blocks. As a result of privatiza-

tion, restitution and acceptance by the authorities of the capitalist rule that an individual's income determines the quality of housing occupied, new structures of social segregation have appeared and homelessness, practically absent from the old East Berlin, is now widespread (see Haussermann 1996: 228–30). No wonder that the term *die Wende* ('the change' or 'the U-turn') became almost as commonly used in post-Wall Berlin as the word *perestroika* in Gorbachev's Soviet Union.

Some of the city's quarters, most importantly the centre of the old East Berlin and the neighbourhood of the Wall, have changed so much in the last decade that they are hardly recognizable. These include Alexanderplatz, which before the Second World War was Berlin's bustling centre and after the war became East Berlin's most important square, and has now been completely redeveloped; and Potsdamer Platz, where in recent years Sony has built its European headquarters. Interestingly, although the Wall was demolished, no other building was erected to replace it as a new symbol of the united Berlin. The Brandenburg Gate, which formed part of the border between East and West Berlin, in common with other important buildings of the past lost its old connotation as a 'dividing line' between two contrasting political systems. Its new connotations, on the other hand, are multiple and contradictory. It is a place where representatives of the far Right gather to demonstrate against immigration, as well as those who protest against the proliferation of racism in Berlin and Germany. It also became a massive flea market for communist memorabilia: uniforms, medals, icons. On the whole, contemporary Berlin feels somehow devoid of any centre or core – a feature that the films discussed in this chapter acutely emphasize.

The bulk of new Berlin films, including *Night Shapes, Life is a Building Site, Run, Lola, Run, Plus-Minus Null, Little Angel* and *Dealer*, centre on nomads, *gastarbeiters*, refugees, tourists, squatters, outsiders, people without any permanent address or those who are never at home as a result of a hectic life. Many of the films consist of several parallel or intermingled narratives. In *Night Shapes*, which is set during one night, a homeless couple who unexpectedly receive 100 marks from a passer-by look for a place to spend the night, a lonely farmer comes to Berlin seeking a prostitute (or a wife), and a busy businessman takes care of a small black boy from Angola after wrongly accusing him of stealing his wallet. The last group of characters consists of some young punks who first rob the farmer of his bag full of condoms and then steal and burn the businessman's car. The film is set during the night when the

17. *Night Shapes* (1998), dir. Andreas Dresen

Pope visits Berlin. This event, however, has no impact on the spiritual lives of the characters. They watch with complete indifference his numerous images on television. For many of them, the Pope's visit is only a nuisance – it adds to the homeless couple's difficulty in finding a cheap hotel and causes traffic jams, which prevent the characters from reaching their destination in time.

All of these people are uprooted or disenfranchised. The Angolan boy has nobody in Berlin apart from a cousin working as a cook in a bar, who failed to show up at the airport. The businessman is divorced, lives by himself and has no time for socializing. The homeless woman is divorced and has a child who was taken away from her by the social services. She is afraid that the same fate awaits her second child whom she is now carrying. The young prostitute befriended by the farmer has no true connections with anybody; her sole interest is in earning enough money to feed her heroin habit. The stories are inconclusive. Although for the characters the night is adventurous and full of encounters with people who could change their lives, metaphorically and actually in the morning they are still where they were the evening before: the lonely farmer returns to his home village, the prostitute looks for another client, the homeless people must spend the next night without any guarantee of shelter, the businessman has to return to his hectic job. The film conveys a deep sense of futility and of the immense potential of good-will wasted. The symbol for this is the farmer's asking the prostitute to write him a letter when she has already thrown away his address.

A similar pattern of narratives and human destinies is revealed in *Plus-Minus Null*. The main character is Alex, a young, divorced builder, socially and romantically involved with two prostitutes, Svetlana, who is an immigrant from Bosnia, and Ruth, who used to live in East Berlin and worked as a nursery nurse. Each of the characters is a victim of change – Alex messed up his personal life, Svetlana became a casualty of the war and the grave economic situation in Bosnia, while Ruth lost her job as a result of *die Wende*, which brought rationalization of employment and, consequently, massive unemployment in the former GDR. All of them try to change their lives in order to feel independent of their adverse circumstances. Svetlana wants to marry a German man, which is a precondition for remaining in Berlin indefinitely; Alex and Ruth want to set up a business; all of them dream about earning enough money to regain their lost dignity and self-confidence. As in *Night Shapes*, however, their efforts are in vain. In the end all of them are where they started – Svetlana waits at the railway station for a train to Bosnia, Alex's business plans end up as a fiasco, Ruth returns to her work on the streets. As the title suggests, the total result of their efforts is zero. A similar story is included in *Dealer*. The main character, Cam, who is a Turkish immigrant, encouraged by his girlfriend tries many times to break with his past as a small-time drug dealer. His boss, Hakan, promises him that he will run a bar, but does not keep his word and is eventually shot dead. Cam tries to work as a dishwasher in a restaurant, but poor wages and hard work prove too much for him and he returns to drug dealing. In the end he is caught by the police and threatened with deportation to Turkey.

Run, Lola, Run also consists of several narrative strands, but they all feature the same characters, Lola and her boyfriend Manni. In each of the parts Lola runs to find money for Manni, who has just lost on a train 100,000 marks, which he received for an illegal car deal. He risks being killed by his boss if he does not deliver the money in twenty minutes. Each part ends differently: in the first, Lola and Manni are surrounded by the police and Lola is shot dead by a policeman; in the second, Manni is killed by a truck seconds before Lola hands him money stolen from the bank where her father works; in the last, she manages to obtain the money, which she wins in a casino, almost at the same time as Manni recovers the bag from the beggar who took it. The very fact of using this device, reminiscent of the structure of Peter Howitt's *Sliding Doors* (1998; see Chapter 8) – although Tykwer executed the plot with more wit and energy – reveals the same message as *Night Shapes* and *Plus-Minus Null*: life in Berlin is as open and unpredictable as a game. Success depends more on luck than on politics or personal qualities such as will and determination. The message is conveyed by the mottoes of the films. One of them reads: 'The end of the game is its beginning.'

In contrast to earlier films set in Berlin, international politics, the struggle for freedom, the victory of socialism, or the fight against terrorism, play little part in the characters' lives. What they experience is the lack of intervention of the state to sort out the citizens' problems (which was the case in the old GDR) and lack of any great idea to enthuse the people, particularly the young. History also ceased to matter: 'the Wall' seems not to exist in the characters' vocabulary. In this respect cinematic Berlin differs largely from representations of Warsaw and Moscow, in which communist history has had a crucial impact on the city's image, character and problems. The political void is typically filled by violence – either random acts of social disobedience and petty crime, or large-scale crime, organized by the mafia. Theft, drug dealing, drug abuse and anti-social behaviour are usually committed by those who are less than thirty years old. They either belong to a specific youth sub-culture, marked by distinctive clothes, hairstyle and language, or are immigrants, usually from Turkey, the former Yugoslavia or Poland.

In spite of having problems with the law, the disenfranchised, 'ex-centric' characters are treated by the filmmakers with understanding, sympathy and tenderness. In most of the films the camera privileges their point of view and seems to relish their mischief. Some of the films even convey the message that the 'others' are the saviours of Berlin. This applies to the boy from Angola in *Night Shapes*, whose presence exerts a positive influence on everyone he meets in Berlin, especially the businessman Peschke (who initially demonstrates mild racist attitudes) – in contrast to the Pope, whose presence in Berlin feels distant and irrelevant. A similar role is played by Svetlana and her Bosnian compatriots in the life of Alex in *Plus-Minus Null*; this young man, confused and lacking in purpose, feels very much at home in the company of people dancing to the songs whose meaning he cannot understand. Kristina, the Greek woman in *Life is a Building Site* who seeks her lost brother, is treated as a 'Christmas gift' by Buddy, a divorced man. On the other hand, the 'decent', white people (predominantly male), who are successful and powerful, are shown in an unfavourable light. The representatives of the authorities, such as the police, the law, bankers, social workers and the Church, are particularly unsympathetic. They are portrayed as weak, over-bureaucratic, hypocritical, selfish and uncommitted to their work. In most cases they are not only unable to help the confused youngsters and foreigners, but add to their misery; the only exception being the main character in *The Policewoman*, who is compassionate, although ineffective in law enforcement. In criticizing the authorities new Berlin cinema has much in common with British social realistic films and the reviewers of *Night Shapes*, *Plus-Minus Null* and *Life is a Building Site* compared them to the cinema of Ken Loach and Mike Leigh (von Thuna 1999: 41; Knoben 2000: 31; Worschech 1997: 33). In the case of *Life is a Building Site* the connection with Loach's films and working-class realism is more direct, for the casting of Ricky Tomlinson as a 'rough diamond', working-class hero – a character he also played in Loach's *Riff-Raff* (1990) and *Raining Stones* (1993), as well as in the television sit-com *The Royle Family* (1999–). Some of the films represent the white male body as an 'area of crisis', which adds to the impression of Berlin as lacking a centre. Hence, both Jan in *Life is a Building Site* and Romeo in *Silvester Countdown*, in spite of being physically attractive, have deep sexual problems. Jan is so worried that he has contracted the HIV virus that he becomes impotent; Romeo is unable to fulfil his girlfriend Julia's immense sexual appetite. In *Night Shapes* the farmer's moral objections to using a teenage prostitute and his lack of self-confidence mean that he returns to his home village without fulfilling his dream of having sex.

In contrast to many East German films made before unification, in which the characters read German books and watched German films in the cinemas or on television, Berlin culture, as represented by the filmmakers, is dominated by American style and content. For example, the characters typically watch on television German imitations of American chat shows and quiz games, and karaoke pubs and clubs are widespread. The walls of the characters' flats are covered with photos of such global icons as Jimi Hendrix, Tom Cruise and Madonna, but no

German actors or pop stars are shown. Even the German language is saturated with English words and expressions, and *gastarbeiters* often use English to communicate with each other, as well as with Berliners. The centres of mass consumption, such as a supermarket in *Life is a Building Site*, are depicted as cultural centres, with singers performing for the customers. The old cultural centres, on the other hand, such as an archaeological museum in the same film, serve as sites of consumption – a large pharmaceutical company organizes a lavish reception there.

The disappearance of German culture is not a new phenomenon in German film – it was the main theme of the New German Cinema, constructed at the beginning of the 1960s by Alexander Kluge, Wim Wenders, Jean-Marie Straub and Rainer Werner Fassbinder (see Elsaesser 1989; Wenders 1999). Yet representation and evaluation of Germany's Americanization and surrender to consumerism differ in the films made in the 1990s and those made in earlier decades. First, for the characters in New German films, particularly those directed by Wenders, Americanization is an important issue. Bruno in *Im Lauf der Zeit* [Kings of the Road, 1976], noticing that he cannot get rid of a pop song from his head, says: 'The Yankees colonized our subconscious.' However, the very fact that he does not take this colonization for granted suggests that the task of changing the Germans into Americans is not yet complete. By contrast, in the films made in the 1990s nobody shows any astonishment in the face of American cultural dominance. Second, films such as *Abschied von gestern* [Yesterday Girl, 1966], directed by Alexander Kluge, and *Kings of the Road* referred to and promoted a certain ideal of German culture, either through their narrative content or through their style. Most often they pointed to the classical German cinema of Fritz Lang and Detlef Sierck (Douglas Sirk) and the romantic works of Goethe, Kleist and Fontane as a tradition which should be learnt from and followed by new generations of Germans. The young East Germans of the 1990s, as represented in the films considered, on the other hand, seem to have no cultural baggage to carry into the new era.

The importance of 'others' lies in making up for the disappearance of the old German and Berliner culture and for Germany's Americanization and subordination to consumerism. Against the background of the absence of what Wenders would identify as 'German culture', the culture of immigrants from Bosnia, Turkey or Africa, as revealed in singing, instrument playing and dancing in a pub or by a bonfire, feels very genuine, spontaneous and innocent. It is not surprising, then, that 'true Berliners' who cannot afford to participate in consumerist pleasures, for example Alex in *Plus-Minus Null*, try to adapt to the culture of the incomers. Unlike some recent French or British films which stress the cultural gap between the incomers or ethnic minorities and the white population of European cities, the Berlin films tend to emphasize the similarities between the culture of the native Berliners and those of the ethnic minorities. For example, although many of the characters are probably Muslims, there is no reference to their religion. Social class and personal circumstances (a significant number of men in the films cannot marry the women whom they love because they are already married), and not religion or colour of skin, seem to be the major factor in dividing Berliners or bringing them together.

The absence of any firm geographical and cultural centre in Berlin, as represented in the films, is paralleled by the lack of a stable home on the part of their characters. Practically all the places in which the characters live are only poor substitutes for homes. Alex in *Plus-Minus Null* lives in a container on a building site, the Bosnian refugees in the same film live in a kind of hostel, Ruth lives in a dilapidated flat with the wallpaper peeling from the walls and a broken shower. The teenage prostitute in *Night Shapes* does not even have a place of her own. She takes her clients to hotels paid by the hour and spends the rest of the night with a group of drug addicts in an extremely chaotic flat, probably a squat, where there are not enough beds for everyone. The homeless couple in the same film live in a cardboard box and dream not even about a home, but about a night spent in a cheap hotel with clean sheets and a shower. When in the end they find such a hotel they are overwhelmed by joy. The businessman in *Night Shapes* has a large flat, but he is hardly ever there and the place seems deserted. The central couple in *Life is a Building Site* make love each time in a different place: in the flat of Jan's dead father, in the place of a friend, in the flat of Jan's sister, in a hotel. Some of the characters, such as Alex in *Plus-Minus Null* and Peschke in *Night Shapes*, seem more attached to their cars than to their homes. In addition, many of the characters, even if they do have a place to live, have their real home somewhere else – in Bosnia, Angola, Poland or another German town. Their homes are also incomplete in the sense of their families being broken up. There is a certain irony in the fact that the programme of rebuilding and expanding Berlin is accompanied by enormous homelessness and poor housing, and those who build the new Berlin, like Alex in *Plus-Minus Null*, are completely excluded from enjoying the fruits of their own labour (Knoben 2000: 45). In this respect, the Berlin films of the 1990s are reminiscent of Lang's *Metropolis*, where the population of the city was neatly divided between the poor workers who built it and worked for it and those who enjoyed the results of their work.

Most of the people in the films have insecure, part-time or low-status jobs – such as a builder, a cook and a barman – or are unemployed. Many characters are also employed in the black economy: drug dealing, cigarette smuggling or selling stolen cars. The occupation most often represented in Berlin films of the last decade is prostitution. The frequency with which prostitutes are portrayed reflects the fact that, along with Amsterdam and Hamburg, Berlin is the biggest centre of the sex industry in Europe, attracting hundreds of women from both Germany and former communist countries, such as Poland, Russia, Bulgaria and Yugoslavia. Prostitution signifies the economic and emotional instability of life after the collapse of the Wall, as exemplified by the previously mentioned character of the ex-nursery teacher Ruth in *Plus-Minus Null*. Secondly, prostitution (as Jean-Luc Godard highlighted in many of his films) encapsulates Western capitalism, where nothing is for free. It is worth noting that, instead of concentrating on the sensational and dramatic aspects of the lives of prostitutes, and sentimentalizing their lives, which is typical of American cinema, the German directors depict prostitution as ordinary and mundane, in a manner reminiscent of Godard. Thus, we often see the prostitutes counting money and keeping their accounts. The proliferation of prostitutes (and their clients, who are typically white and affluent) further suggests a crisis of white masculinity.

The majority of films discussed in this chapter are shot largely on location and use many devices, such as long takes, high-angle and panoramic shots, that allow us to see a lot of Berlin. Furthermore, the narratives are constructed in such a way that characters are forced to wander large distances, running, walking and using various means of public transport, examples being Lola in search of money for Manni in *Run, Lola, Run* or the homeless couple looking for a cheap hotel in *Night Shapes*. However, the city that they encounter in their journeys resembles more often an imitation of big cities in foreign films or the simulacra of the city spaces used in computer and video games, than the Berlin known from earlier cinematic representations. This effect results not only from the factors previously described, but also from the visual style and narrative structures employed by the directors. For example, the

Berlin found in *Plus-Minus Null* looks very much like Hong Kong in the films of Wong Kar-Wai, due to the grainy images, to the unnatural, fast or very slow movements back and forth within the same shot and to extremely wide-angle shots. In some scenes it feels as if we are watching a play of lights and colourful patches rather than solid objects. We can also notice a striking similarity in the visual style of *Plus-Minus Null* and *Wonderland*, directed by Michael Winterbottom and set in London (see Chapter 8). In all the films the purpose of such a technique seems to be to create an impression of the chaos and alienation of the con-temporary metropolis. *Plus-Minus Null*, *Night Shapes*, *Sara America* and *Run, Lola, Run* also share with the cinema of Wong Kar-Wai and with Winterbottom's *Wonderland* a fragmented narrative structure.

Sometimes Berlin also resembles cities in films whose authors borrowed from earlier cinematic representations of Berlin or made references to this city. For example, the night club where a teenage prostitute takes a farmer in *Night Shapes* looks almost exactly like the Club Berlin in Martin Scorsese's *After Hours*, set in New York. The similarity is reinforced by the narrative – the farmer feels as alien and lost in this milieu as the protagonist in Scorsese's film who becomes lost in the arty SoHo district of New York. In *Silvester Countdown* Berlin is to be found somewhere else – in Warsaw. Here a young Berlin couple bursting with sexual desire encounter a huge sign that reads 'Berlin' and find a multitude of sex clubs, which they supposedly lack in Berlin. Such a juxtaposition of Berlin and Warsaw is obviously paradoxical, if not ironic, as Berlin is a much larger centre of the sex industry than Warsaw and many Polish women go to Berlin seeking employment in the sex business.

Conclusions

The films discussed in this chapter concentrate on the instability of contemporary Berlin: the fundamental change in Berlin's architecture and image, the disappearance of the old social structures and institutions, resulting in the lack of financial and social security for large groups of people and in the high level of crime. Many of the phenomena are depicted as serious problems in the lives of Berliners, yet the films rarely offer any solution to them. There is no doubt that their authors sympathize with those who are the victims of the situation and who are marginalized in Berlin: foreigners, the unemployed, the homeless, the young and those employed in the black economy, but their films lack the political commitment that we find in the films of Ken Loach, to which many of them are compared. In a fashion, which can be described as postmodern, they limit themselves to depicting the state of things, instead of proposing how to change them. Most importantly, they do not suggest a nostalgic retreat into the past or the resurrection of some mythical 'German identity' as a way of overcoming the present problems. The past is forgotten and erased. In this respect, they are very different from the New German Cinema of Wenders, Kluge and von Trotta, who in the 1960s and 1970s lamented the disappearance of a genuine German culture. For the German directors born in the 1960s, such as Tom Tykwer, Andreas Dresen, Eoin Moore, Thomas Arslan or Roland Suso Richter, some of whom were not born in Germany or came from families of immigrants, the only culture that matters, that is genuine, is the one that actually exists – and Berlin, with its cosmopolitanism, mutability and corelessness, is its centre and epitome.

7

Cleansing the City and the Country: Moscow in the Films of Pavel Lungin

R ussian cinema of the 1990s is renowned for its pessimism. Films of both historical and contemporary subjects portray all kinds of human suffering in a world that is utterly hostile and ugly. The majority of critics explained this preoccupation by referring to Soviet/Russian reality: for Russians both the past and the present day were difficult, even tragic, so no wonder their cinema reflected this situation. The emphasis on the dark side of Russian life also seems to reflect the new circumstances of the film industry – political censorship has largely disappeared, so artists are at last free from having to promote a system which was always inefficient and resulted in abject failure. Moreover, filmmakers, especially the young and those supported by Western producers, seem to assume that concentrating on the shocking aspects of Russian reality will grant them critical and commercial success (see Stiszowa 1997).

Whatever the reasons, the fact is that the films of the 1990s are on the whole much grimmer than those produced in any earlier period of Russian cinematic history. Large Russian cities, and Moscow in particular, become in the films of the 1990s sites of all possible pathologies and the epitome of the whole, tormented country, which neither resisted the change to democracy and the free market economy, nor liberated itself from the legacy of communism. This is true of two films by Pavel Lungin set in Moscow in the early 1990s – *Taxi Blues* (1990) and *Luna Park* (1992) – which are regarded as models of postcommunist Russian cinematic production. They are at the same time 'city films', in the sense of presenting people and problems specific to the big city, and 'national films', as they accurately capture the mood at the end of the old system and the resulting political and moral vacuum all over the country. Yet, in spite of being grim and dark, Lungin's films are not nihilistic, as they offer a clear, distinctive message of what Russian citizens should do to remedy their current misery.

The City in Russian/Soviet History and Cinema

At the turn of the twentieth century Russia was still essentially a rural country – in 1897 less than 10 per cent of its population lived in cities. Following the October Revolution, the pace of urbanization in Russia and the USSR was faster than anywhere else in the world at the time, and in the years 1930–40 the rate of urbanization in Russia was probably the most rapid ever experienced in human history (Lewis and Rowland 1976: 206–7). The communist authorities neither had any strategic urbanization plan, nor did they try to preserve the status quo, but embarked on an extensive programme of industrialization, whose inevitable result was the expansion of existing towns and the construction of new ones (Lewis and Rowland 1976: 210–11). Many of the new factories and cities were built at huge human cost in remote areas, such as Siberia and the Far East. Yet, industrialization was regarded as the end that justified any means, even the misery and death of millions of people. Accordingly, the cinema, which Lenin and his successors regarded as the most powerful tool of communist propaganda, had the task of acknowledging the achievements of the citizens of the Soviet Union in the industrialization of the vast country, and of encouraging them to even greater efforts. Many of the greatest achievements of the formalism and early social realism of the 1920s, such as *Chelovek s kinoapparatom* [Man with a Movie Camera, 1929] by Dziga Vertov and *Oblomok imperii* [Fragment of an Empire, 1929] by Friedrich Ermler, as well as 'construction dramas' of the 1930s, such as *Vstrechnyi* [Counterplan, 1932] by Ermler and Sergei Yutkevich, and *Semero smelykh* [The Brave Seven, 1936] and *Komsomolsk* (1938) by Sergei Gerasimov, were products of this spirit. The films often equated the city with a factory and celebrated and commemorated both. Their characters were happy to live in a mechanistic, industrialized world and enjoyed the beauty of the machine that conquered the forces of nature.

At the same time films were made about life in pre-revolutionary Russia, often portraying strikes in capitalist factories, examples being *Stachka* [Strike, 1924] by Sergei Eisenstein, *Mat* [Mother, 1926] and *Konyets Sankt-Peterburga* [The End of St Petersburg, 1927] by Vsevolod Pudovkin or *Trilogia o Maximie* [Maxim Trilogy, 1935–39] by Grigori Kozintsev and Leonid Trauberg. They typically created a dystopian portrait of the Russian city as a place of poverty and exploitation. The machine, sanctified in 'construction dramas', was condemned in 'revolutionary stories' as a tool of people's alienation (in the classical, Marxist meaning of the term) and, particularly in films that presented the origins of the Bolshevik Revolution, as a vehicle of sinister, military production.

What the two kinds of films have in common is a conviction that the factory and the city were loci of conformity, as individuals had to adjust to their rhythms. People in factories performed the same, mechanical tasks, and strikes and revolutions were organized not by individuals, but by masses of people, working in the same place and living in similar conditions.

In the case of Russian cities and Moscow in particular, the conviction that the city is more important than the individuals who live in it was not far from reality. In communist times Moscow was filled with tall monuments, many of them inaccessible to the public, who were limited to admiring them from a distance. The huge tenement blocks, in which thousands of people lived, also looked monumental rather than domestic. Detached or semi-detached houses, on the other hand, were almost nonexistent. Even Moscow's streets, as Mikhail Yampolsky observes, were created not for individuals, but for the masses. 'The arterial roads were uncommonly wide, left turns were prohibited almost everywhere, and even right turns were often not possible. City authorities have diligently replaced above-ground pedestrian crossings with underground ones, and prohibited not only parking, but even stopping along such major roads as, for example, Tverskaia' (Yampolsky 1995: 98). The subordination of the people to an urban project, which was a consequence of a certain social utopia, was particularly striking to foreigners, such as Walter Benjamin who, when discussing the Moscow of the 1920s, observed that 'even the traffic in Moscow is, to a large extent, a mass phenomenon' (Benjamin 1986: 112).

The Second World War added a new meaning to the Russian city, which became a martyr. This was particularly true of Stalingrad and of Leningrad, attacked on two fronts by German and Finnish armies and besieged for 900 days. Films, both documentaries, such as *Leningrad Fighting* (1941) by Roman Karmen, and fictions, such as *Stalingrad* (1943) by Leonid Varlamov or *Battle for Stalingrad* (1949) by Wladimir Petrov, celebrated the heroism of these cities. Numerous films were also made about the martyrdom of Moscow, Sevastopol and other Russian towns.

After the war, the theme of building and defending the city lost some of its appeal. The factory and the city themselves gradually gained more complex and less positive connotations. Some, more daring, directors of the 1960s and 1970s, such as Eldar Riazanov, Yuli Raizman, Gleb Panfilov, Georgi Danelia and Lana Gogoberidze, mostly through the genre known as *bytovoi*, which can be translated as 'contemporary drama', drew attention to various pathologies of city life, such as alcoholism, corruption, loneliness, poverty, family breakdown and, in the case of women, difficulties in combining work with home-making. Andrei Tarkovsky, although he did not deal overtly with problems of industrialization, and even did not refer directly to Russian reality, created in his famous science fiction *Stalker* (1979) a powerful image of industrialization ended in disaster.

Yet it could be argued that the idea that the city, and Moscow in particular, is somehow more important and better than the countryside survived in Soviet cinema and in other areas of culture until the beginning of the 1980s. In fact, the idea was quite close to reality – the living standards and the level of personal freedom were much higher in the cities, especially in Moscow, than in rural regions. Gyorgy Enyedi explains it as follows:

> In theory and in practice Marxist governments were biased in favour of the cities ... The cities enjoyed advantages in the allocation of development funds by the central planners. Socialist governments were suspicious of the countryside, where the farming population, suffering from heavy taxes, compulsory deliveries of foodstuffs and collectivization, was reluctant to support ambitious programmes of industrialization. (Enyedi 1996: 113)

Consequently, migration from the country to Moscow was regarded as a major social advance by millions of ordinary Russians. At the same time, Moscow, as happened to other European capitals, represented in the cinema the country as a whole. It was assumed that what was true of Moscow, was also true of the whole Soviet Union.

One of the most famous post-Second World War Russian films to portray life in Moscow was *Moskva slezam ne verit* [Moscow Does Not Believe in Tears, 1980] by Vladimir Menshov. The film was a box-office hit and, as a measure of its international success, received an Oscar for Best Foreign Film. *Moscow Does Not Believe in Tears* encapsulates the general idea of Moscow as a place of opportunities, but also shows the dangers and shortcomings of city life – the favourite theme of Russian films made during *perestroika* and after the collapse of communism. It portrays the lives of three provincial girls, Katya, Luda and Tonya, who in the late 1950s come to Moscow looking for love and success. Initially they share the same accommodation in a workers' hostel and work in various factories. After almost twenty years Katya indeed achieves success, although not without much work and determination, becoming the director of a large factory in Moscow and acquiring a spacious and rather elegant flat.

The best indication of the strength of the myth of Moscow as a place of golden opportunities is represented by the words of Luda: 'Moscow is a lottery. Every day you can win something.' Luda, however, is not the one to win, but to lose – her sportsman husband becomes an alcoholic and she ends up with a mundane job in an ironing service. Moreover, Menshov contrasts the country with the city in a way that shows the country as a healthier and happier place to live. We refer here to the fact that Tonya, who ends up marrying a countryman like herself and living in the country with her in-laws, thus missing all the opportunities to which Luda aspired and which Katya fulfilled, is ultimately regarded as the luckiest one.

Taxi Blues – The End of a Working-class Utopia

Taxi Blues was produced when the Soviet Union was still in existence but, according to both film critics and the director himself, it focuses on what happened after *perestroika* – the collapse of communism (Ponarin 1990: 18–19; Ledochowski 1990: 24). 'Films are produced over a long period, therefore one must make a movie about what will happen tomorrow,' said the director, Pavel Lungin, to explain the premise of *Taxi Blues* (Sitbon 1991: 44–5). Lungin, who before his directorial debut worked as a university lecturer and a scriptwriter, wrote the screenplay of *Taxi Blues* to be made by Lenfilm, the big Soviet production company. Yet, as a result of a series of coincidences, the script was shown to the French producer Marin Karmitz, known for financing the films of such *auteurs* as Alain Resnais, Louis Malle, Claude Chabrol and Krzysztof Kieslowski. Karmitz found the story attractive to Western audiences and decided to produce the film (Ponarin 1990: 17–18). The fact that Lungin with *Taxi Blues* subsequently received the award for Best Director at the Cannes Film Festival in 1990 proves that he was right.

The inevitable end of the old communist system is conveyed through the story of a strange friendship between a taxi driver, named Vanya Schlikov, and a saxophonist, Locha. They meet for the first time when Locha, with a group of friends, cruises Moscow by night in Vanya's taxi. Locha is looking for excitement, but when his friends leave, he asks the cabby to wait while he disappears into a tenement block, apparently to look for money. After some time the driver realizes that he will not be paid and leaves, hoping for revenge. Subsequently, he finds Locha and takes away his precious saxophone but, instead of selling it, forces the musician to repay his debt by working as his servant. Locha moves into Schlikov's flat, but resists the pressure to become a diligent worker. Eventually, discovered by an American jazz musician visiting Moscow, Locha leaves Schlikov for good, to embark on a successful career in the USA.

According to the renowned Russian film critic Andriej Plachov, the Moscow depicted in *Taxi Blues* resembles Las Vegas (Plachov 1990: 35). If this opinion is at all justifiable, it is conveyed only in the first scene of the film, when Vanya Schlikov drives his taxi through the centre of the city. The main, wide street is well lit and decorated with banners and neon signs, the sky is illuminated by fireworks, and the pavements are full of people. Yet, even this image conveys more the socialist seriousness than the search for fun, with which Las Vegas is associated, as the street is decorated with large posters of Lenin, and the colossal illuminated letters on the imposing buildings read CCCP (for Union of Soviet Socialist Republics). The people all look in one direction – at the sky. We can guess that this is no ordinary day, but a national holiday, presumably the anniversary of the October Revolution. The whole scene strongly recollects the description of Moscow given by Walter Benjamin – Moscow is made for the masses, not for individuals. Once Schlikov leaves the centre, the view changes completely; the city becomes dark, empty and anonymous. The block into which Locha disappears is so

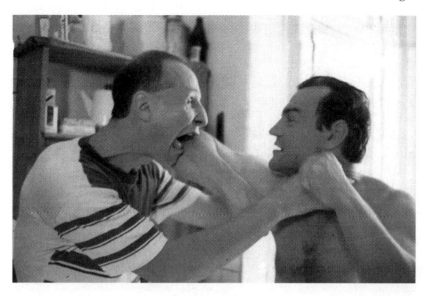

18. *Taxi Blues* (1990), dir. Pavel Lungin

huge that it will take days, if not weeks to discover where he lives. This
grim, depressing image, rather than the view of the 'flashy centre', will
dominate the rest of the film. Even the centre of Moscow in subsequent
scenes will lose its resemblance to Las Vegas, becoming empty and
dark.

Lungin portrays Vanya Schlikov as a man who tries to make the most
of his limited opportunities. He works hard, doing many extra hours in
his taxi, and pays a lot of attention to his fitness and personal hygiene.
He takes a shower every day, changes his clothes after work and uses
special, homemade exercise equipment. His 'bodyguard' musculature is
the best testimony to his health and fitness. Vanya also strives to make
his flat tidy and cosy, decorating it with posters and magazine cutouts.
Once Locha moves in, he persuades his artistic companion to follow
his example and even provides him with expensive food high in vitamins.

Yet, Vanya's efforts to create a clean, healthy environment are undermined by the age and poor quality of the building, as well as by his
own, working-class habits. His tiny 'bachelor's apartment' consists of
small dark rooms, filled with gym equipment, bunk beds and cardboard
boxes, functioning as cupboards. The rooms look more like corridors
or train compartments than proper rooms. There is little privacy in the
tenement block, as each kitchen is shared by more than one family and

19.   *Taxi Blues* (1990), dir. Pavel Lungin

serves also as a drying room, the telephones are in the corridors and there is a custom of leaving the doors open. Schlikov's neighbour, Netchiporenko, an old man of conservative, anti-Semitic views, spends more time in Vanya's flat than in his own, cooking for both of them, talking about the past and filling the flat with the ambience of a neglected bachelor. The taxi driver has even less influence on his wider environment, as the neighbouring, dingy streets serve as an area to collect industrial waste and are used by the local people to play cards and musical instruments, drink vodka, sing, dance and defecate. Schlikov's appeal to the shopkeeper to stop selling vodka to the queuing drunkards is in vain and Vanya is even attacked by a group of drunkards. It is also obvious that the council pays no attention to the state of the pavements and streets; there are holes and puddles of water on the streets even when it is not raining.

Locha brings Schlikov only disappointment; although he reluctantly agrees to carry the suitcases of Schlikov's passengers and to wash his taxi, he does so neither attentively nor properly. Moreover, after taking a bath one day he leaves the tap running and floods the neighbouring flats, causing extensive damage. Ultimately, Schlikov's attempts to stay clean and force everyone else to be clean only emphasize his inability to overcome the grim environment.

The majority of the exteriors and interiors used in the film give the impression of irreparable neglect and dilapidation, one example being the abattoir where Schlikov's girlfriend is employed. Even more than Schlikov's flat, this looks like a tangle of corridors and of poorly lit, dirty rooms. There are no separate areas for clerical work and for slaughtering, nor for work and for rest. Consequently, people eat their meals among the pigs' carcasses and office files, which appears grotesque and surreal. Hardly anyone there works; whenever Schlikov visits his friend there is a party going on, with people drinking alcohol. It also looks as if most of the meat processed in the abattoir is sold to the workers' 'friends' and on the black market. The taxi depot where Schlikov keeps his taxi and the music studio where Locha prepares for his concerts all resemble abandoned factories – huge, grim and run-down. The atmosphere in the depot is similar to that of the abattoir; the prospect of entertainment seems to be the sole motive why people work. Moreover, people party as if there will be no tomorrow – they hardly talk, only drink heavily, as if to forget their drab reality. An even more surreal view is provided by the converted train where Locha lives before he moves in with Schlikov. Vanya, who looks for Locha there, opens various compartments only to find people heavily drinking and partying, completely oblivious to the outside world. All places give an impression of transience, typical for a country caught between two political and economic systems, but the purpose or even direction of the change is not clear.

The impression of in-betweenness is conveyed not only by what is shown, but also by what is not. The old symbols of socialist 'progress', such as factories, machines and chimneys and communist propaganda are either scarce or not fulfilling their role. Similarly rare are the new signs of capitalist consumerism that flooded Moscow in the last years of *perestroika*, since when they have become a constant element in the urban landscape (see Condee and Padunov 1995). The space in *Taxi Blues* is hardly 'westernized'; there are no adverts on television or on the streets, and the only billboard featured in the film shows Locha's American concert. Graffiti, regarded as among the most powerful tools to articulate new ideas in Russia and Eastern Europe, are anaemic and unimaginative: minute and colourless 'Reebok' and 'BBC' inscriptions on the wall. Flashy consumer goods, such as a man's dressing gown in garish colours or a female dummy, eventually appear in Schlikov's flat, but he did not buy them in Moscow but received them as a gift from

Locha on his return from America. The gadgets, as Karen Jaehne notes, look extremely inappropriate among the simple furnishings (Jaehne 1991: 52) and this is precisely Locha's point – he gave them to his ascetic friend to make him look ridiculous. Schlikov at first finds the gifts funny, but soon wants to get rid of them, finding them a 'polluting' influence.

The motifs of dirt and cleansing are profound in *Taxi Blues*. First, there is a literal cleansing – keeping one's body clean and one's environment tidy. Cleansing also has a metaphorical meaning, as it refers to getting rid of people who 'contaminate' society, to cleansing one's culture of 'dirty' elements. Such an idea is characteristic of totalitarian regimes, including Stalinism. One recollects the gulags where people who did not fit the Stalinist ideal of society were incarcerated because of their social background, political views or ethnicity. Cleanliness in both senses is close to Schlikov's heart; he wants himself and everyone around him to remain pure. Obviously, such a project presupposes a certain ideal of culture and society. Vanya Schlikov's ideal is that of a homogeneous society, consisting of people like himself: hard-working, truly Russian and communist. Most forcefully he conveys his ideal to a group of young people who approach his taxi asking to hire it, by accusing them of having delicate hands and eventually beating them up. Schlikov despises artists in particular, whom he accuses of living at the expense of the working classes, and Jews for being physically weak and over-privileged by the communist authorities. Unsurprisingly, Schlikov feels utter contempt for Locha, a Jew and an artist (a trait he shares with many famous Russian filmmakers, including Sergei Eisenstein and Friedrich Ermler). Although it is never made explicit, Locha's interest in jazz might be another reason for regarding him as non-Russian and unworthy. Jazz was always treated with the utmost suspicion in Russia (see Eagle 1992; Jaehne 1991). Some party officials considered jazz as 'legitimate', being the music of the black proletariat, but the opinion prevailed that, as Maxim Gorky put it, 'jazz represented a capitalist manipulation of savage and degenerate sexual impulses' (Eagle 1992: 252).

Although Vanya's attitude to Locha is saturated with unacceptable ethnic and class prejudices, the saxophonist does nothing to indicate that these prejudices are unfounded; on the contrary, he confirms them by being totally irresponsible, selfish and reckless. In the director's own words, his two main characters signify two sides of Soviet/Russian culture: European and Eurasian. Locha, who is physically frail, but

intelligent and talented, personifies Europe, while muscular, hard-working Schlikov stands for Eurasia (Sitbon 1991: 45). Lungin assumed that
the victory of communism signified the triumph of Eurasian aspects
of Russian over European culture.

From a postcommunist perspective, which is undoubtedly adopted
by the majority of viewers, it is Vanya Schlikov, with his plain features,
coarse manners, old-fashioned flat and working-class values, rather than
Locha, who does not suit society. The taxi driver's unattractiveness and
the obsolescence of his values are obvious even to his girlfriend, whom
he invites to a party, but who immediately abandons him for a flamboyant musician. Locha also ignores Schlikov – he eats his meals and
drinks his alcohol, but afterwards moves to another room without even
thanking him for his hospitality. There is an analogy between Schlikov's
situation and that of millions of ordinary working-class Russians, who
in subsequent years were also abandoned and forced to move to the
margins of Russian society. Their privileged position (if not in reality,
at least in official political discourse) was taken over by businessmen,
media people and members of the mafia as a result of various factors,
such as the gradual diminution in importance of heavy industry and the
introduction of a market economy. Moreover, they ceased to be a
coherent group and became socially fragmented and politically dis-
oriented.

Another powerful image of Schlikov's redundancy is conveyed in the
scene in which he waits for Locha, who at this stage is a world-renowned
celebrity, to return to Moscow from New York. The saxophonist,
accompanied by a large entourage of groupies, climbs into an elegant
western limousine and simply fails to notice his old companion who is
waiting for him in his old-fashioned Volga, dressed in his best Sunday
clothes. Again, this image can be regarded as symbolic of the predicament of millions of Schlikov-like people (or, perhaps, even of Russia
as a whole) who in the late 1980s and in the 1990s waited in vain for
western interest and recognition.

Although Vanya regards himself as morally superior to Locha and
bemoans the decline of his motherland, his own activities exacerbate its
parlous state, thus undermining his high moral position. For example, he
boosts his own income as a taxi driver by selling alcohol at night when
the shops are closed and draws Locha into this illegal trade. The very fact
that Schlikov operates largely at night, when most people are asleep,
suggests that he ignores cultural and even natural norms. Accordingly,

there is an element of arrogance in his belief that he can serve as an example to his peers. Schlikov is also inconsistent; on the one hand he dislikes art and frivolity, as well as showing contempt for western ways, on the other, the news of Locha's success in America completely changes his attitude to his old friend – he becomes very proud of him, forgiving all the disappointments the saxophonist brought him.

Lungin shows that in late-communist Russia there is only a narrow distinction between cleansing and destruction. What looks at the beginning like putting things in order, finishes with rampant annihilation. An example is the party that Schlikov organizes for Locha. Schlikov puts a lot of effort into preparing the food and decorating the room but, offended by the saxophonist, who is unwilling to appreciate his effort, gets drunk and knocks over a table, spilling food everywhere. He also rapes his girlfriend Christina to punish her for preferring Locha to himself and, at another party held in his honour at the abattoir, he makes a frenzied attack, for no reason shouting at everybody and destroying the guitar with which Christina entertains the guests.

The climax of Schlikov's frenzy is his final attempt to stop Locha, who decides to leave after only a short stay, to join the groupies accompanying him on his trip back to Moscow. From Locha's point of view the decision is perfectly rational – Schlikov was never his 'natural' friend, so no wonder the saxophonist feels no obligation to keep him company. We can even be surprised that Locha decides to visit the taxi driver at all. For Schlikov, however, Locha's departure before the party even starts, when the table is full of food and alcohol, is deeply insulting. Consequently, Vanya stops a nearby taxi, throws out the driver and starts to pursue what he thinks is Locha's car. He crashes into the car, killing the driver, who – to his stunned disbelief – is not Locha, but an unknown Japanese. In the closing titles we read that the stories of Schlikov, Christina and Locha all finished reasonably happily: Schlikov set up his own taxi company and bought a Mercedes, Christina married a millionaire and became a businesswoman, and Locha made more hit records before dying of excess alcohol consumption. Yet, in the light of what was presented, the outcome of the film must be regarded as utterly ironic, a travesty of the Hollywood-style ending, completely at odds with Russian late-communist reality.

Schlikov's muddled personality, his intolerance and violence, his crude manners with women, as well as his obsession with physical fitness and work are reminiscent of Travis Bickle in *Taxi Driver* (1976) by Martin

Scorsese (see Ponarin 1990). Both men have an ambition to introduce order into their social environment, to – as Travis puts it – 'clean the city of the scum', without being orderly themselves. Moreover, in both cases it is suggested that their frustration results not only from their own shortcomings, but also from a failure on the part of society, or the state in which they live. Travis was traumatized by the Vietnam War, where he acquired his xenophobia and violence; Vanya was cheated by an ideology which promised him a privileged place in society, and left him marginalized and forgotten.

There are significant differences between the environments in which Travis and Vanya operate. Scorsese's New York is very colourful and alive, both during the day and at night, it is a city that never sleeps. Moreover, it is accessible, full of night bars, restaurants, cafés and cinemas working twenty-four hours a day. Much is going on simply on the streets, political meetings take place in public squares, prostitutes seek clients and quarrel with their pimps, people chat in front of the bars and cinemas, or simply hang out. It is also a place of opportunities, people of different social backgrounds can meet there, albeit sometimes only for a short time. For example, Travis manages to strike up a friendship with Betsy, who is good-looking, educated and sophisticated, and the presidential candidate for the USA is a passenger in his taxi.

Moscow, on the other hand, feels utterly alienating and desolate, both during the day and at night. Lungin's film features few places of public entertainment, such as cinemas, restaurants or clubs. The only café shown in *Taxi Blues* serves as a background for Locha's illegal vodka sales, thus only emphasizing the dysfunctionality of Russian entertainment venues. All parties and gatherings take place in private or semi-private spaces: in people's flats, in factories, in shop queues, on the nearby streets. There is little chance to meet anyone new, particularly from different social backgrounds. One cannot even imagine Schlikov carrying any prominent figures of Russian life in his taxi; his car seems to serve only people like himself who live on modest incomes in drab houses. No one has the relaxed gait and demeanour characteristic of New Yorkers. Paradoxically, although there were relatively few car owners in Moscow in the 1980s, Scorsese's New York of the 1970s feels more like a city of *flâneurs* than Lungin's Moscow. The Muscovites' clothing is also grey and uniform in comparison with the abundance of colours and styles one can see on the streets of New York in Scorsese's film. It looks as if the long years of disapproval of any sign of nonconformity

made Muscovites unable to express their individuality. *Taxi Blues* is shot
in dark, 'dirty' colours, with the only addition of red, all adding to the
impression of grimness, sadness and violence in Russia's capital city.

In contrast to earlier cinematic portrayals of Moscow and other
important Russian cities, whose authors tried to portray the urban space
as an aggregate of well-known sites – famous streets, bridges, buildings
and monuments – *Taxi Blues* lacks this quality. The centre of Moscow
rarely features in Lungin's film and most spaces do not have any speci-
ficity; even the few monuments that appear in the shots are unidentifiable.
Moreover, it is impossible to appreciate any connection between different
locations, all appearing to be separate, discrete. On the whole, this
supports the concept conveyed by the narrative that Moscow became
socially and historically fragmented. This is, of course, another sign of
the failure of communism as a utopia of togetherness, social inclusion
and wholeness.

The Moscow in *Taxi Blues*, being huge in area and almost empty, is
nothing like a modern or a postmodern metropolis, suffering from
overcrowding, excessive traffic and pollution. Yet, in contrast to the
director of the previously mentioned *Moscow Does Not Believe in Tears*,
Lungin does not present any of Moscow's 'anti-metropolitan' features,
such as proximity to the countryside, as an asset. The landscape of
Moscow's outskirts, which Schlikov visits, apparently trying to sell
Locha's saxophone to the Gypsies who live there in caravans, is even
more depressing than images of central Moscow. The dirt, poverty and
general anarchy are even more extreme than anywhere else in Moscow.
The place has the backwardness of the periphery and none of the
redeeming characteristics of nature.

Luna Park – The Excesses of the Carnivalesque

In *Taxi Blues*, the desire to put the clock back, to return to some form
of communist utopia (which never existed in reality) by re-educating
those who pollute society with their inappropriate attitudes and lifestyles,
was the small-scale plan of one disorientated individual. In *Luna Park*
it becomes a major project shared by a large number of mainly young
people, who carry it out systematically and ruthlessly.

In the film's opening scene the two meanings of cleansing coincide:
the literal and the metaphorical. A crowd of muscular young men,
resembling western skinheads, answer their leader's questions in unison:

20.   *Luna Park* (1992), dir. Pavel Lungin

'Who are we?' – 'The Cleaners!' 'What are we cleaning?' – 'Russia!' The role of the 'dirt' in this scene is played by western civilization, symbolized by cans of Coca-Cola. The Cleaners crush them with their hands before attacking another group of young people: a Hell's Angels-style gang who arrive at the battlefield on motorcycles. The fight is brutal and neither group has any respect either for the lives of their opponents or for their material surroundings. We see burning motorcycles being thrown from the top floor of apartment blocks, cars being burnt and demolished and an enormous iron gate used by the skinheads to attack their enemies. They use metal rods and chains to strangle each other. The scene finishes when the skinheads' leader sits on a bulldozer and the machine moves among the fighting people, collecting piles of earth and anything that stands in its way. In its barbarity, the fight resembles that between the Russians and the Teutonic Knights in *Alexander Nevsky* (1938) by Sergei Eisenstein. Paradoxically, the young skinheads, athletic, bare-chested and almost entirely blond, look more German than Russian. One German reviewer even describes the leader of the group, Andrei, as a 'Russian Siegfried' (Greuner 1993: 32).

A typical, huge Soviet 'palace' (which also featured in *Taxi Blues*) serves as a backdrop to the fight. There were several buildings of this type built in Moscow during the Stalinist era and one was built in

Warsaw as a 'gift' from the Russian people to their Polish 'friends' (see Chapter 5). Tall, imposing, monumental and often surrounded by social-realist sculptures, the 'palaces' became the most distinctive and enduring achievements of Stalinist architecture. The juxtaposition of the 'palace' with the post-Soviet act of destruction is, in our opinion, not accidental. It suggests a similarity between the Stalinist project of a new beginning for Russian history and the missionary zeal that inflames Lungin's skinheads. Indeed, it can be argued that the skinheads are the spiritual children or grandchildren of those who built social-realist palaces. However, in contrast to Stalinists, who were interested not only in destruction but also in construction, for the film's characters 'cleaning' seems to be the ultimate goal. The fact that the palace remains, while everything around is levelled to the ground, can be interpreted as a sign of the robustness of past architecture and past values which the buildings embodied. A low-angle shot is employed in this scene, strengthening the impression of the palace's powerfulness.

The next scene takes us to Luna Park, a cross between a funfair and a circus, situated on the outskirts of Moscow. Here the fascists introduced in the previous scene meet, and some even seem to live here. Luna Park is nothing like a modern theme park; the equipment is dilapidated and old-fashioned, and there are few visitors. The small audience who come to see a clown perform consist only of some soldiers and a few adults with children, leaving most of the seats empty. Nobody laughs at the mediocre performance and some viewers even sit with their backs to the actors. The leader of the show is Aljona, who is also the manager of Luna Park, the mother and lover of the skinheads' leader, Andrei. She also takes the role of the main ideologist of the group and initiates their racist attacks. Her ideology is first revealed when she describes to her young followers her dream about a stone crying because of the great danger that threatens Russia. The stone advises her to build a hermitage that will be visible only to true Russians. This tale refers to the situation of the fascists: the cellar where they meet is like the hermitage, isolated from the outside world and unknown to those who do not belong to their circle of Russian nationalists.

Encouraged by Aljona and led by Andrei, the skinheads ransack Moscow's restaurants. Their aim is to intimidate, humiliate and steal money from their Jewish owners. Hot jelly is poured in their faces; they are also forcibly carried in a wheelbarrow and beaten up. In addition, their restaurants are marked with the Star of David, presumably to inform the visitors that they sit in a 'contaminated' place. All these scenes of harassment bear strong similarities to images of Jews being intimidated by the Nazis before the Second World War. Against the background of the frightened and humiliated people, Andrei and his friends look particularly strong and Germanic. As with the Nazis, the Russian fascists hate Jews both because they regard them as racially inferior and because they are rich and successful. Indeed, the restaurant raided by Andrei and his gang is full of people enjoying themselves. It might also be suggested that the skinheads hate them because they represent the market economy, which is at odds with the socialist ideals that appeal to the skinheads. Andrei and his comrades also target gays, intending to rid Moscow of homosexuals for reasons similar to their desire to get rid of Jews: because Russia has nothing to gain from them. Andrei's comrades tell two young gays kidnapped at a rock concert and imprisoned in the cellars of Luna Park about young working-class women living in provincial Russian towns and waiting to be impregnated to give birth to a new generation of Russians – they can not fulfil their 'patriotic duty' because men like them refuse to do their bit. Fascists also despise homosexuals because they regard them, like the Jews, as physically weak and feminine.

To convince her son that the Jews do not deserve their privileged position, Aljona tells Andrei about her own, tortuous career. She was once a young gymnast and singer about to take part in a competition for young artists. Shortly before the event one of the judges, a famous Jewish composer, invited her to his home, where he seduced her; during the competition he did not repay her for her 'service', but slighted her for lacking talent. Aljona tells Andrei that the judges at the competition, where she did badly, were almost all non-Russians: Jews, Georgians, Tartars. This reinforced her belief that foreigners, not Russians, governed Russia, the Russians being reduced to second-class citizens in their own country. In spite of her nationalism, Aljona seems to be more fascinated with German culture than with Russian traditions. Evidence of this is her love for the music of Richard Wagner, regarded as the perfect embodiment of German culture. Telling Andrei about her 'romance' with the Jewish composer, Aljona reveals to him his own background as half-Jewish – the composer was his father. This leads Andrei to look for his father and for his own true identity. Andrei's pursuit allows the director to show various aspects of life in contemporary Moscow.

Luna Park serves as the main setting in the film; it is the place from

21. *Luna Park* (1992), dir. Pavel Lungin

where Andrei begins his journey to find his father and to where he keeps returning. It is a liminal zone. 'Liminality' indicates borderline, marginality, 'in-betweenness'; moments of discontinuity in the social fabric, in social space and in history. Liminality is associated, for example, with places of religious experience, with the seashore and the 'carnival-esque' (see Shields 1991). One sense in which Luna Park belongs to this category is geographic – it is situated between the city and the country-side. On one side of the funfair we see a forest, on the other tenement blocks and factories. Luna Park gets the worst of both worlds; on the one hand it is dirty, polluted, full of alcoholics and various kinds of drop-outs, on the other, it is provincial and far from the centre of Moscow – at night it is almost impossible to get away from it. The liminality of Luna Park manifests itself also in its structure, in which margins are used much more than the centre; almost everything that happens here takes place either high in the air, on the roller-coaster, or on various sorts of merry-go-round, and in its enormous bunker, where Andrei and Aljona have their meetings with their comrades.

Luna Park is also a site of the carnivalesque, as defined by Mikhail Bakhtin, as it includes the temporary suspension of hierarchical ranks and liberates its participants from the norms of etiquette and decency imposed on them at other times (Bakhtin 1984: 5–10). The skinheads who stay in Luna Park do not obey any rules of etiquette and defy any authority and social control. We see them displaying their physiques to each other, drinking champagne out of the bottle, shouting and laughing loudly. The fact that the majority of scenes are shot when the characters are in frantic movement, going up and down on the roller-coaster or on the go-carts, increases the impression of carnivalesque freedom, joy and madness. Although in constant motion, Luna Park is on the whole static and claustrophobic, as the movements are circular – the go-carts cannot escape their confines and the roller-coaster cars always return to the same point from where they started their journey. Cinematography strengthens the feeling of dizziness, circularity and claustrophobia, as the camera usually assumes the point of view of someone on a roller-coaster. A similar function is played by the sharp, MTV-style montage, which, by emphasizing the motif of roller-coasters and merry-go-rounds, gives the impression that there is no escape from Luna Park.

The carnivalesque is also often the site of violence and excessive, wild sex, forbidden under normal circumstances. Rob Shields, for instance, when discussing the liminal qualities of English seaside resorts, refers to the phenomenon of the 'dirty weekend', when respectable married men indulge in extra-marital sex (Shields 1991: 105–12). In Luna Park this forbidden sex is primarily between Andrei and Aljona; its wildness results from being incestuous.

On the other hand, Luna Park is not a typical or true liminal space because liminality presupposes that normality exists beyond its borders. For example, the Victorian holiday at the seaside resort was extraordinary because the rest of the year was ordinary, lived according to the 'rationalised regimes of industrial labour' and subordinated to social control, imposed by law, customs and religion (Shields 1991: 84–7). The difference between Luna Park and the rest of Moscow lies only in the degree of abnormality. All the places that Andrei visits when searching to find out who he is, are sites of decline, disorder and violence. First, we see him visiting a register office to find his birth certificate. In its corridor a wedding party in taking place, with people drinking alcohol and dancing to the accompaniment of a small orchestra. On the same corridor people are sitting and waiting on the benches to be seen by various clerks and a worker is putting nails in the wall. Everybody is lost in his own affairs and oblivious to the presence of others.

Similar scenes take place in the flat of Naoum Kheifitz, Andrei's father. The flat is huge and was once very elegant, as suggested by some furniture and souvenirs, among them a marble bust of Kheifitz himself, made during Stalinist rule. At the time of Andrei's first encounter with his father, however, Naoum uses his flat not only as a place to live but also to boost his meagre pension, as he rents it to anybody who is prepared to pay. The composition of his 'guests' is grotesque in its heterogeneity and incompatibility: old ladies' clubs, musicians of different sorts, protesters of various nationalities, foreign television journalists, whores and their clients, and eventually Naoum's own friends. The scene looks like a never-ending party.

It turns out that, for Naoum, who is well remembered for his past flamboyant lifestyle, partying is now a way to earn extra cash. He offers his services as a professional entertainer to the organizers of weddings and celebrations in honour of retired workers. He also entertains schoolchildren. Andrei, who accompanies Naoum to some of the events, is forced to meet and drink with people whom his gang would like to dispose of: ethnic minorities and other 'polluters' of Russian society. There are also parties in the flat of Andrei's mute bootlegger friend (or relative) whom he approaches to get a gun. The general impression is that the whole of Russia has stopped working in order to join in a celebration of some sort. The only site of labour visited in Lungin's film is a steelworks where Andrei's aunt is employed as a manager. Even she, however, complains that people in her factory no longer work and reminisces with nostalgia about the time of communism, when competition in production was a way of life. The shift from working to playing is suggested by setting one of the parties in a trolleybus, which the retired driver, for whom the event is being organized, used to drive. Although the usual purpose of the parties is to commemorate someone, the participants behave as if their aim is to forget; drinking alcohol is what these events are all about. Consequently, the parties are not particularly joyful and they often end in violence – tables are turned over and people are abused or even beaten up. There is also much promiscuous and 'indecent' sex around, as suggested by a prostitute and an Arab businessman who visit Naoum's flat. On another occasion, after a night spent at his father's flat, Andrei finds himself in bed with a stream of different people: women and men, old and young, people of different ages and colours of skin.

Lungin shows that the Cleaners' perception of themselves as the saviours of Russia is arrogant and unreasonable. They cannot serve as an example to be followed by the rest of the nation because they are like the rest of it, only worse – more violent, lazy and regressive. They are even inconsistent in their attitude to ethnicity. This is shown in a humorous episode in which they discuss Arnold Schwarzenegger; the skinheads utterly admire the Austrian-American symbol of machismo (their club in Luna Park is decorated with his photographs) but at the same time they cannot accept him as a Westerner with a Jewish name, so they invent a ridiculous story, according to which he is of Russian background. By the same token, as the skinheads cannot serve as an example to ordinary people, Luna Park cannot be an example for Moscow, because it is similar to Moscow, only more extreme in its vices. It can be argued that the funfair serves as a metaphor of contemporary Moscow, or even of the whole of Russia.

The huge gulf between the ambitious project of cleaning the city and the poor quality of the 'Cleaners' reminds us of *Taxi Blues*. The only difference lies in the fact that Schlikov in *Taxi Blues* had some redeeming features; he was hard-working and serious. The neo-Nazis in *Luna Park*, on the other hand, seem to have nothing positive to offer. The only exception is Andrei, who at a certain point strikes up a friendship with his witty and charming, albeit irresponsible, Jewish father, deciding to break with his old friends, his mother and his own past. The film ends with Andrei destroying Luna Park with a handful of grenades and then leaving Moscow with his father by train, heading for Siberia.

Lungin is not unique in presenting Russia as a site of the carnivalesque. Anna Lawton, Svetlana Boym and Andrew Horton single out a whole group of films made in the 1980s and 1990s that confirm such an image of Russia, particularly movies directed by Yuri Mamin, such as *Neptune Festival* (1986), *Fountain* (1988) and *Sideburns* (1990) (see Lawton 1992; Boym 1993; Horton 1993). The difference between *Luna Park* and the films by Mamin lies in their approach to reality. Mamin's portrayal of Russia is hugely exaggerated and grotesque, his narratives and settings have only metaphorical, not literal meaning. Moreover, as Lawton suggests when discussing his films in a chapter entitled 'Peering into the Future', they refer to the possible future of Russia rather than to its present (Lawton 1992: 215–19). Lungin's film, on the other hand, although not completely devoid of exaggeration, demonstrates that taking part in a carnival is a way of life for ordinary, contemporary Muscovites.

As is *Taxi Blues*, *Luna Park* is also full of references to western cinema. The film reminds us most of the Australian *Romper Stomper* (1992) by Geoffrey Wright. Both movies are convincing portraits of ethnic conflicts in contemporary towns (in the case of *Romper Stomper* between the white inhabitants of Melbourne and Chinese immigrants) and both show the ultimate defeat of the racist 'Cleaners'. There is also some affinity between *Luna Park* and films by the Hong Kong director Wong Kar-Wai. The ending of Lungin's film, which emphasizes the dystopian character of the city and the redeeming force of nature, is particularly similar to the ending of Wong's *Days of Being Wild* (1990). In Wong's film, set partly in Indonesia, the main character also leaves the city by train, trying to escape his tragic fate and heading into an unknown future. The high-angle shot of a train going through the wild countryside, used in the closing episodes of both films, can be interpreted as a distancing device – against the background of the vast expanse of tall trees the characters appear small and meaningless. In the case of *Luna Park*, the image of nature hardly touched by human affairs is also, in our opinion, a source of optimism; as long as Russian people have somewhere to run away to from the city life, they have a chance to start again.

Conclusions

It is often assumed that the contemporary city is a locus of fragmentation and difference. This diagnosis to a great extent can be applied to Lungin's Moscow, along with some other cities discussed in this book. His two films portray Moscow as devoid of any cultural, historical or even geographical centre. We also do not recollect any other Russian film presenting such a variety of races, nationalities and cultures, as *Taxi Blues* and *Luna Park* do, with their Jews, Arabs, Asian Muslims, blacks, Japanese, Eskimo-like people, western foreigners and, of course, Russians.

The emphasis on difference and fragmentation is deliberate; it allows Lungin to highlight the growing gap between, on the one hand, the reality of ethnic and cultural diversity and of increasing fragmentation in both Moscow and the former Soviet Union as a whole, and, on the other hand, the project of an ethnic and cultural cleansing and of a strong centralism in which many Russians and even the Russian state indulge. The clearest testimony to this gap is to be found in the prolonged wars in the Asian republics of Chechnya and Dagestan and the significant popularity of extreme nationalist movements. In *Taxi Blues* and *Luna Park*, Lungin does not refer directly to most of these phenomena, but provides us with an insight into their social and psychological background and gives his diagnosis of the current situation. It feels as if the main problem of present-day Russia is not its social and ethnic differentiation and fragmentation, but its resistance to change, its search for unrealistic and violent alternatives in the name of a return to some kind of utopia of ethnic, social and cultural purity – a purity that in reality never existed. In short, the solution that Lungin proposes is to stop cleansing the city and the country, and to accept instead reality as it is.

III

Case Study: Great Britain

British Cities since the 1980s and Their Cinematic Representation

The last part of our book will be devoted to the cinematic representation of the cities of one country: Great Britain. Against the
backdrop of 'Old Europe', Britain has changed immensely in the last
two decades, particularly as a result of socio-economic and political
transformation, brought about by the governments of two prime min-
isters: the Conservative Margaret Thatcher and New Labour Tony Blair.
In the decade during which she was prime minister, Thatcher, who
became the epitome of the New Right, managed, as John Corner and
Sylvia Harvey observe,

> [To] 'roll back' the state and public sector, to reduce public spend-
> ing, to minimize both public provision and public intervention in
> the market, and to return all profitable enterprises to the owner-
> ship and control of private shareholders through an extensive
> programme of denationalization ... Their adoption in Britain has
> facilitated ... a decrease in manufacturing industry, growth in the
> financial and leisure service sector, growth in the proportion of
> self-employed in the workforce, a growing trade gap, mass un-
> employment, and the development of a low-wage sector of the
> economy. (Corner and Harvey 1991: 3)

The changes introduced by Thatcher, and continued by John Major, had an almost immediate and profound effect on the state and image of British cities and urban life (more so than on the countryside, which only recently experienced an upheaval, due to such 'by-products' of Thatcherite politics as bovine spongiform encephalopathy). First, they strengthened the position of London as the richest city in Britain and as the political, economic and cultural centre of the country. London under Thatcher also consolidated its status as one of the centres of global capitalism and the new information economy, in conjunction with New York and Tokyo. Not surprisingly, most of the existing literature on the postmodern European urban environment refers to London. For instance, much has been written on the process of concentration of corporate activities in central London and the consequent increase in speculative building that has resulted in the regeneration of the City.[1] Thatcherite policies also resulted in the decline and marginalization of many other British towns, particularly those in the North and West, whose wealth came from heavy industries such as coalmining and shipbuilding.

Another important result of Thatcherite policies was an increasing divide between poor and rich areas in British cities, as well as social fragmentation. Again, nowhere else is this phenomenon more visible than in London, which contains some of the richest and poorest areas of England. However, the Thatcherite legacy is not only the loss of national standing of the poorer cities and the further decline of 'sinking', working-class estates; as Franco Bianchini and Hermann Schwengel observe, the situation of British cities since Thatcher gained power is full of paradoxes and contradictions: urbanism and anti-urbanism; Europeanization and Americanization; regeneration and further decline; the new interest in active citizenship and the erosion of local autonomy (see Bianchini and Schwengel 1991).

So far, the most significant political change brought about by the government led by Tony Blair (who in many ways continues the work of his Conservative predecessors) is devolution in Scotland, Wales and Northern Ireland, introduced as a vehicle to increase democracy in the parts of Britain that had the strongest regional identity and greatest dislike of central government, and thus strengthen the unity of Great Britain. The most visible result of this transformation is, however, an increase in Scottish and Welsh nationalism and a pressure for ever greater political independence from England. It is difficult to establish at this stage if devolution affected more those living in the cities than in the country, and in what way life in Edinburgh and Cardiff has changed since they became the sites of new regional parliaments.

Are these political and social changes reflected in contemporary urban British cinema, or are other factors, particularly those which can be described as purely cinematic, more significant for the image and character of British towns as they appear in the cinema of the 1990s? In order to answer this question we decided to look at films set in four British towns that are very different in terms of their size, geographical location, history and character: London, Edinburgh, Swansea and Blackpool.

8

London: Fragments of a Metropolis

London in Cinema

To summarize the history of London in cinema seems almost an impossible task. The difficulty results from the large number of films set in London and the variety of features, often contradictory, which the English capital reveals in these films. Having said that, we will argue that some of the faces of London are more distinctive and memorable than others, and that certain types of representation of London were dominant in particular periods of cinematic history, usually following the changes that took place in discourses larger than 'London cinema': British cinema, as well as world cinema.

Thus (to limit ourselves to the war and postwar period), in the 1940s and the early 1950s London was typically portrayed as an ensemble of small communities belonging to the larger community of England, examples being Ealing productions such as *Fires were Started* (1943), directed by Humphrey Jennings, *Passport to Pimlico* (1948) by Henry Cornelius and *It Always Rains on Sunday* (1947) by Robert Hamer. The bird's-eye view of London that opens many films of this period, followed by a shot of the part of the city where the narrative is set, emphasized this 'community inside a community' perception of London. However, while the films made during and immediately after the war conveyed the feeling of national and local unity, later films emphasized the danger of destruction of communities by selfish, young individuals, the archetypal example being *The Blue Lamp* (1949) by Basil Dearden. The 1960s are primarily associated with 'Swinging' London, as represented, for example, in *Darling* (1965), directed by John Schlesinger, *Catch Us If You Can* (1965) by John Boorman, *Georgy Girl* (1966) by Silvio Narizzano and *Wonderwall* (1967) by Joe Massot. In these films Londoners are usually affluent, liberal, hedonistic and at ease with themselves. There is no longer any need to forge a community; communities, if they exist at all, are short-lived, ad hoc creations, and their purpose is not mutual support but fun. This also applies to the working-class 'sub-genre' of 'Swinging' London, as portrayed in *Alfie* (1966) by Lewis Gilbert or, to a certain extent, *On the Buses* (1971) by Harry Booth. The 1970s can be regarded as a transitional period in the representation of London, between the swinging and careless 1960s and the depressing 1980s, best encapsulated by *Performance* (1970), directed by Nicolas Roeg and Donald Cammell and the largely forgotten *The Optimists of Nine Elms* (1973) by Anthony Simmons. The most important influence shaping cinematic London of the 1980s and early 1990s was Thatcherism. In terms of representing the city, the main purpose of numerous films of the period, such as *Riff-Raff* (1990), directed by Ken Loach, *My Beautiful Laundrette* (1985) by Stephen Frears, *Meantime* (1983) and *High Hopes* (1988) by Mike Leigh, *Sammy and Rosie Get Laid* (1987) by Stephen Frears, *London Kills Me* (1991) by Hanif Kureishi, and *Mona Lisa* (1986) by Neil Jordan, was to demonstrate the deep social polarization of London: London of the rich and selfish, and London of the poor and helpless. With the exception of *Riff-Raff*, this is also presented as a city of alienation, where people of different classes and, indeed, of the same class meet only in times of conflict.

Apart from films showing contemporary London, almost every decade produced a number of movies constructing the city's historical or mythical image. Particularly worthy of attention is the recurring interest among British and American directors in Victorian, or more precisely Dickensian London.[1] In his investigation of the cinematic uses of Dickens, Jeffrey Richards draws attention to the changes that have taken place over the years in the way London has been depicted in the adaptations of Dickens's novels. Discussing the early adaptations, particularly *David Copperfield* (1913), produced by Cecil Hepworth and directed by Thomas Bentley, Richards emphasizes the scarce use of London locations and imagery, compared with images of rural England. He states: 'It is ironic that although Dickens was a distinctly urban writer, who was most at home in the teeming streets of London, he is being constructed here as a pastoralist' (Richards 1997: 332). Post-Second World War adaptations of Dickens, such as *Great Expectations* (1946) and *Oliver Twist* (1948), directed by David Lean, *Nicholas Nickleby* (1947), directed by Alberto Cavalcanti and *Scrooge* (1951), directed by Brian Desmond Hurst, 'restored the darkness to the Dickensian vision and retold the stories in a shadowy, atmospheric, chiaroscuro Dorean London, far removed from the bright, pastoral imagery of 1930s Dickens' (p. 341). The 1970s brought many musical versions of Dickens, which showed a London of 'well-scrubbed, well-drilled cockney urchins dancing up and down picture-postcard streets' (p. 347). In the films made in the 1980s, Dickens's novels and, consequently, Dickensian London were a vehicle to show disgust or admiration for Thatcherite London and Britain (p. 349), an example being *Little Dorrit* (1986), directed by Christine Edzard. According to Andrew Higson, Edzard's film provides a 'tasteful urban pastoral' vision of London, where even poverty is picturesque (Higson 1993: 114).

Since the late 1950s cinematic London has become increasingly heterogeneous and fragmented, both as a physical space and as an assembly of human relationships. Ethnicity and class, and the combination of the two, are the main factors in this process. The first is highlighted in *Sapphire* (1959) by Basil Dearden, *To Sir, with Love* (1966) by James Clavell, and, more recently, *Young Soul Rebels* (1991) by Isaac Julien. Class as an aspect that divides London is emphasized most famously in films such as *Poor Cow* (1967) and *Riff-Raff* by Ken Loach and *Meantime, High Hopes* and *Secrets and Lies* (1995) by Mike Leigh. Probably the most complex vision of London's society is shown in the 1980s films by Stephen Frears and Hanif Kureishi, *My Beautiful Laundrette* and *Sammy and Rosie Get Laid*, where the criteria of the division of London are class, ethnicity and even sexual orientation.

It is almost banal to say that cinematic London changed because real London also experienced transformation. For example, many old buildings and estates have been destroyed and new ones have been built, certain quarters became gentrified, while others lost their middle-class status. However, cinema's reaction to these transformations is not simply one of imitation. While some directors try to document changes in London's social and cultural geography, others attempt to immortalize or revitalize past associations of certain quarters of London. This last phenomenon is particularly common in contemporary, or more precisely, postmodern cinema, examples being *Lock, Stock and Two Smoking Barrels* (1998) by Guy Ritchie, which represents East End London as it looked in the 1960s (or, rather, as people might imagine it looked at the time) or, to a certain extent, *Notting Hill*, which will be the subject of a more detailed examination in a later part of this chapter.

It would be unfair to talk about London in cinema without mentioning the contribution of particular directors. In our opinion, the most distinctive and enduring in capturing the popular imagination, both in Britain and abroad, is the London of Alfred Hitchcock, portrayed in such films as *The Lodger* (1926), *Blackmail* (1929) and *Frenzy* (1972). It is a place, as Peter Hutchings observed, for the activities of the libido, where streets are metaphorically and literally littered with 'ripped whores' (Hutchings 1986: 370). Another director who has given us a distinctive image of London is Mike Leigh; his is a city of grey, depressing suburbs and depopulated, alienating working-class housing estates. Some of the most interesting portrayals of London were produced by foreign directors, such as Jules Dassin's *Night and the City* (1950), Roman Polanski's *Repulsion* (1965), Michelangelo Antonioni's *Blow-Up* (1966), Jean-Luc Godard's *One Plus One* (1968) and Jerzy Skolimowski's *Moonlighting* (1982). They made London look more cosmopolitan, both by introducing foreigners as main characters and by showing London as a locus of international debates, problems and conflicts, as well as a place of mystery and ambiguity, where well-known streets and people gain unexpected, often comical or sinister features. For example, in Godard's *One Plus One* the Black Panthers and international communists present their ideology; in Skolimowski's *Moonlighting* we see Polish *gastarbeiters* renovating an expensive house during December 1981 when martial law was introduced in Poland. Their input into London's discourse also includes showing London in ways in which cities were represented in other cinematographies. Thus, in Jules Dassin's *Night and the City*, London becomes a 'noir city', in many ways similar to the cinematic New York of the 1940s and 1950s. London in *One Plus One* is fragmented and dehumanized in the way Paris was in many of Godard's own films, an example being *Deux ou trois choses que je sais d'elle* [Two or Three Things I Know about Her, 1966].

What is striking in the whole history of London cinema is how rarely it is depicted as a city of strollers, as opposed to other European metropolises, such as Paris (an archetypal city of *flânerie*, thanks to, among others, Baudelaire and the French New Wave), Rome or Dublin. We rarely see people in films walking the streets of London and when they do, it usually ends badly for them – they are raped, mugged or

killed, and their bodies are disposed of in the Thames, as shown in
Corridors of Blood (1958) by Robert Day or Hitchcock's *Frenzy*. The image
of London as unfriendly to strollers can be explained by various interconnected factors. Patrick Keiller, the director of the critically acclaimed
pseudo-documentary *London* (1994), quotes Alexander Herzen, the exiled
Russian socialist who arrived in the city in 1852, who said, 'There is no
town in the world which is more adapted for training one away from
people and training one into solitude', and suggests that this opinion is
as valid in the 1990s as it was in the 1850s. According to Keiller, 'London
took a wrong turn in the nineteenth century. Cities became the site of
modernism, but Britain chose the suburban, perhaps through governments' fear of the mob, or of socialism, and London became a place
to pass through, not to linger in' (Yates 1994: 55). This suburban and
'anti-*flâneurian*' character is reminiscent of many other cities in the
English-speaking world, particularly the USA, and manifests itself in
the lack of a distinctive, well-defined centre and of clear pedestrian
routes, even if it can be argued that London has several 'centres' around
which Londoners stroll and to which they relate.

Cinematic London is not a place conducive to strolling perhaps
because since the eighteenth century English writers and artists, such as
Dickens and William Hogarth, have portrayed London as a dangerous
place, particularly for women and outsiders, due to a large number of
Jack the Ripper-type serial murderers, as well as common criminals,
drunkards and beggars. These figures gained a firm and prominent
place in the national psyche, and cinema, being its perfect mirror,
reflected this perception of London. The best examples are films by
Hitchcock, such as *The Lodger*, in which London is populated by serial
killers from Sunday tabloid stories. By contrast, we find far fewer urban
murderers in the cultural history of Paris, Moscow or Dublin. The
closest to London in this respect are Berlin and Prague but, in contrast
to London, their sinister features were associated only with a particular
period in their histories (the 1920s and 1930s).

Another factor is the famous London rain and fog. The industrial
revolution produced much pollution and smog, reducing visibility and
discouraging people from walking. London, as James Donald observes,
is not the only city that has suffered the dire effects of pollution in
modern times, but London's fog has become almost symbolic of the
city, again largely thanks to art and literature, most notably the work of
Turner, Dickens and T. S. Eliot (Donald 1999: 2–3).

The remaining part of this chapter is concerned with two facets of London revealed in the cinema of the 1990s: 'posh' and 'chaotic'. They are very different, but have one important feature in common: they are the images of fragments of a metropolis, rather than portraits of the whole city. Before we begin, it is worth emphasizing that our analysis does not attempt an exhaustive examination of cinematic London in the 1990s. As previously mentioned, cinematic London has many facets, and London in the 1990s has even more than in earlier periods.

Posh London: *Sliding Doors* and *Notting Hill*

Notting Hill (1999), directed by Roger Michell, contains many scenes set in the second-hand bookshop run by William Thacker – the main character in the film. William is visited here several times by a famous movie star, Anna Scott, who is the film's main female protagonist. On her first visit she is shown browsing. William notices that she is concentrating on a coffee-table book about Turkey and advises her to avoid such a colourful volume and to buy a more practical guidebook instead. He claims that somebody who has actually been to Turkey wrote the one that he recommends. Anna, however, chooses the book written by an author who, according to Thacker, has never visited the country. Her choice epitomizes the way in which London is portrayed in the two films discussed here. Their directors know very well what the real London looks like and are aware of the connection between a London address and the social status of the people who live there. Yet, for the sake of increasing their attractiveness to foreign audiences, they are prepared either to conceal their knowledge of London's 'social map' (as in *Sliding Doors*) or, in a bolder way (as in *Notting Hill*), to contradict it.

Sliding Doors (1998), directed by Peter Howitt, begins with a bird's-eye view of London, including such well-known sites as the Houses of Parliament with Big Ben on the river Thames. This type of opening was characteristic of many earlier films set in London. In *Sliding Doors*, however, there is no district, estate or street to be approached. After the first shot there is a cut to the flat where the main characters, Helen and Gerry, live. Helen, who works as a PR executive, is about to leave for work while her boyfriend is still in bed. Then action switches to the Embankment tube station, from where Helen walks to her modern office in a large, glass building. That day she is fired and her life takes on two parallel incarnations. In the first she catches the tube home and finds her boyfriend in bed with another woman. Consequently, she leaves him, falls in love with another man, James, and sets up her own, successful PR company. In Helen's second incarnation, the tube doors shut before she manages to board and there are no more trains going in her direction. She tries to get a taxi, but is mugged and injured, is taken to hospital and comes home only seconds after Gerry's lover, Lydia, has left. In this incarnation, Helen stays with Gerry almost till the end of the film, taking a job as a waitress.

Helen and Gerry live in a large, immaculate white terraced house, with solid marble pillars. We see Helen and Gerry's neighbourhood only briefly and we never learn what lies beyond the neat white houses, as if the filmmaker wanted to prevent us from placing the characters on a geographical and social map of London. The whole film is much more concerned with interiors than exteriors. Interiors signify the characters' social status and interests. Helen and Gerry's furniture is soft and comfortable and the whole interior looks warm and welcoming. Compared with the real London, the rooms are surprisingly large, suggesting considerable affluence. Although Gerry is meant to be an intellectual, there are few books or ornaments. On the whole, the house is middle-class rather than 'arty'. The immaculate whiteness of the walls of the apartment of Gerry's lover Lydia and the sculptured bust that decorates it, combined with the spare presence of ultra-modern furnishings, suggests that she is a rich follower of fashion (one can imagine that the modern look of her flat was secured by a professional interior designer). The cold, minimalist setting of Lydia's apartment contrasts most with the informal, friendly warmth of the house of Helen's friend, Anna, where Helen moves after discovering Gerry's infidelity. Eventually, we have a snapshot of the house where James, Helen's new man, used to live. This looks like an aristocratic property, with extremely high ceilings and a large, old portrait on the wall.

Helen is the breadwinner for both herself and Gerry, whose only occupation is writing a novel. His lifestyle and pattern of work do not change when Helen loses her supposedly well-paid PR job. There is never any talk of Gerry finding a job, either in the version of the story in which Helen stays with him, or in the one in which she leaves him. There is also no discussion about them moving to a smaller house. On the whole, Helen's catching or not-catching the tube influences only the romantic lives of the characters, not their living standards or social milieu. This unwillingness to represent the characters in terms of their class and financial status may be explained by the author's desire to portray them at the same time as very ordinary and very attractive. Moya Luckett justly argues that Howitt's film 'reconciles two economic and social experiences, effacing class through images and illusions' (Luckett 2000: 98). She also suggests that this attitude is reminiscent of the way the issue of class is treated by New Labour.

In contrast to the interiors, the exteriors in *Sliding Doors* are scarce and lacking in any distinctive features. The fact that the characters live in London seems to have little to do with their attitudes or lifestyle. They are neither victims of city solitude, as are, for example, the characters of Antonioni's films of the 1960s, nor 'people of the world', whose eccentric, urban tastes can be fulfilled only in the most trendy parts of the metropolis. Helen and her friends' pastimes of visiting cinemas and libraries, rowing, or going to pubs and restaurants, are not particularly metropolitan, or urban, but plainly middle-class. People living in other parts of the country or, indeed, in many other countries, could do similar things in their leisure time. There is also never a case of the protagonists enjoying their city, lingering in London, being *flâneurs*. Their attitude to their home town is purely pragmatic – for them, it is a place where they work, meet friends, make businesses, but it is never a character in its own right. Helen and her friends not only do not allow London to dominate them, but make no attempt to introduce their local culture to London. The international and multinational cast of the film – Anna being Irish, James Scottish, Lydia American, Helen being played by an American actress and Gerry by an Irishman – has practically no impact on any aspect of the film, and the national and regional differences between the characters are obliterated.

Peter Howitt gives no clues as to the location in London where his characters live, nor about the distance between places that they visit. They are shown using the underground and, even more often, taxis, but on no occasion can the precise itinerary be deduced. The journeys are cut short and no recognizable buildings or monuments appear in the frame. What we see are mainly shops, such as Boots, which can be found on the high street of any British town. When the characters are shown walking, they are filmed in close-middle shot, which again makes the setting unrecognizable. On the rare occasions when the protagonists appear in a long shot, thus enabling us to see a wider background, as in the scene when Helen and James chat on a boat on the river, the background with a bridge and some buildings is blurred. We cannot tell if they are in London, or in any other town. The most persistent element of the setting is a milk bar, situated in a caravan-like structure, where Helen and James meet. Such bars, with neon adverts of Coca-Cola, often feature in American films, but are rare both in the real London and in British films. Other public places that the characters visit, such as office buildings, an Indian restaurant, pubs and cafés, look either anonymously international, or are more reminiscent of their American equivalents than of London buildings.

On the whole, London in *Sliding Doors* is 'neutered' – lacking any recognizable features, and hardly significant from the point of view of the characters or the plot. According to Pierre Sorlin, the 'neutering' of cities in films (which he proposes to call the 'destruction' or 'negation' of cities) is a wider phenomenon, typical of European cinema since the late 1960s, citing in particular films such as *Blow-Up* (1966) by Michelangelo Antonioni, *Two or Three Things I Know about Her* (1966) by Jean-Luc Godard and *Alice in den Städten* [Alice in the Cities, 1974] by Wim Wenders (Sorlin 1994: 132–3). Indeed, in comparison with the bulk of films from earlier decades, the films Sorlin mentions are imprecise when identifying the location of the plot and uninterested in creating any connection between the town and the characters. However, it is worth stressing that, in comparison with *Sliding Doors*, the films that Sorlin discusses contain much local atmosphere. It can be suggested that the tendency he describes deepened over the years. Sorlin explains the phenomenon of the 'negation of cities' by the desire of European directors to present towns as anonymous and lacking in local features, uniform products of global capitalism, 'increasingly humdrum expanses crossed by indifferent drivers and damaged by greedy developers' (Sorlin 1994: 133). We agree that by ignoring the particular features of Europe's most distinctive cities, European cinema, including the film discussed here, increasingly reflects the international, even global character of European towns. However, there is an important difference in the attitude towards the city in *Alice in the Cities* on the one hand and *Sliding Doors* on the other. The directors of these two films are much more optimistic about urban life. They do not show the contemporary metropolis as a locus of alienation, but as a place of excellent opportunities, where everybody, irrespective of their material status and personal situation, can find somebody friendly and compatible. Several critics argue that London in some films of the 1990s, including *Sliding Doors*, is so unrealistic because it uses a fairytale-like location (see Murphy

2001). Peter Matthews, who also notices that the London of *Sliding Doors* is 'neutered', explains it by the fact that the film was aimed at American viewers. He claims that 'the assumption seems to be that US viewers, while happy to entertain a generic vision of England, will be put off by too rich a display of cultural otherness' (Matthews 1998: 56). Again, this is a feature that differentiates *Sliding Doors* from the previously mentioned films by Antonioni, Godard and Wenders, which were directed primarily at European, sophisticated, art-house audiences.[2]

In Howitt's movie, the scarcity of distinctive locations, combined with the lack of reference to any typical English customs, results in the impression of the characters' shallowness and the 'cultural vacuum' that they inhabit. The overtly postmodern technique of breaking the narrative into two intertwining parts, thus undermining the realism of the film, enhances the feeling that it portrays neither Londoners, nor Americans in London, but inhabitants of an artificial and flat 'cinema-land'. In contrast to *Sliding Doors*, *Notting Hill*, as the title suggests, is set in one of the most distinctive areas of London. Notting Hill was previously known in the cinema as a place where immigrants, especially of African origin, would settle. Accordingly, it was a place of modest prosperity and frequent ethnic tensions, as revealed in *Sapphire* by Basil Dearden and *Otley* (1968) by Dick Clement. Nowadays, however, it is one of the most fashionable and safe parts of London, with almost exclusively white residents. Aristocrats, politicians and numerous media people have their houses here. Many of these celebrities know each other and even exchange their spouses and partners, providing valuable material for newspaper and magazine gossip columns. In short, Notting Hill, as Nick James observes, is a quintessential '*Hello!*-land' (James 1999: 21). The last relic of the old period of multiculturalism is the carnival, held in August each year. In Michell's movie Notting Hill is the setting for a love story between William Thacker, the divorced proprietor of a second-hand travel bookshop and Anna Scott, a famous American movie star. They meet for the first time when Anna visits William's shop incognito. After that, they meet on numerous occasions in London, but only briefly, as Anna has to return to Hollywood. Eventually, after a series of trials and tribulations and mutual misunderstandings, they unite for ever, and set up house in Notting Hill.

The pre-credit sequence contains a montage of images presenting Anna (played by Julia Roberts) as a global celebrity. 'We see Julia Roberts step into a flashgun arena; Julia Roberts fixing her smile's pearly crescent;

Julia Roberts trading mutual bedazzlement with the press, her faun's eyes wary, on the edge of controlled alarm; Julia Roberts the silent, soft focus of so much clamour for glamour, dressed as transformed gamine, a latter-day Audrey Hepburn in precise *Breakfast at Tiffany's* chic' (James 1999: 20). Anna's constant change of dresses and hairstyles, the continuous smile on her face, as well as the view of hundreds of photographers registering her every move, convey the impression of the artificiality and one-sidedness of her life and, by the same token, of the whole world in which she operates. This is a world in which surface matters more than substance and where everything, even a smile, has its price. The silence of these sequences reinforces the impression that Anna is only a perfect surface and a precious commodity, not a whole human being.

From the first Hollywood sequence the action moves to Notting Hill, where William is on his way to work. The short journey is accompanied by his voiceover describing Notting Hill with unusual tenderness; as his 'favourite bit of London' and a 'village in the middle of the city'. The village metaphor returns in the film many times, both through the narrative and dialogue, as well as visually. Unlike the artificiality of Hollywood, Notting Hill, as a proper village, is green and sensitive to the weather. On his way to and from work William passes numerous stalls selling fresh fruit, vegetables and fish. In Notting Hill the change of seasons is marked by the summer flowers being replaced by Christmas trees and then by cherry branches, covered with white blossom. The whole surroundings of the market change, in rhythm with the products sold on the stalls: sun is replaced by rain, then by snow and again by sun. This is shown most vividly in a scene in which the whole year passes as William strolls through the market, musing about his beloved Anna. The village character of Notting Hill is enriched by large, communal gardens, such as the one which William and Anna come upon on their way from the house of William's friends. They climb a tall fence and find themselves in the middle of a huge area of trees, bushes and grass, reminiscent of the 'secret garden' of Frances Hodgson Burnett's classic tale and of Agnieszka Holland's film, *The Secret Garden* (1993), based upon it. The high-angle shot used at the end of this scene enhances the perception of the park being like a limitless sea of greenery. The park also has a human quality – a bench, dedicated by a husband to his deceased wife, placed where they used to rest together. Unlike William, who takes such views for granted, Anna feels very moved by the naturalness of the garden and the imagined lifestyle of the people who live in its environs. The clearest expression of her admiration is the idyllic image that closes the film: pregnant Anna and William rest on a bench, presumably in the same park. He reads a book, she lies with her head resting on his knees. Anna adapts to the rural tranquillity of Notting Hill not only in her behaviour, but also in her style. In William's company she discards her make-up, her hair falls loose, her clothes become simple and comfortable, with floral patterns, unlike the tight stiff costumes and designer dresses that she wore in the films and on official engagements.

The village quality of Notting Hill is also a consequence of the fact that, according to William, its inhabitants form a tightly-knit community. William himself has been living there for many years and many of his friends have their houses nearby. He meets them in the local restaurants and visits them regularly; he never has to use private or public transport, but walks to their homes. His bookshop is more a place to drop in and kill time than somewhere to do serious shopping. Notting Hill is unlike a typical modern metropolis because there is no room there for global capital and multinational ventures. The entrepreneurship is on a modest, local scale: fruit stalls, restaurants, bookshops and 'not so genuine' antique dealers. The pace of life is slow, adjusted to the apparently modest expectations of the inhabitants. William does not even have a car and we see an old bike squeezed in the narrow corridor of the house. The apparent superfluity of a car also suggests that Notting Hill is self-contained and that one can meet one's most important needs without the necessity of going further. It is worth remembering that self-containedness was a feature of pre-modern city life and that post-modern architects, after half a century of following the concepts of Le Corbusier, returned to it (Harvey 1990: 39–40). Accordingly, in its self-containedness, being a place of living, work and leisure, Notting Hill can be regarded as a model of postmodernity.

Michell's film follows the pattern of a 'prince and Cinderella' story, only with the gender roles reversed. William's residence in Notting Hill is meant to increase his credentials as an impoverished Londoner. His job plays a similar function, evoking associations with George Orwell, who worked in a second-hand bookshop and described his experiences in *Keep the Aspidistra Flying* (1936). The fact that William has to take a lodger, an eccentric Welshman named Spike, in order to pay the bills, adds to the impression that William lives 'a million miles' from the world of the rich and beautiful Anna Scott. Modesty and even a self-deprecating attitude are also typical of William's friends and his younger sister, Honey. At the party to which William takes Anna, his friend Max describes them all as a bunch of underachievers; hardly anybody in this circle seems to have a decent job or salary, and most are haunted by bad luck in their personal lives. Yet, the notion of Notting Hill as 'loserland', which William and his friends promote, is contradicted intertextually by common knowledge about the true status of Notting Hill as a 'village of millionaires'. After the film's première, numerous reviewers commented on the disparity between the social status of the characters in Michell's film and the financial reality of the inhabitants of Notting Hill. One could summarize such questions as: 'How could William Thacker afford such a posh address?' The concept of Notting Hill as a 'humble village' is also constantly undermined by images of its exteriors and interiors. The terraced houses, which William passes on his way to friends, are immaculately clean and lavish. There is little traffic and no industry, pollution or rubbish in sight; instead there is much greenery. The open-air cafés and restaurants are full of middle- and upper-class people, conspicuously enjoying good life. The parties, which Max and Bella organize for William and his sister, are also lavish and stylish. When William leaves his friends' house in the morning, we see a typical image of upper-class life – a man, probably a dog-walker, walking several pedigree dogs on the street. Although Notting Hill seems to be far from the metropolitan bustle, at the same time it is situated a comfortable distance from the luxurious hotels where Anna would stay while visiting London. The whole portrayal of the locale is constructed around the idea of 'urban pastoral', understood as a place combining the best features of both worlds: rural and metropolitan. Unlike the films previously discussed, camera angles, positions and movements are often used not only to follow the narrative, but to reveal the pleasures, even splendour of the setting, thus enhancing the idea, conveyed by the film's title and revealed in William's inner monologue, that Notting Hill is a character in its own right. The visual splendour, contradicted by the characters who are self-deprecating about their social status and lifestyles, is reminiscent of British 'heritage films' of the 1980s and 1990s, which are often regarded as the epitome of 'Thatcherite cinema'. As Andrew Higson observes, at the level of narrative and dialogue these films often condemned Victorian/Edwardian materialism, but at the level of spectacle admired the lifestyle of the English upper classes (Higson 1993:

110). The casting of Hugh Grant in the role of William Thacker enhances the impression that Notting Hill is a posh part of London and that he is a typical upper-class resident.

Against the background of the house of William's friends and other properties shown in the film, William's home looks rather small and untidy. Still, it is cosy and stylish and there is no hint of the council flats typical of Ken Loach's or Mike Leigh's films. Moreover, in spite of his humble situation, William displays an aura of nonchalance and cultural superiority over Anna. For example, he treats her cinematic career with mild contempt. When she rehearses for her new role as a junior officer in the Pentagon, he comments that the level of prose in the script is far from Henry James (who, in spite of being American, was enchanted by the English landscape and way of life). Interestingly, Anna later shoots *Wings of the Dove* in London, indicating the seriousness with which she has treated her English friend's opinion. William also shows disregard for the whole media culture. When Anna is in total despair, finding that hordes of reporters are waiting for her to leave William's house, he tries to console her by telling her that 'today's papers will be tomorrow's rubbish'. On another occasion, when he learns about her relationship with another Hollywood actor, he observes with bitter irony: 'My whole life ruined because I do not read *Hello!*' Again, we can assume that such an attitude (contrasting with the manner in which real inhabitants of Notting Hill society and Hugh Grant himself treat the media) results from the conviction that life for the sake of media coverage is not worth living – in contrast to the true, natural life led by the inhabitants of Notting Hill. The gap between William's self-deprecating attitude and his real social position serves to fulfil the basic premise of a romantic comedy, which is the initial disparity between the status of those who are in love. At the same time it promotes a vision of London (and England) as a cosy, idyllic and provincial land, associated with Ealing comedies. Such an image does not threaten the superiority of America (on the contrary, it acknowledges it), but offers a pleasant 'holiday' alternative.

In his inner monologue, which opens the film, William conveys the impression that Notting Hill is a place of nonconformity and fun, where people are not ashamed to indulge in idiosyncratic interests and tastes. This impression is further strengthened by the choice of secondary characters, particularly William's unemployed lodger, Spike, who never shaves or combs his hair, sports T-shirts with slogans such as 'Fancy a fuck', and nonchalantly dismisses William's romantic problems by comparing them with such issues as third world debt. Another example of the unconventional inhabitants of Notting Hill is William's sister, new-age, red-haired Honey. In spite of these examples of people who do not fit into the money-obsessed, conformist society, Michell's Notting Hill feels (perhaps predictably) very different from previous literary and cinematic portrayals of the place, such as Colin MacInnes' 1959 novel *Absolute Beginners* and *Performance* by Nicolas Roeg and Donald Cammell. In MacInnes' book and Roeg and Cammell's film the neighbourhood of Portobello is a dangerous and adventurous place, where one can easily lose one's life simply on account of being there, and where people are not afraid to experiment, not only with alcohol and drugs, but also with their innermost selves, their identities. Against this background, Michell's Notting Hill looks very middle-class and conservative. The film's director confessed in an interview that for five impoverished years in the late 1970s and early 1980s he rented a flat there, when it was a raffish, rundown hippie ghetto, and that he would buy potatoes and parsnips for 'ghastly soups' from the Portobello Road market traders featured in his film. He also admitted (thus acknowledging that in contemporary, postmodern times cinema shapes reality more often than mirrors it) that 'it's still one of my favourite places, but it's a shame that Notting Hill is changing and that this film will contribute to that change' (Paton 1999: 13).

Chaotic London: *Beautiful People* and *Wonderland*

Whereas in *Sliding Doors* and *Notting Hill* London can be described as posh, the London of *Beautiful People* and *Wonderland* can be regarded as fragmented and chaotic. Fragmentation and dispersion have been read as alienating features of the postmodern metropolis and, conversely, as positive and liberating. Deleuze and Guattari, whose thought serves as a theoretical perspective for an analysis of these films, are firmly positioned on the positive side of this dividing line. A fragmented urban space accords well with Deleuze and Guattari's idea of a postmodern subject characterized by plural identities and by a displaced and decentralized consciousness. The fragmented city is a promising environment for Deleuze and Guattari's 'deterritorialized' body.

In *A Thousand Plateaus* (1988), the authors distinguish between smooth space and striated space, between nomad space and sedentary space.

The city is, of course, the striated space *par excellence*; but it is also the space from which smooth space is put back into operation, both outside and inside the city itself. 'The smooth spaces arising from the city are not only those of world-wide organization, but also a counterattack combining the smooth and the holey and turning back against the town: sprawling, temporary, shifty shantytowns of nomads and cave dwellers, scrap metal and fabric, patchwork, to which the striation of money, work or housing are no longer even relevant' (Deleuze and Guattari 1988: 481). Such counterattacking spaces are not the only viable way to live smooth in cities. For Deleuze and Guattari, the urban nomad provides an alternative example of a supple use of the city space. 'For example, a stroll taken by Henry Miller in Clichy or Brooklyn is a nomadic transit in smooth space; he makes the city disgorge a patchwork, differentials of speed, delays and accelerations, changes in orientation, continuous variations' (p. 482).

The fragmentation and chaos of the contemporary metropolis can perhaps be seen as a vehicle whereby smooth areas within the highly striated urban space are produced, places in which it is possible for the postmodern subject to live as a nomad. Jasmin Dizdar's *Beautiful People* (1998) and Michael Winterbottom's *Wonderland* (1999) offer the opportunity to test this assumption. These two films present the viewpoints of a semi-outsider and of an insider, respectively, on the same aspect of the multifaceted capital that is London: its chaotic urban environment.

Jasmin Dizdar has described himself in an interview as 'a naturalized British person' who grew up in Bosnia (Ross 2000: 1), and in another as a 'former Yugoslavian' (Champion 2000: 1). *Beautiful People* is his first full-length feature film, and was produced by the British Film Institute. The plot is complicated and features many characters. A Serb and a Croat from the same village run into each other on a London bus and begin to scuffle. Having being thrown off the bus by the driver, the Serb chases his ex-neighbour through central London, under the half-concerned, half-curious gaze of Londoners and tourists alike (two of whom happen to tape the chase). The two Bosnians eventually end up in hospital where they share a room with a Welsh nationalist and are looked after by a strict but capable British nurse. Portia, a young doctor who works in the same hospital, the rebellious daughter of an MP, is embarrassed by her aristocratic, right-wing and snobbish family. One of her patients is Pero, a young Bosnian refugee and ex-basketball player recently arrived in London. Pero is in hospital after a car accident while fleeing from the police, who mistakenly believed that he was menacingly pursuing a woman, whereas he just wanted to return her wallet. The woman with the wallet is the wife of a clumsy, gentle and overworked gynaecologist, Dr Mouldy, from whom she intends to separate, taking with her their reckless twins. Among the gynaecologist's patients is a distressed Bosnian couple who want the doctor to abort the baby they are expecting, the fruit of multiple wartime rapes. A Scottish BBC journalist, Gerry, the father of Chloe, a schoolfriend of the twins', and husband of Kate, an unhappy kitsch artist, is sent to Bosnia as a war correspondent. Griffin, the deranged son of a school headmaster, goes to Holland with his new friends, two hardened junkies, to watch (only on television, mind) an English soccer match; at the airport, after their team's defeat, Griffin, who is under the effect of drugs, falls asleep on a cargo of humanitarian aid and ends up on a UN aeroplane, only to be parachuted into the middle of a Bosnian field. Surviving a rocket attack, he is picked up by a UN truck and arrives, along with the BBC journalist, at an improvised camp hospital where he offers his drugs as an anaesthetic to a man who is having his leg amputated. He then takes charge of a child who has been blinded in the earlier rocket attack.

Each strand of this complicated, occasionally moving and often humorous plot goes in its own particular direction, then changes course unexpectedly, ends up mixing with other strands, and finally finds its solution. Pero and Portia marry despite the reaction of her family – a mix of horror and snobbish tolerance. The BBC journalist who comes back suffering from 'Bosnia Syndrome', which in his case takes the form of a desire to amputate his leg, is cured by a hypnotist with the words 'the leg stays, Bosnia goes'. Griffin finally finds a suitable role for himself, and makes his parents happy at the same time, looking after the little blinded Bosnian. The doctor is left by his wife and his children but finds a partial compensation in sharing his house with the Bosnian couple and their baby daughter. The Serb keeps harassing the Croat, until they seem to find a moment of mutual acceptance during a game of snap shared with their nurse and the Welsh nationalist – this is also the closing scene.

Most of the film is set in London, except for the Bosnian section, which was actually re-created in a club shooting range in Liverpool. Some of the characters are English, namely Portia and her family; the nurse; Griffin, his family and friends; and the doctor and his family. The BBC journalist and his family are from Glasgow; the nationalist in the hospital is Welsh. There are many Yugoslavian characters: Pero; the ever-quarrelling Serb and Croat; the Bosnian couple with their baby daughter. We also meet some immigrants from other countries, such as the wise railway employee from Cyprus who helps the suicidal BBC journalist off the train tracks, or as in Pero's mixed neighbourhood, where a black woman is chased and arrested by the immigration service.

Many ethnic groups, as well as different social classes, are present in *Beautiful People* and, even though mostly unwillingly, are forced to coexist and interact by their spatial proximity, be it that of a London bus, of a hospital room, of a wedding reception or of a school entrance. Nevertheless, we will argue that the characters do not perceive the urban environment as continuous and shared, but – on the contrary – as fragmented and disjointed. Consequently, they frequently see their encounters and interactions as haphazard and coincidental.

Public spaces and private places alike undergo a similar dismember-ment in *Beautiful People*. We will first consider a few of the film's public spaces. In the first sequences, the Serb chases his Croat ex-neighbour through some streets of central London. The camerawork in this scene is representative of the whole film's attitude to London's urban space, in that this space is dissected into a set of fragments that are afterwards artificially associated by a euphoric, hasty and tongue-in-cheek editing. Elements of real street scenes, of anonymous buildings and recognizable symbols such as Big Ben are mixed together in a way that recalls our postmodern fragmented knowledge of cities as created by the mass media, and television in particular. The effect is accentuated by the documentary-like quality of these images, thanks to which they have the look of televisual realism, and by their editing to the rhythm of a fast Slavic pop song that makes them look like a music video. This 'video-clip London' becomes a cultural product of the global society while maintaining its Britishness at the same time. In these sequences, for instance, we are shown Churchill's statue from various perspectives, and in particular his closed fist. A familiar symbol of Britishness and British pride, Churchill will be visually equated with a refugee from an ex-communist country in the final image of the film – the closed fist of the Serb raised during the game of snap played with the Croat, the Welshman and the British nurse.

The scene of the young Bosnian couple and their new-born baby travelling by taxi to the doctor's house produces a similar vision of London. Looking through the car windows, the two characters experience a fragmented but elated vision of a London that looks like an impossible blend of different city areas. The Bosnian couple travel in a smooth city and perceive it as a patchwork, somewhat like Deleuze and Guattari's urban nomad – though it is essential to distinguish between those who are nomads by choice and enforced refugees.

A comparable effect is reached in the filming of the characters' houses. At first the spectator experiences them as a series of separated and highly characterized environments, each representative of a lifestyle and a character's status. Some such places are the doctor's house – a middle-class, detached house with garden, always cluttered and chaotic; Gerry's house – transformed by his wife into a sort of implausible museum of modern art; the headmaster's house – orderly and petit-bourgeois; Portia's family mansion – aristocratic, substantial and refined; and Pero's grotty rooms in a working-class, multi-ethnic block of flats. The other interiors in the film are for the most part hospital rooms: those where the doctor works; Pero's room where he is nursed by Portia; the Serb, Croat and Welshman's room; the room where Gerry begs for his leg to be amputated; and the room where the little blind Bosnian is minded by Griffin. We should also add to the list the camp hospital in Bosnia where Gerry and Griffin witness the amputation of a wounded man's leg.

Despite this initial impression of fragmentation, intended as separation and autonomy (an impression heightened by the fact that the characters live mostly unaware of their proximity to each other), as time goes by the spectator realizes that the film's spaces are either contiguous or unknowingly shared by some of the characters. It is only at the end of the film, for instance, that the doctor's house and the headmaster's are revealed to be side by side. Also, it takes a while to understand that many (if not all) of the hospital rooms belong to the same building. Furthermore, there are countless examples of places in which either some of the characters meet regularly, for instance in front of the school, or unsuspectingly cross each other's path. The spectator's privileged cognitive position in relation to such connections strengthens his or her impression of continuity and networking in the film.

The scene of Griffin's return from Bosnia reinforces the effect of adjacency and criss-cross. First we see him at the airport, filmed with the other passengers by a television crew; then we see the taped scene on the television set in the headmaster's living room. Griffin's parents are unaware of their son's presence on the screen; when he actually enters the room he creates the impression that he emerged from the television set. More than a casual comment on the omnipresence of television in our lives, this episode strongly creates the impression of a seamless juxtaposition of spaces, both real and virtual. *Beautiful People*'s houses are a series of fragments of very diverse interiors patched together by means of the effects of contiguity and intersection.

These remarks on the perception of the urban (and filmic) space by its characters and by the audience suggest a fragmentation of the environment that, however, is not experienced as alienating. It is precisely the adjacency of interior, autonomous spaces on the one hand, and the elated experience of a smooth outdoor environment on the other, that reduce the potential for estrangement in a fragmented city fabric. Thus, the filmmaking works to create an urban environment that is disjointed but not alienating, fragmented but not estranging.

This fragmentation may be seen as deriving from the fact that London in *Beautiful People* is represented as the receptacle of a prior fragmentation, that of postcommunist countries and of Yugoslavia in particular. Pero calls 'former' the Yugoslavia represented on a map in his room. 'This is my former country, my former me. They are all former in Yugoslavia.' The film is full of former people, of refugees who bring pieces of their former lives into London's melting pot, contributing to the effect of fragmentation and plurality.

It is interesting to note that the only section of the film in which space is not fragmented by the editing and by the camerawork is the young Bosnian's home-movie of his wife after their wedding. The film, which he shows to the doctor in his attempt to convince him to abort the baby, shows a happy, younger-looking and smiling woman, still in her bridal gown, who dances for her groom's camera. The environment is presented in a way that suggests wholeness, completeness, unity and happiness. This home-movie is set in a Yugoslavian wood, presumably in times of peace, before the country underwent its final disintegration and became 'former'.

The body in *Beautiful People* is another paradigm of fragmentation within London's postmodern urban environment. The clearest example is that of the severed leg. As already mentioned, Gerry witnesses the amputation of a Bosnian man's leg in a camp hospital. He follows a nurse who carries the severed limb out of the tent and throws it on a pile of human remains. While a mesmerized Gerry stretches his hand out to touch it, he is shot in his own leg. Upon his return to London, he falls into a manic state that is diagnosed as 'Bosnia Syndrome', and described as an obsession with helping people and doing good that brings the sufferer to identify with the victim and see the world through the victim's eyes – and in fact he continues to repeat: 'I saw *it*.' As a consequence, Gerry craves for his own leg to be amputated. He goes to the hospital to ask for an amputation and he is of course thrown out; he takes a prosthetic leg that is lying in the rubbish bin outside the hospital and drags it away. We find him sleeping the morning after with his leg lying purposefully across a railway track. This episode is prepared for and reinforced by many hints, such as the use of the relevant phrase 'break a leg'; Gerry's daughter watches a scene from *The Railway Children* on television in which somebody is lying across a railway track; her mother works on a sculpture in the shape of a man with a missing leg; and later she will find a grenade that her husband has carried in his suitcase, concealed in a sock.

The theme of the amputated leg clearly states that the fragmented body is that of the refugee, the victim of the disintegration of a world, the former body with whom Gerry temporarily identifies. Other characters, refugees for the most part, partake of this bodily disintegration – it is no accident that so many of the film's interiors are hospital rooms. Let us recall the battered bodies of Pero run over by a car, of the Serb, the Croat and the Welsh nationalist who display bruises and bandages throughout the film; but also the raped body of the Bosnian bride; the excavated face of the blinded Bosnian child; and the pierced bodies of Griffin and his friends who inject themselves with heroin. The peril of a final bodily dismemberment is represented in the scene in which Griffin unwittingly stands on a mine in Bosnia.

Luckily, the bomb does not kill Griffin. Pero's head heals rather quickly. The Bosnian bride gives birth to a little girl, and after seeing her she realizes that she is not the enemy and 'becomes' her mother. The Bosnian child is lovingly looked after by Griffin, his family and, at the end, his ex-cynical friends. The Serb, the Croat and the Welshman are going to recover. Even Gerry is cured of his 'Bosnia Syndrome'. The leg stays, Bosnia goes. *Beautiful People*'s 'ethnic', disjointed, former body finds a domicile, although unstable, in the western, fragmentary, postmodern metropolis. The chaos of the city offers smooth spaces within its highly striated environment, places in which some of the refugees can find shelter, at least for a while, as the episode of Pero's black neighbour expelled by the immigration service reminds us. After all, as one of the distinguished guests at Pero and Portia's wedding observes, 'Here in Britain we are a mixed bag too', and he adds, 'I don't think that experimental ideas like ethnic cleansing would catch on here'. Britain's solution – or, shouldn't we say, Western Europe's solution – is less drastic: partial acceptance, but definitely not integration. Pero wants to believe that by marrying Portia he is going to be 'one of them', but he never will be. When at the wedding reception he reaches in his pocket, everybody thinks he is going to pull out a gun – including the (western/white) spectator.

Whereas London's fragmented and chaotic environment is not alienating for the refugees, other characters do find this city alienating – for instance, the overworked gynaecologist; Gerry who, for a little while, looks at the world from the victim's perspective, but without being a victim at all; and stressed-out Kate, who once exclaims, 'What if we start again, buy a croft and go live in peace?' But, as we know, crofts are not an easy alternative, and once Gerry is cured the whole family leaves for a less drastic destination – a therapeutic holiday in Hawaii.

Despite the clear difference between Deleuze and Guattari's nomad and *Beautiful People*'s refugees, Dizdar has filmed London with irony and an elated eye that finds, in its otherwise striated space, some smooth, postmodern, disorganized and encouragingly fragmented areas, in which human destinies float, clash and are reconciled. For some of the characters, namely the victims, chaos can be positive – and that's why the Bosnian couple decide to call their new-born baby girl Kaos. The film's final credits flow over the images of the Bosnian home-movie; unity, harmony and wholeness are, as always, the stuff of memories and films.

Michael Winterbottom's *Wonderland* does not put forward an alternative to the chaos and fragmentation of the postmodern city; unity, harmony and wholeness are not to be found anywhere, including the past. The protagonist of the film is a disjointed family: mother and father live together in their lower-middle-class South London house, but communication between the two is nonexistent, and Eileen never hides her contempt or even her disgust for Bill. The rest of the family is dispersed: Debbie is a separated hairdresser who lives with her nine-year-old son, Jack; Nadia works in a café in Soho and looks for love in the lonely hearts columns; Molly and her partner Eddie, whose baby she is expecting, are going through a crisis; Darren, her brother, left home and is no longer in touch with his family. Even if one evening we see Eileen reordering old photographs of her children, the evidently traumatic event of Darren's departure makes it clear that the family's past, as well, was marked by unhappiness and lack of communication.

The film concentrates on five days, from Thursday evening to Monday morning, normal and at the same time eventful days for many of the characters. After a disappointing date, Nadia meets photographer Tim through an advertisement; her hopes are in vain, as Tim is not looking for a long-term relationship and soon finds another bed partner. Jack is supposed to spend the weekend with his father, Dan, while his mother goes out with her occasional lover. On Saturday father and son go to a football match, but in the evening Dan leaves Jack alone at home with a video and goes to the pub. On Sunday Jack, who was supposed to go to the amusement park with his mother, receives a phone call from her from the hospital, where Molly is in labour. The child decides to go on his own, leaving his father to sleep off his drunkenness. While at the park, Jack is attacked and robbed of his Walkman and his backpack, and ends up at the police station. Eddie, who is confused and scared by the arrival of a new baby, quits his job as a salesperson in a kitchen shop, but hasn't the courage to tell Molly. When she finds out, his reaction is to leave the house and go driving around all night on his scooter. While Molly is having the child, Eddie has an accident and paradoxically ends up in the same hospital, where he meets mother and baby, and asks for forgiveness. Darren, who now lives outside London, has come to visit with his girlfriend for the weekend to celebrate his birthday. He tries to contact his family by phone from the hotel, and on Sunday night he leaves a brief message on his parents' answering machine, while they are at the hospital with Molly.

There are very few other characters in *Wonderland*, the most important of whom is Freddie, a young black man who lives in the parents' neighbourhood, and works in a hi-fi shop near Nadia's café. He is secretly in love with Nadia and regularly eats in her bar, almost unnoticed by the girl. Freddie lives with his family, and is constantly nagged by his mother, who would like him to go out more often.

Though the plot is so clearly focused on one family, it takes some time for the spectator to understand that most of the characters are related. This delay, which reminds us of a similar effect in *Beautiful People*, is caused by the extreme fragmentation of the narrative, one of the characteristics that makes of *Wonderland* a postmodern film. The captions indicating the days of the week are simply not enough to create coherence in the subject matter. Furthermore, most of the characters seem lost in their isolation from the outside world, including from their family. Nadia and Debbie often meet, but they are clearly very different from each other. Molly is not in touch with Nadia, and her relationship with Debbie is rather superficial. Debbie's interest in sex and her social life distract her from her child's needs, and her son is often abandoned to watch violent or brainless television programmes. Even the relationship between the sisters and their parents is very poor. Nadia is in touch with her dad, but never has time to stop and talk to him. Eileen goes to visit Molly, and behaves like a stranger in her own daughter's house. Debbie never meets or talks to her parents. Love relationships are also highly problematic and often a source of pain and disappointment to the characters. Eileen and Bill's marriage epitomizes the unsatisfactory, dried-out relationship of a middle-aged couple who have gradually grown apart from each other. Nadia forces herself through painful dates with perfect strangers. Debbie's relationship with Jack's father is very tense, and with her occasional lovers she acts in an unnatural, overexcited manner. Molly and Eddie seem unable to communicate their fears and expectations, so that when problems surface it is in a disastrous way. Freddie's interest in Nadia, instead of helping him to find a place within society, isolates him further.

The characters also live detached from their environment. They walk the streets of South London (Elephant and Castle) and central London without seeing anything, concentrating on themselves and their personal problems. The city around them is extremely chaotic. Soho and the other central areas that we see are crammed with people. Streets are always busy, we see people begging for money or sleeping on the footpaths, the rubbish piled everywhere. Major roads are full of traffic, and people drive very tensely. Rain often adds to the general sensation of unease. In the southern area where Eileen and Bill live streets are usually empty, but chaos is nevertheless the main feature of the environment, due mainly to excessive noise. This is caused principally by firecrackers habitually exploded for fun by the children of the area, and by Eileen and Bill's loud neighbours. Their dog's constant barking exasperates Eileen to the point that, after yet another night of insomnia, she gives him a deadly dose of rat poison; it is one of the most chilling scenes of the film. The discomfort of living in this area is increased by the lack of privacy in Eileen and Bill's house, whose living-room window is perfectly visible from the dreaded neighbours' backyard. Characters react differently to the chaos of the city: whereas Eileen is deeply affected by it, Bill successfully ignores it; Freddie protects himself from it by spending all his free time locked up in his small bedroom; Debbie seems comfortable with it, but not as much as Dan, who is in his element when confusion reigns or tensions run high; Nadia and Eddie are instead very much absorbed by their own thoughts and problems, and walk the streets as if they saw nothing around them.

Most public places are represented as crowded and chaotic: the many pubs, always packed with people in search of fun, full of smoke, noise and music; the packed stadium, where Jack and Dan go for their Saturday afternoon outing; and the swarming amusement park where Jack gets lost in the crowd. London is represented as a wonderland, an exhilarating and bewildering roller-coaster, a fast-moving spectacle full of lights and noise. Wonderland is the postmodern metropolis presenting itself as a never-ending show that tries to excite and captivate, and hides the problems of everyday life. The characters immerse themselves in this atmosphere, stupefied and lost; the ferment and bewilderment conceal the lack of purpose, communication and happiness in their private lives. This London is a multiracial society apparently without conflict; home-lessness and poverty are evident in the streets and at the same time become practically invisible in the spectacle of the moving feast. In this lower-middle-class family money is not the most pressing issue – a modest prosperity has been achieved; Debbie and Nadia have what seem to be stable jobs; Eddie can just about afford to quit his job, despite the arrival of a new baby; and Dan drives around in a BMW. Petty bourgeois values have a particular appeal for Molly, who lives in a clean and standardized apartment, with a brand-new natural wood kitchen, and a nursery fed with goods from a franchising giant like Mothercare. Debbie and Jack's apartment is the most cluttered and unpleasant in the film, whereas Nadia's is the most alternative-looking. Bill and Eileen's house has the tidy and familiar look of a suburban lower-middle-class residence, one that offers no shelter from the adjoining neighbours' house.

Though a similar story could easily be set in most big European cities, London is the unmistakable milieu of Winterbottom's film. The flavour of both its suburbs and its centre are perfectly captured; the hamburger joints, the pubs and cafés, the hairdresser's shop, the bingo hall, and all the faces are so real-looking because of the particular filmmaking style: Winterbottom used a reduced technical troupe, a hand-held super16 camera, natural lighting, no extras and real locations. With

22.   *Wonderland* (1999), dir. Michael Winterbottom

this technical minimalism, *Wonderland* resembles a documentary on London rather than a fiction film.

> The pared-down approach was not planned in advance, but grew naturally out of the situations the cast and crew found themselves in. 'As soon as we put up a light, people became very aware of us,' Winterbottom explained. The lights were ditched, but then the boom attracted attention, 'so we only used hidden radio mikes'. In the end, the clapper boards were vetoed too, to the discomfort of some of the cast, who felt uneasy about the blurring of the line between reality and acting – just as Winterbottom intended. 'The whole method of filming came from the desire to be able to include in the film a real sense of the city, rather than a re-created version of it.' ('Through the Looking Glass', *Guardian*, 19 July 1999)

The results of this method of shooting are visible both in the 'dirty' and grainy image, and in the realism of the scenes set in public spaces, populated by real-life clients and passers-by. The impression is that of a hectic metropolis in which the never-pausing flow of existence is composed of the chaotic mix of fragments of millions of lives. As Grégory Valens wrote, *Wonderland* makes of fragmentation – narrative, aesthetic and philosophic – an art (Valens 1999: 40). This fragmentation, the film seems to say, is the way life is in a contemporary metropolis. In contrast to other films on London analysed in this chapter, different urban areas are distinguishable, and the true city is clearly visible in the many exterior scenes; characters often use means of transport (car, motorbike, bus, tube and train are frequently seen), and even more often they walk or stop in the street, as does Eddie, who rehearses his speech to Molly on Westminster Bridge, looking towards the Embankment and London Bridge. The urban geography is not disguised; routes from one place to another are repeatedly shown, and the city's panorama is visible several times from Nadia's apartment, or is deliberately shown by the camera. Despite the realism of the urban geography, the effect of fragmentation and chaos prevails, as characters move as if in a trance and rarely is their attention captured by a splinter of external life, a child begging for money in the tube or a man selling copies of the *Big Issue* in the street. The split is not only between the characters themselves, but also between the characters and the city. The camera attempts to link them to each other and to their living environment by performing fast movements back and forth within the same shot, movements that replace the much more classic angle/reverse-angle shot. This experimental feature is used by Winterbottom not only to associate the faces of two characters who talk (or do not talk) to each other, but sometimes – and in a more uncommon manner – to link a building to a face.

This initiative, rather than overcoming the seclusion and the distance of the characters from both other people and the urban environment, succeeds only in highlighting it. Similarly, the hand-held camera, often kept very close to the faces and bodies, has the unmistakable effect of further isolating the characters. But the most striking technical stratagems used by Winterbottom are the slow and fast motion that alter the normal flow of time during strolls or trips by the pensive protagonists. Used to emphasize the distress, more rarely the happiness, of a character, the slow and the fast motion 'accentuate the deconstruction of the narrative, the disintegration of time, the deliquescence of the notions of duration and linearity' (Valens 1999: 41; our translation).

It is in this use of deconstructed, variable time when moving through the city that a resemblance can be found between *Wonderland*'s characters and Deleuze and Guattari's nomads. 'For example, a stroll taken by Henry Miller in Clichy or Brooklyn is a nomadic transit in smooth space; he makes the city disgorge a patchwork, differentials of speed, delays and accelerations, changes in orientation, continuous variations' (Deleuze and Guattari 1988: 482). This phrase perfectly describes the changes of speed in Winterbottom's film. *Wonderland*'s London is so chaotic and fragmented that for some of the characters it can become a smooth space: the city melts away and almost disappears while Nadia walks lost in her own feelings. Her attitude, though, is not that of a *flâneur* who enjoys and dominates the city; rather, it is that of a fragmented subject who shapes the urban environment according to her current state of mind. Amid all this chaos, only Michael Nyman's recognizable and uniform music has the power to keep the narrative and the characters together, to impose an order upon the film's fragmentation.

The portrait of London emerging from *Wonderland* is that of a frenzied city, a permanent spectacle of lights, people and movement. The effects on the city users are at the same time captivating (think of the rapt faces of both adults and children staring at the match or at the fireworks, but also at television) and estranging, as is the case for many of the characters who roam the streets of night-time London almost in a trance. There seems to be no alternative life in this London – only love is regarded by some as the pathway to happiness. In the film's last sequences, Nadia and Freddie meet by chance and walk together towards work, sharing the frame and perhaps the hope of a better, common future. *Wonderland* closes on a note of (feeble) hope, just as did *Beautiful People*, with a moment of pure fun shared by a bunch of dissimilar and even antagonistic characters. In both films, nevertheless, hope is primarily embodied in a new baby who, rather than representing a romantic faith in the future, comes to impose sense on the disorder of life, without expecting to put it in order, as the names of the two girls remind us – Kaos and Alice (in Wonderland).

9

Escape from a Celtic City

O ne of the most significant features of British socio-political life of the 1980s and the 1990s was the upsurge in Scottish and Welsh nationalism. There were many factors contributing to this phenomenon, one of the most important being Scottish and Welsh resistance to Thatcherism. The opposition to Thatcherite policies and economics resulted from the devastating effect they had on the lives of people in Scotland and Wales (as well as in the North of England), such as high unemployment and increasing inequalities. Moreover, the feeling of political alienation was increased by the fact that, in spite of strong support for the Labour Party among the Scottish and Welsh population in consecutive general elections, the Conservatives retained a majority at Westminster. Consequently, a new spirit of regional unity was forged, which was articulated in the aspiration to have parliaments in Scotland and Wales, an aspiration that was fulfilled after the Labour Party won the general election in 1997 (the Scottish Parliament and the National Assembly for Wales). Devolution has been accompanied by an increase in the popularity of the nationalist parties in both Scotland (Scottish National Party) and Wales (Plaid Cymru).

The rise in Scottish and Welsh nationalism was followed by, and to a certain extent influenced, popular culture, including cinema, and there is a widespread perception that the last decade of the twentieth century was a particularly good time for the Celtic film industries. For example, David Berry writes with reference to Welsh cinema of the 1990s: 'Wales is in the throes of its most invigorating creative film period since William

Haggar delighted crowds with his shows in the British cinema's first decade' (Berry 1994: 9). The boom experienced by the Scottish and Welsh film industries is partly the result of heritage films and costume dramas (often made with American money and with American, Australian or English actors playing the main roles), such as *Rob Roy* (1994) by Michael Caton-Jones, *Braveheart* (1995) by Mel Gibson, *Rebecca's Daughters* (1991) by Karl Francis and *The Englishman Who Went Up a Hill and Came Down a Mountain* (1994) by Chris Monger. Yet, it was contemporary urban films that increased interest in and drew attention to Scottish and Welsh cinema. This chapter will be primarily concerned with cinematic representations of a Celtic City, as an arena for the debate about Scottish and Welsh identity. We decided to look in detail at two films that were particularly successful among British and foreign audiences and are regarded as pivotal in capturing the mood in Scotland and Wales in the 1990s. These are *Trainspotting* (1995), set in Edinburgh, and *Twin Town* (1997), set in Swansea.

Urban Kailyard

Cairns Craig argues that Scottish literature is constructed within the framework of two discursive positions: Tartanry and Kailyard. The Tartanry discourse is articulated through connection with the Jacobites and the myth of heroic and Romantic Scotland, as popularized by Walter Scott's *Waverley* (1814). This is 'a world that has not been demeaned by modern civilization and is still in touch with the nobility which we associate with classical antiquity' (Craig 1982: 8). In the Kailyard discourse, on the other hand, as immortalized by J. M. Barrie in his *Auld Licht Idylls* (1888), Scotland is a 'world of grotesquely impoverished human potential', whose inhabitants are 'backward, parochial, narrow-minded and utterly incapable of becoming conscious of the values by which they are being found comic' (p. 8). This Scotland is a place to escape from, 'a cultural wasteland whose values are inimical to the imagination' (p. 9). What Scott and Barrie have in common, according to Craig, is the depiction of Scotland from the outside and the rejection of both Tartanry and Kailyard as social and cultural ideals. As Craig puts it, 'by both authors the reader is invited into a Scottish world only to have revealed its hollowness, its inadequacy to the complex reality of modern life' (p. 9). Colin McArthur, in his seminal essay 'Scotland and Cinema: The Iniquity of the Fathers', transfers Craig's argument from literature to cinema, suggesting that Scottish cinema is also dominated by Tartanry and Kailyard. Most often cinematic 'representations of Scotland and the Scots offer Tartan exteriors and Kailyard mores' (McArthur 1982: 41). According to McArthur, by adjusting to the regressive Tartanry and Kailyard discourses, the bulk of films about Scotland neither depict the lives of Scottish people accurately, nor provide them with a useful ideal for the future. Consequently, he advocates a Scottish cinema that would oppose Tartanry and Kailyard, being contemporary, urban and made by insiders.

Trainspotting, based on the best-selling novel by Irvine Welsh, published in 1994, was heralded as a film that not only fulfilled the conditions McArthur outlined, but also showed Scotland as it had never been seen before (O'Hagan 1996: 8). In our opinion, however, the film not only breaks with many traits typical of earlier cinematic representations of Scotland, but also demonstrates the difficulties of constructing a discourse conveying a new Scottish identity, which is meant to replace the old Tartan and Kailyard stereotypes. The film was made by the same team that produced the immensely popular and critically acclaimed *Shallow Grave* (1994): director Danny Boyle, scriptwriter John Hodge and producer Andrew Macdonald. Although in *Shallow Grave*, as Moya Luckett observes, 'representation of Edinburgh departs from the kind of long-shot, bird's-eye view iconography commonly used to introduce cities in cinema' (Luckett 2000: 93), the film provides us with a distinctive image of Edinburgh, understood both as a physical entity and as a way of life. It shows a gentrified, imposing and alluring Georgian New Town and its young, well-off and sophisticated inhabitants. *Shallow Grave* also underlines its Scottishness by reference to tartans and kilts, the Scottish television channel, even Scottish food. Yet, the references are subtle, Scottishness is never overtly discussed in the film and there is a hint of irony in the way it is represented. For example, the main character of the story, Alex, played by Ewan McGregor, celebrates Hogmanay at a charity ball, clad in a plain jacket and tartan trousers, which is a travesty of the traditional tartan costume. His 'tartany' image can also be regarded as a foretaste of the scornful attitude to Scottishness that will be typical of Mark Renton, McGregor's character in Boyle's next film. In common with *Shallow Grave*, *Trainspotting* revolves around the lives of a group of friends living in Edinburgh: Mark Renton, Sick Boy, Spud, Tommy and Begbie. All of them are unemployed and addicted to hard drugs, with the exception of Begbie, who is addicted to violence. The main character and narrator of the story is Renton, and his attempts to break with both his drug habit and his friends fill most of the narrative.

The film begins with an image of Renton and Spud running through the centre of the city, from Princess Street towards the Royal Mile, two of the most touristy routes in Edinburgh, where many famous historical buildings and monuments stand. Yet, in the images of Brian Tuffano, the streets are grey and dirty and there is no trace of the kilt-wearing bagpipe players who assemble near the railway station and the National Gallery to attract tourists. Edinburgh Castle, which, as David Bruce observes, features prominently in almost every film set in the Scottish capital (Bruce 1996: 80), as well as other imposing buildings of the city, are not shown at all. Instead, in the background we see some ugly blocks of flats and nondescript walkways. In the course of the film Boyle returns to the centre of Edinburgh and again this is shown in the same grey, nondescript way, with no space for spontaneous, unstructured activities. The most noticeable buildings are shops, such as Marks and Spencer and John Menzies, which can be found on any British high street. Their inclusion can serve as a metaphor for the restricted use of the city centres during the Thatcher era as 'centres of well-ordered consumption' (Bianchini and Schwengel 1991: 220).

The decision to show the city centre in such an unappealing way can be seen as a form of criticism of Thatcherite urban ideology and policy. Primarily, however, the way in which the centre of Edinburgh is captured in these episodes undermines the 'heritage' image of Edinburgh that prevailed in the history of Scottish cinema. John Hill observes that in another well-known Scottish film, *Gregory's Girl* (1980), which is set in Glasgow, the director Bill Forsyth 'challenges conventional Scottish imagery and does not seek to reveal any "essential" or even distinctive Scottish identity' (Hill 1999: 243) – and the same can be said about Boyle's attitude to Edinburgh. Yet, unlike Forsyth, who in *Gregory's Girl* was able to show Glasgow as a distinctive, unique place, albeit defying stereotype, Boyle tries to obliterate the differences between Edinburgh and other British, or indeed, European cities. As far as the centre of Edinburgh is concerned, it could be any town or even, as Moya Luckett suggests, rather Glasgow or Manchester than Edinburgh (Luckett 2000: 92).

The centre of Edinburgh is the setting for only a small portion of the film. Renton, Spud, Sick Boy, Tommy and Begbie live in an even grimmer, more nondescript part of the city, consisting of apartment blocks and ugly, dilapidated terraced houses. This is, anyway, what we see in the relatively rare moments when the characters are shown near their houses. Although the narrative is more fragmented in the literary original than in Boyle's film, the space, paradoxically, feels more coherent and clearly articulated in the novel. Every location is described by Welsh in detail. For example, we learn not only that Renton lives in Leith, but more precisely that he stays on Montgomery Street, and that the windows of his one-room apartment overlook the Links. Similarly, according to the book, every drug dealer serves a particular local community; thus 'Mother Superior', who is based in Tollcross, covers 'Sighthill and the Wester Hailes schemes', while Mike Forrester sells drugs primarily to the 'Muirhouse–Leith mob' (Welsh 1993: 6). Welsh also includes information about which bus to take in order to get from one place to another, and how long a particular journey lasts on a bus, as opposed to in a taxi. The precision with which Welsh describes the setting in *Trainspotting* (in common with his other novels and short stories, including *The Acid House* and *Malibu Stork Nightmares*) and the connection between the layout and culture of Edinburgh, is one of the main ways in which his books convey such a strong sense of Scottishness. For example, Welsh demonstrates that there is a distinctive hierarchy of council estates, as well as among the inhabitants of an estate. By contrast, in the cinematic *Trainspotting* no street names or even city quarters are revealed. As a result, only those viewers who know Welsh's book well can guess that the film is set on the Muirhouse estate. The scenes shot outdoors are so brief and their *mise-en-scène* is so shallow that on the first viewing it is difficult to deduce if the characters live in a very run-down part of Edinburgh, or in a more respectable neighbourhood. Similarly, on the streets there is never anyone else apart from the main characters, no passers-by to establish the social status of any given neighbourhood. The pervasive sense of community found in Welsh's book and in many earlier British films that made references to Thatcherite Britain, such as *My Beautiful Laundrette* (1985) by Stephen Frears, or *Rita, Sue and Bob Too* (1986) by Alan Clarke, is absent in Boyle's film. On the other hand, this 'shallow' mode of representing the city, characteristic of *Trainspotting*, became the norm for later British films, particularly those set in the East End of London among the criminal underclass, such as *Lock, Stock and Two Smoking Barrels* (1998), directed by Guy Ritchie and *Love, Honour and Obey* (1999), directed by Dominic Anciano and Ray Burdis.

Apart from their addiction to drugs, the common denominator

between Renton, Begbie, Sick Boy, Tony and Spud in Welsh's book is the fact that they come from the same council estate. The estate also encapsulates a particular way of living and even the state of mind of Welsh's characters. In their social circle they are known as 'schemies', while politicians and sociologists would describe them as victims of 'social exclusion'; their opportunities for geographical and social mobility are very limited. They are poorly educated, therefore cannot find a satisfying job, and have no car, therefore must rely on poor public transport. As a consequence of this predicament, Mark in Welsh's novel rarely visits his girlfriend, Kelly, simply because she lives too far from his flat and he is usually too short of cash to get there by taxi. In the Britain of the 1980s the car became not only a symbol of affluence and upward social mobility, but also of the individualism promoted by the Thatcher government, in the face of which public transport declined. Therefore, those without access to a car were doubly marginalized from the mainstream of society, both physically and symbolically. In Welsh's book, living on a housing estate also results in being denied access to high-quality food and relying on cheap take-aways of fish and chips and curry. Finally, it means having no hope, assuming that the future will be as bad as the past, if not worse. However, according to Welsh not all the connotations of a council estate are negative. As a social environment he treats it with a certain ambivalence as, on the one hand, living on the same council estate gives his protagonists a sense of belonging, but, on the other, it increases the difficulty they experience in breaking their destructive connection with each other.

The issue of 'regional geography' and its consequences in terms of making particular social and cultural choices, such as hanging about with the same group of people and supporting a particular football team, was excluded from Boyle's film. Similarly, the significance of living on the same housing scheme was greatly reduced. Boyle never shows the tortuous attempts to overcome the limitations of the housing estates, where buses and taxis are always scarce. Instead, when Mark decides to buy heroin, he sinks through the floor in a surreal fashion and finds himself immediately in the drug dealer's flat. Generally, we do not even know if Mark, Spud and Tommy spend most of their time in each other's company because of their addiction to drugs or because they live close to each other.

Similarly, in comparison with the literary original, in the film less emphasis is placed on the issue of class. Being working class is a

23. *Trainspotting* (1995), dir. Danny Boyle

characteristic of the generation of Mark Renton's parents and their friends; the younger generation, on the other hand, is somehow beyond class. This is most obvious in the case of Mark, who feels totally out of place when visiting smoky pubs and bingo clubs with his parents, and who eventually gets a rather middle-class job as an estate agent. There is also a strong contrast in the iconography of the interiors of his parents' house and his own home. The former is cramped, old-fashioned and in bad taste. Mark's flat, on the other hand, with Munch-style graffiti on the wall and minimal furnishings, seems quite sophisticated. It could just as well belong to a working-class, as to a middle- or even upper-class person. The touch of surrealism increases the difficulty of placing Mark's physical environment according to a particular class.

Moreover, the class solidarity, typical of the older generation, is replaced among Renton and his friends by selfishness – an attitude that Thatcher excused, even promoted. Danny Boyle admits that in his film the problem of class was neglected, arguing (unjustly, in our opinion) that: 'The book isn't an examination of class. Anybody who wants to make it out to be that has their own particular axe to grind' (Macnab 1996: 11).

The general message of the film is that there is something wrong with Edinburgh as a whole, rather than with its particular geographical region or social class. The whole city is 'sick' and 'dirty', with dilapidated walls covered with abusive graffiti. The same aura of neglect can be detected in the smoky pubs and other public spaces. Dark colours, used in the majority of scenes, add to the impression of neglect. Moreover, as Philip Kemp notes, 'lavatories figure prominently in *Trainspotting*' (Kemp 1996: 53) and they are not at all elegant. The toilet where Mark loses his two suppositories ('the worst toilet in Scotland', as the subtitle indicates), can compete for the 'honour' of the ugliest, dirtiest toilet ever shown in cinema. A toilet might also be regarded as a metaphor for Edinburgh and perhaps for the whole of Scotland. As a toilet, Edinburgh is a place where waste, literally and metaphorically, is disposed of and stored: smelly, unpleasant, shameful (by way of contrast, in the part of the film set in London there are no toilets). Begbie, Mark and the other friends also use the toilets as a trap for moneyed tourists – Begbie attacks them there, threatening them with a knife and mugging them. By the same token, Edinburgh is a place that outsiders should avoid. On the other hand, it could be argued that a toilet is somehow liberating, a place where one can find relief and 'be oneself'.

Trainspotting is set mainly in interiors. According to Danny Boyle, the main reason for this was the film's modest budget of 1.7 million pounds.

> I believe that to make a film on this scale on location, even if it wasn't on a grim housing estate, is almost impossible ... The only way we could make it – especially with 230 scenes in the film – was to do as much of it in the studio as we could. This decision, stylistically, affects the rest of the film. (Macnab 1996: 10)

Indeed, it affects the film's look, narrative and ideology. The emphasis on interiors adds to the nondescriptness of the city portrayed, and suggests that the characters, particularly Mark, avoid leaving their own places and exploring a wider environment. They are completely withdrawn; their ultimate dream, as various surreal scenes show, is to hide inside the house, or even in bed, or beneath the floor – to sink and disappear. At the same time they can not hide – their friends and family always find them. At a certain point Mark even regrets that he did not go to jail, as his friend Spud, who was caught stealing with him, found solitude and peace there. Mark's situation can also be read as a metaphor for Edinburgh as an enclosing, suffocating environment, which evokes associations with 'Kailyard', a discourse according to which, as was previously mentioned, Scotland is parochial and claustrophobic. The main difference between the earlier (literary and cinematic) incarnations of 'Kailyard' and the image created by Boyle lies in the fact that the traditional 'Kailyard', as the name suggests, is connected with rural Scotland, while in *Trainspotting* it is primarily urban. Moreover, Boyle widens the boundaries of Kailyard – in his film the term can refer to Edinburgh and to the whole of Scotland.

In the majority of films, both contemporary and historical, Scottish nature is romanticized and stands for everything of which the Scots are proud. In *Trainspotting*, it symbolizes Scottish backwardness and failure to achieve nationhood. This notion of Scottishness is encapsulated when Mark and his friends leave Edinburgh to visit the Highlands. Tony (the only member of the group who does not take drugs at this stage) encourages them to climb Ben Nevis by appealing to their national pride. Yet Tony's words, 'Look how beautiful Scotland is', and the image of the dramatic mountains leave Spud and Sick Boy unimpressed and for Mark they serve as a catalyst for his most ferocious attack on his country. Mark tells them that he does not hate the English, because they are 'wankers' – Scotland was even unable to find a 'decent nation to be colonized by'. After his outburst the friends rush home without climbing Ben Nevis, to inject themselves with heroin. For Mark this is his first contact with drugs for some time. It can even be suggested that the encounter with 'bonnie Scotland' is a factor in Mark's return to drugs; he must take heroin to ease the pain resulting from his realization of how miserable his country is. The anti-romantic attitude to nature, which Boyle proposes, also contrasts with that in numerous earlier films, set in towns and revolving around the lives of members of the working class, such as the New Wave classics *A Taste of Honey* (1961) and *The Loneliness of the Long Distance Runner* (1962), both directed by Tony Richardson, and *A Kind of Loving* (1962), directed by John Schlesinger. In these films the city represents entrapment and the countryside offers a chance of escape, albeit usually for a short time. Boyle's characters, on the other hand, have no illusions about the liberating impact of nature, they are 100 per cent city creatures. Boyle also avoids viewing Edinburgh from a hill, which was typical of New Wave's representations of cities. As a result, his Edinburgh gives the impression of being fragmented and elusive, impossible to grasp or conquer (which was often the dream of ambitious working-class heroes of earlier British films).

When Mark is not hiding, he is running away. He runs from the store detectives, the police, his parents and even his friends. This demonstrates that his life in Edinburgh is not very happy and it gets worse as the film progresses: the death of his friend Alison's baby daughter, Spud's imprisonment, Mark himself overdosing and being taken to hospital. Eventually, Mark reaches the conclusion that the only way to improve his existence is to leave Edinburgh and go to London. He is also encouraged to move by his teenage lover, Diane, who claims that his life is frozen in time: his favourite music, films, even drugs are all outmoded. On Mark's arrival London is portrayed as a montage of tourist attractions: London Bridge, the National Gallery, Carnaby Street, Piccadilly Circus, red buses and policemen on horses. In contrast to the scenes set in the centre of Edinburgh, which are medium shots with no angles, in the London section long shots prevail and angles are used extensively, allowing us to see the imposing London buildings in full. The takes are extremely short, giving the impression of speed and dynamism, even dizziness. This impression is further strengthened by the loud music. Paradoxically, although only a fraction of Boyle's film is set in London, we see many more of London's well-known landmarks than we do Edinburgh's.

Mark finds London very welcoming. Guides and tourists on special buses wave to passers-by (and to the film's viewers), children feed pigeons and smile straight at the camera, and friendly policemen help lost tourists to find their way; in contrast to Edinburgh where policemen are shown only chasing thieves. Cafés and streets are full of people of different ages and colours of skin, who seem to live in perfect harmony. There are no images of people working, only of those who are resting and enjoying themselves. The colours of the streets are bright, with red dominant, and the sun is shining, unlike in Edinburgh, which in *Trainspotting* always has dull weather. There is also an impression of space, of fresh air, contrasting with the claustrophobia of Edinburgh. John Hill suggests that in this episode 'the film cheerfully evokes the most cliched images of London in an ironic inversion of the touristic imagery which commonly accompanies the arrival of an English character in Scotland' (Hill 1997: 252). For Mark, London is a place of golden opportunities, offered by Thatcher's government, and he gets a job there that epitomizes the Thatcherite economy: as an estate agent. He is shown thoroughly enjoying himself in this role and his persuasive skills and experience in cheating people, as well as his general cynicism, seem to be a factor in his job satisfaction. The social and geographical environment in which Mark operates in London is very different from his Edinburgh's milieu.

He deals mainly with middle-class people and his own elevation to the middle class is signified by his new appearance, typically wearing a shirt and tie. All this suits him well. In an inner monologue Mark confesses: 'For the first time in my life I felt almost happy.'

One can ask why Mark never tried to earn his living through 'proper' work in Edinburgh and to achieve happiness by abiding by the law and other standards of mainstream society. The answer is made clear when Mark's friends visit his London flat. Begbie comes first, looking for shelter on the run after a robbery, then Sick Boy invades his apartment, hoping to start a new career in London as a pimp. Their presence not only disrupts Mark's orderly and peaceful life, but fills Mark with disgust and fear. His friends not only live in his apartment and eat his food, but also sell his belongings, spend his money and cause him trouble at work. Begbie and Sick Boy's 'invasion' and their sponging on Mark can be interpreted as a metaphor for England being sponged on by Scotland, a notion shared by a significant number of those living in the South East and one which Scottish nationalists find particularly offensive.

From the very beginning of the film, Mark shows that he is intellectually superior and stronger in character than his friends. In London this distance seems even greater, as Mark becomes more annoyed and exasperated by their behaviour than he ever was in Edinburgh. Moreover, all of them look provincial and seem lacking in self-confidence when they try to do business with London drug dealers, to whom they sell a large supply of heroin that they bought from some Russian sailors. Mark fails to build a new, 'orderly' life for himself in London, as he failed to in Edinburgh. However, the reason for this is not London per se, but its proximity to Edinburgh. Being in London, Mark is exposed to the influence of his mates, epitomizing all the vices and malaise of his old town. Ultimately, Mark runs away from London, as he did from Edinburgh, choosing life abroad after he betrays his friends and steals their money. Although he commits a deeply immoral act, he does not lose our sympathy because Boyle is able to convince us that Mark has no other option if he wants to survive and succeed. We might guess that Mark will flourish far away from his old friends, while those who remained in Edinburgh will sink even further.[1]

Pretty Shitty City

Unlike Scottish cinema, which is typically placed in the context of Tartanry and Kailyard, historians of Welsh cinema have made no attempts to discuss it in terms of a few dominant paradigms representing Wales and its people. However, David Berry in his *Wales and Cinema* identifies problems pertinent to Welsh cinematography, which are similar to those uncovered by Colin McArthur in Scottish cinema: a pre-occupation with Welsh myths, rather than with its reality; a limited choice of settings, such as a colliery and the most picturesque and touristy corners of rural Wales, at the expense of showing urban life; cliched portrayals of women; and, crucially, the domination of Welsh cinema by outsiders, particularly Englishmen and Americans. As Berry puts it: 'For years Welsh people have been forced to see themselves on screen as often uninformed visiting film crews have seen them. All too frequently the view offered has told us more about the film-maker than about Wales' (Berry 1994: 11). *Twin Town*, together with some other films made in the 1990s, including *Gadael Lenin* [Leaving Lenin, 1993], directed by Endaf Emlyn, were heralded as the beginning of a more indigenous Welsh cinema, in the same way that *Shallow Grave* and *Trainspotting* were regarded as the first chapter of a new Scottish cinema.

The director of *Twin Town*, Kevin Allen, played a small role in *Trainspotting*. Ben Thompson, who wrote a review of *Twin Town* for *Sight and Sound*, suggested that Allen 'borrowed' many ideas from *Trainspotting*, such as the choice of setting, narrative devices, symbolism and the type of characters (Thompson 1997: 54). The action of *Twin Town* takes place in Swansea and the main protagonists, Jeremy and Julian Lewis, known in their city as 'the twins' (although they are only brothers), in common with their counterparts in Boyle's film are unemployed and unruly. They fill their time stealing cars for joyriding and exchanging drugs with the local pensioners. As long as Jeremy and Julian keep a safe distance from Swansea's business 'moguls', their behaviour is generally tolerated. The situation changes when they try to force a wealthy local businessman, Bryn Cartwright, to pay their father compensation for breaking his leg while working on one of Cartwright's construction sites. Their mutual revenge leads to the death of the twins' parents and their sister, and to Cartwright's subsequent murder.

In contrast to *Trainspotting*, which opened with an unflattering image of the centre of Edinburgh, *Twin Town* opens with a view of Swansea as tourists might imagine a typical Welsh seaside resort and in a way which is reminiscent of many films set in Wales. First, we see a bird's-eye view, including the sea surrounding Swansea on one side and green hills on the other. Then the camera takes a closer look at the seaside pleasures, showing girls running with miniature windmills in their hands, boys playing rugby, holidaymakers walking with plastic bathing toys or enjoying a ride in a horse-drawn carriage, and old people waving to the camera. The colours are gaudy, with plenty of reds, greens and yellows. The slow motion used in this scene prevents us from missing any of Swansea's numerous tourist attractions and gives the impression of a happy and tranquil place. This impression is strengthened by the gentle, 'retro' music – 'Downtown', sung by Petula Clark. The syrupy image of a 'tourist paradise' is so complete and the impression of the camera's presence so vivid that it creates the suspicion that the author is providing us with a very self-conscious and ironic representation of Swansea. The fact that the first scene is strongly reminiscent of the beginning of another film set in a small town, *Blue Velvet* (1986) by David Lynch, awakens further suspicions that Swansea's happy and appealing surface hides a rotten and hideous core, as did the American Lumbertown where Lynch's postmodern classic was set. The mood of the next scene, showing the Lewises joyriding, is in complete contrast to the opening of the film, confirming the suspicion that Swansea is not all tranquil, happy and safe. The dynamic soundtrack reaffirms this feeling. In the course of the film we see a Swansea that oscillates between extremes: serenity and noise, beauty and ugliness, naturalness and artificiality, affluence and poverty – and sometimes also combines and reconciles them.

Some of the contrasts coincide with geographical differences. Unlike *Trainspotting*, where the topography of Edinburgh was hardly conveyed and the city looked homogeneous, with the centre sharing many of its characteristics with working-class housing estates, in *Twin Town* the emphasis is put on the geographical and social heterogeneity of Swansea. This contrast is made apparent by the large proportion of the film shot on location, and by the extensive use of long shots. Apart from the touristic seaside boulevards, there are glimpses of Swansea's quiet, semi-rural suburbs where the only distraction is the noise of the cars driven by the Lewises and the local policemen. In a different part of the town, or perhaps outside the town altogether, the millionaire Bryn Cartwright has his huge estate, surrounded by high fences and closed-circuit TV cameras. We also see the lively centre of Swansea, particularly busy at night, when people gather in their hundreds in the restaurants, pubs and clubs. Eventually, there are nondescript, rather ugly outskirts of the town, with a ring road and road works and a kind of shantytown – a caravan park, where the Lewis family live and where most of the film's narrative is set. The place is also on the edge of Swansea and looks almost like a self-contained village, with children playing near the houses and no cars in sight. Not far from the caravan park stands a large, old, disused factory with tall, smokeless chimneys – a reminder that Swansea once was, and no longer is, an industrial town, a notion that is also conveyed through the choice of characters. All of them work in new (post-Fordist) service industries of entertainment (massage parlours, karaoke clubs), property developments and drug dealing, and nobody is employed in the old (Fordist) industries of manufacturing and trade. The fact that the factory is visible from the Lewises' caravan only suggests that they are the main victims of the Thatcherite revolution and of the general decline suffered by the Welsh economy in the 1980s. The absence of old industries and the huge contrast between the standard of living of the working class, as represented by the Lewis family, and the obscene luxury of Swansea's entrepreneurs, are not the only indicators of the film's time. Another is the close tie between money and state institutions, represented by the police. Instead of serving the whole community of Swansea, the policemen are on Cartwright's payroll, helping him to arrange his illegal drug deals. They are also biased against the working-class underdogs – when they are not involved in their dodgy interests, they are chasing Jeremy and Julian, whose crimes are relatively harmless in comparison with their own and those of Cartwright.

The material constraints that the Lewis family experiences are reflected in their humble possessions and in their occupations. The father, Fatty Lewis, accepts the badly paid casual work on the construction site, claiming that it is better than earning nothing. His daughter, Adie, adds to her wages as a receptionist in a massage parlour by means of occasional prostitution, and she dreams about saving enough to be able to leave Swansea; the 'twins' are unemployed and their mother is a housewife with no income. Nobody in this family is a member of a trade union or belongs to any organization or informal community based on common work experience. In contrast to *Trainspotting*, where Mark Renton and his friends did not work mainly because they chose to be idle and were never bored, in *Twin Town* the lack of work is regarded as a despicable predicament. Jeremy and Julian seem virtually unable to fill the time at their disposal; a surplus of time is also the main reason why they take drugs and steal cars. Yet Allen rejects treating his heroes simply as hapless victims of economic and political oppression. This is especially true of the older generation: living in a caravan seems to suit their romantic and anarchic spirit. Fatty Lewis makes miniature boats in bottles and knows many stories of life at sea, his wife plays a pianola and sings. Moreover, there is a certain flamboyance and exaggeration in the design of their caravan, reminiscent of the camp interiors where the characters of John Waters's films used to live. The gaudy clothes and shiny make-up of Adie Lewis and her mother are also reminiscent of the kitsch appearance of Waters's characters.

Kitsch is not limited to the impoverished Lewises. The family home of the millionaire Cartwright is as tacky as that of the poor Lewises, only on a grander scale, with numerous vulgar ornaments and an American-style swimming pool. Cartwright also shares Fatty's interest in miniature vehicles, playing for long hours with his child's model railway. The Cartwrights' crude taste and crude manners suggest that they are nouveaux riches, whose style and social status have not caught up with their material circumstances – a typical characteristic of Thatcherite economy and culture. One of the funniest and most poignant images of the Cartwrights' estate is a bird's-eye view shot that includes their enormous garden. From a distance it looks like a pasture, complete with a sheep grazing on the grass. However, on closer inspection it becomes clear that this is not a sheep, but Mrs Cartwright's poodle. This image can be read as a sign that in recent years agriculture in South Wales has diminished as much as manufacturing, and of the huge expansion in power in Wales of people like the Cartwrights.

As Moya Luckett observes, *Twin Town* displays conflict between England and Wales through the use of various visual means:

> The mise-en-scene interrogates questions of national identity and local pride as in the scene where two characters (one of them leaning against a statue of Noddy, a symbol of imperialist English children's culture) are waiting outside Swansea Station and see 'Ambition is critical' inscribed in the pavement. The older one tells his friend that this is a response to Dylan Thomas's edict that Swansea is 'the graveyard of ambition' … Visible behind them is a bilingual British Rail sign with the English text (in darker letters)

24. *Twin Town* (1997), dir. Kevin Allen (copyright © 2002 by Universal
Studios. Courtesy of Universal Studios Publishing Rights, a division of
Universal Studios Licensing, Inc. All rights reserved)

placed above the Welsh, suggesting the hegemony of British identity while highlighting Wales' linguistic difference and its battle for
bilingual public signs. (Luckett 2000: 93)

English is not the only culture, or even the main culture, that threatens
the Welsh way of life. American and global culture, created and circulated
through the mass media, are also culprits in its dilution and gradual
disappearance. This phenomenon is reflected, for example, in the name
given by the Lewises to their dog – Cantona (a French footballer who
played for Manchester United) – or the Cartwrights naming their huge
estate 'Ponderosa', after the famous American TV series *Bonanza* (whose
protagonist is also called Ben Cartwright). All the characters also seem
to prefer Indian food to Welsh cuisine – the Cartwrights dine in an
Indian restaurant and Fatty Lewis's wife brings in naans and curry when
he is in hospital. Welsh or, more precisely, Swansea culture also suffers
from within; it is stagnant, almost dead, with no signs of development
or revitalization. The main subjects of the protagonists' references to
Welshnessness are bygone traditions, past Welsh achievements and the

heroes of earlier generations. Thus, for example, we see an orchestra of schoolchildren, walking suburban streets, clad in traditional Welsh costume and playing Welsh music. This image, although demonstrating the respect of the new generation of Welsh for their national heritage, also suggests the poverty of contemporary culture. The soundtrack contains many hits from a repertoire of Welsh pop stars of the 1960s and 1970s, such as *In the Summertime* by Mungo Jerry and one of the characters, 'karaoke king' Dai Rees, models himself on Tom Jones. The new Welsh hits, on the other hand, are hardly included in spite of the fact that in reality the Welsh were very successful on the British pop and rock scene (examples being Catatonia and Manic Street Preachers). Fatty Lewis, the most patriotic character in the film, identifies Welsh and local culture with the male voice choir of which he is a member. His conviction can be regarded as a bad prognosis for Swansea culture. The members of the choir are almost all old, it is suggested that their performances have a very limited audience, and the choir is, of course, all male. Moreover, there is a strong association between the male choirs and the Welsh mining industry. David Berry observes that 'there was hardly a mining picture in the forties and fifties without a choir scene or a moment when colliers expressed their camaraderie in song' (Berry 1994: 11).[2] As the mining industry has been practically nonexistent in Wales since the 1980s, the music of the male choir represents a dead culture.

In contrast, a karaoke competition, held at the largest Swansea nightclub, seems to be the most exciting event for the inhabitants of the whole city. The club is completely packed with people of all ages and sexes, enthused by watching others recycling old, well-known songs. In Allen's film, karaoke is the most potent symbol of the replacement of genuine Welsh culture by one that is neither English nor American, simply fake. No wonder that Fatty is a staunch enemy of karaoke. Another example of the internal threat to Welsh culture is its literal privatization by the ruthless nouveaux riches who use it to their own advantage, rather than for the benefit of the whole community. An example is the situation of rugby, regarded as Wales's national sport. In *Twin Town*, rugby pitches and clubs belong entirely to Bryn Cartwright, who is a drug dealer and a dodgy property developer. One has little doubt that, in spite of his claims about his love of rugby, he does little to raise the profile or social appeal of the sport. On the contrary, it is suggested that Cartwright's rugby is as corrupt a business as his other deals. Cartwright's symbolic and literal appropriation of rugby also marks the further marginalization of the Swansea working class, which used to constitute the bulk of rugby players and spectators. Welsh language is noticeable on bilingual signs, but not spoken by any of the film characters, not even by the patriotic Fatty Lewis. The absence of live Welsh language contrasts with Hindi, which is spoken by the waiters working in the Indian restaurant. The Indians use their native language to exchange rude comments about their Welsh guests – something that the Welsh cannot do with their English neighbours, with whom they share a common language.

The most prominent Welshman mentioned in the film is Dylan Thomas. The poet, born in Swansea in 1914, is presented as somebody who was both critical of and tender towards his home town. In one particular scene policeman Greyo tells his pal Terry that Thomas once described Swansea as an 'ugly lovely town'. Thomas's and Greyo's words, however, are ridiculed and distorted by Terry, who proposes labelling Swansea as a 'pretty shitty city'. Terry, who is Scottish (his crude manners and arrogant attitude to people are almost identical to those of Begbie in *Trainspotting*), has no sympathy for or understanding of Swansea or Wales – for him, Swansea is provincial and Welsh people are utterly stupid. His pal, Greyo, who is more responsible and perhaps even interested in his country and proud of it, is unable to challenge Terry's scornful attitude to Swansea. On the whole, there is no contemporary Dylan Thomas in sight, able to understand and discuss the contradictions and complexity of the Welsh national/urban character without prejudice or cheap sentimentality. Perhaps Allen reserves such a role for himself; the fact that Thomas was involved in filmmaking (during the Second World War he wrote scripts for several poetic documentaries produced by the London-based Strand company and the previously mentioned *Rebecca's Daughters* is based on his screenplay) confirms this opinion.

Although, unlike *Trainspotting*, *Twin Town* is full of references to Welsh traditions and history, it treats them differently from the British 'heritage films' of the 1980s and early 1990s, which are regarded as crucial examples of postmodernism in British cinema. Rather than indulging in sentimental nostalgia (regarded as an important element of postmodern culture), Allen critically examines the role of the past in the country's present. More generally, he shows how lessons from the past are irrelevant when trying to solve the current problems of Wales, how inadequate are past traditions (such as language, music, literature, working-class customs) in forging a new unity of Welsh people. At the same time, Allen fails to

25. *Twin Town* (1995), dir. Kevin Allen (Copyright © 2002
     by Universal Studios. Courtesy of Universal Studios
     Publishing Rights, a division of Universal Studios
     Licensing, Inc. All rights reserved)

notice any signs of a new Welsh culture, which the approaching devolution was supposed to celebrate and strengthen.

As *Trainspotting*, *Twin Town* ends with the image of the escape of the
main protagonists: after losing their whole family and achieving their
revenge, Jeremy and Julian decide to head for Morocco. They are not
the only people in the film who leave Swansea – Cartwright's wife also
decides to escape from her home town after her husband's death. In
each case, escape seems to be the only chance for the characters to
achieve a better life; staying in their home town probably means utter

misery, or even death. The escapes shown in *Trainspotting* and *Twin Town* complete the bleak vision of the Celtic City offered by these films, as a hapless victim of the Thatcherite revolution, a sick, decadent place, lacking any distinctive identity or sense of community, with no past traditions to be proud of, and no future to look forward to.[3] What is even more depressing in their representation is the conviction that the cities cannot rectify their own problems and that, left to themselves, they will sink even further (in reality this was contradicted by devolution in Scotland and Wales). Directly, as in *Trainspotting*, or indirectly, as in *Twin Town*, these films promote London/England/foreign countries as a better place than a Celtic City. However, paradoxically, the low opinion of urban life in Scotland and Wales as conveyed by Boyle and Allen might be the reason why their films gained such popularity in Britain and abroad, particularly among young viewers. In contrast to many other British films, particularly the 'heritage cycle' of the 1980s that concentrated on the picturesque aspects of English urban and country life, they were perceived as realistic, unpatronizing and even liberating, in tune with the experiences of many young people who dream about escaping from their home towns.

10

The Eternal Postmodernity
of Blackpool

So far, we have argued that cities in films look postmodern either as a result of their cinematic representation (or, more precisely, of that component of the representation that signifies the difference between reality and its image), or because over the last few decades the cities themselves gained some postmodern features due to such phenomena as post-Fordism or postcommunism, features that the films reflect. We will argue that Blackpool is a different case. Its cinematic postmodernism not only follows the changes that affected the 'real' city in the last decades, and the postmodern style of the cinema of the 1980s and 1990s, but, to a large extent, results from the fact that Blackpool was always, in a sense, postmodern. By that we mean that many of the features commonly associated with postmodernism already existed there and were identified by historians before the term 'postmodernism' began to be widely used.

Blackpool – Postmodern Before Postmodernism

Blackpool, situated on the north-west coast of Lancashire, was the most popular holiday destination for the British working classes for over 100 years. As John K. Walton and John Urry observe, this status seems to have as much to do with its convenient geographical location, as with

British social and economic history. Its route to pre-eminence began in the nineteenth century – the age of industrialization and urbanization and, following these, of regular holidays for the working classes and of mass tourism (see Walton 1978; Urry 1990; Walton 1998). The towns of south and east Lancashire, where the cotton industry was concentrated, such as Manchester, Blackburn and Preston, grew in a particularly rapid manner. Similarly, the demand for leisure by the working-class inhabitants in these towns was greater than in any other part of the country. Blackpool, for its location by the seaside, was regarded as an excellent place to spend a holiday and was easy to reach by train; consequently, crowds of mill workers visited it every year. However, these features alone, as Walton observes, do not entirely explain why Blackpool was chosen by factory workers and ignored by 'respectable tourists', as nearby Southport became a resort for the better off around the same time. An important factor was that Blackpool began as a community of small freeholders. No large resort was so dominated by small, family-run lodging houses as Blackpool. 'There was no room for a planned, high-class estate to grow up on the landowner's own terms, for Blackpool's small freeholders were understandably more concerned with making the maximum profit from a cramped parcel of land than with improving the amenities of the resort as a whole' (Walton 1978: 63).

'As a result, the whole central area became an ill-planned mass of smaller properties, boarding houses, amusement arcades, small shops and the like, with no space for the grand public buildings, broad avenues and gardens found in Southport' (Urry 1990: 23). At the same time, Blackpool did not possess the scenic attractions necessary to appeal to the middle-class tourist market (see Walton 1978: 43). A substantial part of the pleasures it offered to tourists were artificial: funfairs, piers, the Winter Gardens and the Blackpool Tower. Their roots were often foreign – their inventors borrowed ideas from abroad, were financed by foreign capital or even physically brought the attractions from overseas. For example, the Blackpool Tower, which opened in 1894, was an imitation of the Eiffel Tower in Paris and the Pleasure Beach, an open-air amuse-ment park financed by an Anglo-American syndicate, was Blackpool's answer to the various 'parks' at Coney Island in New York (Walton 1998: 93). Blackpool also became famous for its live entertainment: music-halls, theatres and circuses. Many of the shows boasted artists of national and international fame. There was also room for charlatans, pseudo-artists and freaks of all kinds. To the present day Blackpool has an image as the greatest freak-show in Britain. Artists from diverse social backgrounds seemed to prosper, performing side by side, something that was hardly possible in other parts of a generally class-ridden England. Although Blackpool catered particularly for the working classes, some of its attractions also lured members of the middle class. For example, as Walton argues, 'The [Blackpool] Tower was inclusive in its embrace: it welcomed curious middle-class pleasure-seekers as well as "factory folk" ... and this reflected the town's enduring concern to retain as many middle-class visitors as possible' (Walton 1998: 92).

Since Victorian times, the 'pearl of the Lancashire riviera' and 'Eldorado of the North', in common with other British resorts, was also associated with sexual promiscuity (Walvin 1978: 72; Shields 1991: 105–12). It was a place where tourists had the chance to forget themselves by indulging in erotic pleasures that were unavailable in the rest of their lives. Again, this behaviour was as typical of the working classes as it was of 'respectable gentlemen', who enjoyed the candid pleasures of 'dirty weekends'. No wonder that, as James Walvin notes, 'the resort posed dilemmas for morally sensitive Victorians' (Walvin 1978: 72). At one point Blackpool became very popular among homosexuals and today a whole district is dominated by gay bars and clubs.

John Walton argues that Blackpool signifies an extreme diversity of British culture: high and low, middle and working class, respectable and disreputable, local and cosmopolitan (see Walton 2000). This diversity is of a special sort: anti-hegemonic, tolerant, democratic. The necessary condition for the harmonious coexistence of different strains of British culture is Blackpool's cultural openness, which seems to result from two interconnected factors. First, Blackpool constitutes – to use Rob Shields's expression – 'the Other pole to a great cultural centre' of England (Shields 1991: 3); it is widely regarded as a place on the geographic and social margins of the country, left behind by politicians and moralists as unworthy of their attention. Second, its culture is shaped more by its visitors and those who cater for their tastes than by the rest of its population. Consequently, many films present Blackpool as somehow different from the rest of Britain and focus on visitors, rather than residents of this seaside resort.

Various features of Blackpool – the chaotic architecture and small-scale urban design, an inclination to artificiality and love of kitsch, the mixture of high and low art, tolerance of sexual promiscuity and homosexuality – have postmodern connotations. Accordingly, it can be argued that Blackpool represented postmodernity as early as the beginning of the twentieth century, long before the term was coined in the English language. The resort can also be regarded as postmodern in the sense of containing objects that are literally post-modern. We refer here particularly to its most conspicuous feature – Blackpool Tower. The Tower is a postmodern building, because it imitates a quintessentially modern building, the Eiffel Tower, erected for the 1889 Paris Exposition. Moreover, the grand scale and provocative nature of this imitation and the character of the object duplicated (the fact that the Eiffel Tower epitomizes not only modernity, but also Paris and France), makes the Blackpool Tower an object of camp, at least in the eyes of contemporary viewers.

The passage of time added new postmodern features and connotations to those that existed for most of the twentieth century. For example, as John Urry observes, in the 1970s and 1980s, when British seaside resorts began to decline, their managers started to look for new ways to seduce tourists. They appealed particularly to their desire to recycle old images and feelings. As Urry puts it, 'Piers and towers now stand for nostalgia, for the "theme" of the old seaside holiday' (Urry 1990: 34). Besides the nostalgia for the seaside holiday of days gone by, Blackpool evokes a new or 'wider' kind of nostalgia – that for a traditional working-class culture as it is represented in books such as Walter Greenwood's *Love on the Dole* (1933) and Richard Hoggart's *The Uses of Literacy* (1957). It could be suggested that its working-class image was the reason why, after winning the general election of 1997, the (New) Labour Party decided to abandon Blackpool as a venue for their annual conference.

On the other hand, as Urry points out, the general decline of the British seaside resort that began in the 1970s, although to a certain degree affecting Blackpool's ability to attract tourists, also helped to establish its new identity. He writes: 'Blackpool has generally tried to construct itself as irreducibly modern as a cosmopolitan, international leisure centre, the "Las Vegas of the North", having less now to do with its previous Lancashire/Northern/working class associations' (Urry 1990: 35). Tony Bennett notes: 'In Blackpool everything is new no matter how old it is' (quoted in Urry 1990: 35). Keith Waterhouse adds: 'It would have been, in all its gaudy tattiness, the greatest show on earth. It still is, outvulgarized only by Las Vegas' (quoted in Urry 1990: 36). Such terms as 'cosmopolitan', 'irreducibly modern', and 'gaudy' are part of the postmodern jargon, suggesting contemporary Blackpool's post-modernity.

Is Blackpool as it is represented by filmmakers – cosmopolitan, global, irreducibly modern, gaudy, Las Vegas-like, kitsch and camp; or is it rather Lancashire/Northern[1]/provincial/working-class? Some of these divisions might even prove artificial or superficial, as is suggested by Jeffrey Richards who, when discussing the phenomenon of the stardom of the Lancashire actors Gracie Fields and George Formby, claims that 'both indicate the truth of Patrick Joyce's contention that it was possible for people to be simultaneously loyal to family, street, country, nation and Empire: Formby and Fields embodied such multiple loyalties' (Richards 1997: 258). Moreover, is it possible to detect any trajectory in the way Blackpool was represented by subsequent generations of filmmakers? The remaining part of this chapter will try to answer these questions.

Cinematic Blackpool

The first feature film set in Blackpool was made in 1927. This was a silent box-office hit, *Hindle Wakes*, directed by Maurice Elvey, based on the popular play by Stanley Houghton, published in 1912. The best measure of the success of the play and the film was the fact that *Hindle Wakes* was twice more adapted for the screen: in 1931 and again in 1952. The story centres on a strong-minded, independent Lancashire girl who rejects the offer of marriage to her boss's son. Only a part of Elvey's film is set in Blackpool, but the seaside resort plays an important role in the narrative, serving as the setting and catalyst for the romance. In Elvey's film, Blackpool is a place where people abandon their normal inhibitions and let their sexual energy explode. This has much to do with the sheer anonymity of the place, as incomers heavily outnumber Blackpool's resident population. Elvey shows that people are more inclined to indulge in forbidden pleasures when among strangers. The sea also plays its part in helping people to 'forget themselves'. Blackpool is constructed as a liminal space, on the borderline between nature and culture. Although Elvey's film emphasizes the adventures of the main characters, rather than exploring the surrounding environment, one can identify some elements of Blackpool's cultural landscape that will be pertinent to later films set in this city. Particularly worth attention are the traces of 'bogus orientalism' in the shape of snakes and fake Arabs found on the Pleasure Beach and in the Blackpool streets.

The motif of Blackpool as a place of sexual freedom, expressed by those whose sexuality is otherwise repressed, is also an important theme in *Oranges are Not the Only Fruit* (1990), a BBC series, adapted by Jeanette Winterson from her own best-selling novel and directed by Beeban Kidron. This production, only a small part of which is set in Blackpool, casts as the main character Jess, a Lancashire lesbian, brought up by her evangelical, sexually repressed mother. On a trip to Blackpool, the forbidden love between Jess and her friend Melanie blossoms and it is suggested that Blackpool's atmosphere is a contributing factor.

Basil Dean's musical comedy, *Sing As We Go* (1934), in common with *Hindle Wakes*, foregrounds Blackpool's role as a place of refuge from the boring and monotonous life of the Lancashire factories. This time, however, the refuge is not from work, but from enforced idleness as a result of the closure of the mill. The film presents the adventures of a young working-class woman, Grace, played by Gracie Fields, who specialized in playing strong, working-class heroines (Richards 1984: 181–3; Richards 1997: 258–66). After losing her job in the cotton mill, closed as a result of the depression, Grace goes to Blackpool to work as a waitress in a boarding house. However, her employment lasts only a few days; after pouring a bowl of rhubarb on the head of a guest who offended her, Grace is fired and embarks on a series of other jobs, mainly in what today would be called the tourist industry, and is involved in a series of tragicomic adventures. She sells ice-cream, works as a clairvoyant's assistant, performs in a freak-show, participates in a bicycle race and a beauty contest. Her adventures are an opportunity to show off Blackpool's charms: music-halls, circuses, funfairs, beaches, trams, roller-coasters, piers and the Blackpool Tower. Grace's stay in 'the jewel of the Lancashire riviera' ends when the mill reopens.

By the choice of characters and narrative, Dean's film largely conforms to the provincial/working-class image of Blackpool. For example, the modesty and self-containedness of Blackpool tourism is emphasized by Grace's arrival by bicycle. Grace herself is a typical Northern working-class girl with a good sense of humour. She is not afraid to make a fool of herself, but she also notices and instantly ridicules anything that is pretentious, snobbish and false. Jeffrey Richards regards this down-to-earth attitude to life as a typical Lancashire trait (Richards 1997: 255–8). Although Grace befriends Phyllis, a middle-class girl from London, she spends most of her time in the company of other working-class people. There is the impression that the whole resort is full of Grace's work-pals, all speaking with Lancashire accents, eating fish and chips and indulging in the simple amusements offered by the Pleasure Beach. There are also some middle- and upper-class people in Blackpool, such as Hugh, a manager at the factory where Grace worked, and Sir William Upton, an industrialist who has the power to save the mill. However, they come to Blackpool mainly for business and do not partake in the vulgar attractions on offer; they remain distant observers of the working-class people who wallow in Blackpool's pleasures. For example, Sir William remarks: 'I'll take a stroll through the Pleasure Beach. I haven't seen one of these things for years.' Later on he is astonished to learn that Hugh wants to stay in Blackpool longer than is strictly necessary for business.

Dean shows that in the 1930s the holidays of the working classes were as institutionalized as their work, conforming to the picture painted by John K. Walton in *The Blackpool Landlady*. The boarding houses are visited by whole cohorts of holidaymakers, arriving in Blackpool by train. The same groups come to the same house and stay for a fixed period each year, usually one or two weeks. They have meals in the same place and at the same time each day and they all go together to the beaches and funfairs. There are also many activities to enjoy collectively, such as races, competitions and processions. The portrayed communal character of life in Blackpool conforms to the idea of the North as *Gemeinschaft* in contrast to the *Gesellschaft*-like South (Hall 1997: 209). *Sing As We Go* is shot in black and white. The lack of colour reaffirms another popular stereotype of the North – as bleak, colourless, cold and rainy. Indeed, although it is the holiday season, it rains both in Grace's home town and in Blackpool. The most persistent and powerful image of Blackpool in Dean's film is the crowd. Crowds are everywhere: at the funfair, at the circus, in the music-hall, on the beach, in the streets, in the boarding house. In many places people must queue for what they want. The large number of visitors is the main reason for the impression of chaos and carnival. It can also be assumed that togetherness, communality and 'cosiness' attract the working classes to Blackpool and discourage the more individualistic middle and upper classes.

Andrew Higson suggests that, on the one hand, the very setting of the film in Blackpool was a factor in *Sing As We Go* being practically unexportable and restricted to working- and lower/middle-class audiences, and, on the other hand, the parochialism and 'working-classness' of the narrative and characters reinforced the status of Blackpool as a parochial/working-class resort (see Higson 1995). Yet, not everything in *Sing As We Go* is Northern and working-class. First, Blackpool is saturated with fake orientalism: men in Arab clothing walk the streets and the funfairs boast attractions from all over the world. Second, as Hugh's example demonstrates, even those initially sceptical about Blackpool's ability to amuse members of different classes, eventually give in to its charm.

Divorcee Helen, her teenage daughter Jo and Helen's boyfriend, Peter, are also visitors to Blackpool in *A Taste of Honey* (1961), directed by Tony Richardson almost thirty years after the production of *Sing As We Go*. They speak with Northern accents, come to Blackpool from nearby Manchester and can also be described as working class. They do almost exactly the same things as the characters in *Sing As We Go*: riding the roller-coaster, visiting the freak-show, eating fish and chips on the streets and buying cheap souvenirs. However, one can also detect some changes in their pattern of holidaying, as they come to Blackpool only for a day trip, travelling by private car and having no particular itinerary, confirming the impression that after the 1950s holidays to British seaside resorts become more ad hoc and fragmented (Urry 1990: 33–5).

Typical of the British New Wave films, *A Taste of Honey* is shot in black and white. Again, it endorses the myth of the North as 'Darkshire': glum, severe and bleak (Gaskell 1848, quoted in Shields 1991: 210). Blackpool is even more rainy and windy here than in Dean's film. In comparison with *Sing As We Go*, there are also fewer 'exotic' attractions in Richardson's Blackpool. However, it is difficult to establish whether the cause is the conscious decision on the part of the film's author to portray Blackpool as conforming to a certain stereotype of Northernness, or simply the fact that there was no time to reveal all of Blackpool's many attractions (in contrast to *Sing As We Go*, which was almost entirely set in Blackpool, the Blackpool part in *A Taste of Honey* lasts less than six minutes).

The narratives of *Bhaji on the Beach* (1993), directed by Gurinder Chadha, and of *Funny Bones* (1994), directed by Peter Chelsom, in common with the films previously mentioned, revolve around visitors to Blackpool. They come from further afield than their cinematic predecessors and their ethnic identity and social background are different from those of the characters in *Hindle Wakes* and *Sing As We Go*. In *Bhaji on the Beach* they are a group of Indian women from Birmingham and in *Funny Bones* an American stand-up comedian from Las Vegas. The group of Indians in Chadha's film is very heterogeneous in terms of age and identity, encompassing three generations of British Indians – elderly Asian immigrants and those representing the generations of their children and grandchildren. In addition, one of the visitors, Rekha, came to Britain from Bombay with her businessman husband and another, Hashida, is followed by her West Indian boyfriend. Among them is Bina, a shop assistant with Marks and Spencer; Asha, a newsagent with a university degree; Hashida, an A-level student about to start medical school; Ginder, a young housewife who sacrificed intellectual ambitions for a family; and a couple of teenagers, Ladhu and Madhu. Hashida's boyfriend, Oliver, is an art student and the leader of the group, Simi, runs the Saheli Women's Centre, which includes the shelter where Ginder stays with her son. Virtually none of the characters in Chadha's film works in textile factories or heavy industry, which for over a hundred years provided the bulk of Blackpool's holidaymakers. On the contrary, those who are not housewives work or are preparing to work in the service industries. This reflects the particular professional interests of British Asians and their social advancement, but also mirrors the economic and social changes that began in the 1970s and gained momentum in the post-Fordist Thatcher era: consumerism, deindustrialization, the shift from production to a service economy. There is much irony in Chadha's portrayal of Indian women, an irony that relies on the gap between the traditional image of Indians, held by outsiders and even by the characters themselves, and the postmodern reality of their lives, marked by globalization and cosmopolitanism. For example, the most westernized person among the visitors, the one who can be described as 'more western than westerners', is Rekha, the only true Indian in the group. She comes to the gathering wearing full make-up and Chanel clothes and has a copy of *Hello!* magazine under her arm. Her companions, who bring with them boxes of traditional Indian food, are treated by Rekha with chewing gum on their way to Blackpool and, on their way home, with a souvenir cake in the shape of female breasts.

Before the excursion to Blackpool begins, Simi introduces its purpose to her companions, saying: 'It is not often that we women get away from the patriarchal demands made on us in our daily lives, struggling between the double yoke of racism and sexism … This is your day, have a female fun time.' Thus, Simi suggests that Blackpool is a place where an escape from racism and sexism is possible, probably in contrast

26. *Bhaji on the Beach* (1993), dir. Gurinder Chadha

to many other British towns and cities, where their yoke is as prevalent as in their native Birmingham. Indeed, Blackpool proves to be a place where many of the old patterns of behaviour, imposed on Chadha's heroines by Indian traditions and their relative isolation from English culture, can be abandoned. This refers particularly to the contacts with white men. The first to find a white male companion in Blackpool is the 'progressive' Rekha. She is followed by the teenagers who meet two burger-sellers of their own age, keen to have fun with the girls. Then Asha, who seems to be a faithful follower of Indian traditions, including sexual morals, befriends a white man – an oldish, gentlemanly actor, Ambrose Waddington. Eventually, all the women, with the exception of Hashida, end up in a women-only night club, where the main attraction is the performance of a group of male strippers. Not all the women are equally eager to liberate themselves from the yoke of racism and patriarchy. The older women mainly keep to their familiar Indian ways and are outraged by the frivolity and irresponsibility of their younger companions. However, even they seem to be more open to foreign cultures and more tolerant in Blackpool than when at home. This is reflected in the night-club scene, where they only pretend to be outraged by the male strip show.

Among the short encounters between the Indian women and white men, of particular interest is that between Asha and Ambrose, as he raises the question of Blackpool's old and new identities. Ambrose claims that contemporary Blackpool is in a state of decline, its degradation measured by the number of closed or empty theatres and music-halls. This deplorable state results from the spread of television, which replaced or marginalized live entertainment and which the thespian regards as anti-cultural. Ambrose takes Asha to an empty theatre where they both imagine a show. The fact that it is only a dream emphasizes the difference between Blackpool's past and present. The resort's decline is likewise mirrored by Ambrose's own history – in the past he appeared on Blackpool's best stages, now he is reduced to performing on the streets, for casual and often uninterested tourists. Ambrose also declares that Blackpool is no longer true to itself and instead has become cosmopolitan and hybridized, which he regrets. This cosmopolitanism is reflected in the cheap orientalism and, to a greater extent, in the Americanization of Blackpool, for example in the burger-sellers who look like poor imitations of cowboys. Ambrose compliments Asha by telling her: 'You are genuine, you are ethnic.' Ironically, the fact that Asha came to the pearl of Lancashire riviera and let herself be entertained by an Englishman is a sign that she is not so 'genuine and ethnic' as he assumes and it is thanks to people like her that Blackpool lost its ethnic (English) purity. It must also be recollected that the old Blackpool of *Hindle Wakes* and *Sing As We Go* was not as culturally pure as the nostalgic artist suggests. In fact, pseudo-Arabs walked the streets in earlier films and freak-shows were full of monsters from all over the world.

The Blackpool re-created by Ambrose's nostalgia is juxtaposed with the town as experienced by the Indian women. What is striking in this Blackpool is its ability to provide everyone with what they want, satisfying all tastes. For delicate, melancholy Asha, Blackpool is like an oriental garden, full of flowers and birds; for Ginder and her little son it is a funfair; for the teenagers it is a network of fast-food restaurants. Even Oliver finds something interesting in Blackpool – an exhibition of contemporary art. Moreover, everybody enjoys the pleasures of the sea.

Most of the visitors regard Blackpool as very Indian. Rekha even claims that it looks exactly like Bombay. Indeed, in contrast to the black and white of *Sing As We Go* and *Taste of Honey*, it is bright, colourful and gaudy, almost like the setting of a Bollywood film. Andrea Stuart notices: '*Bhaji*'s aesthetic quality is certainly borrowed from Bombay: with its vivid colours and cartoon-like set-ups, it has that overblown but energetic crudity that could only have come from the Indian film industry or American super-hero comics' (Stuart 1994: 27). However, not everything is in the eye of the beholder. For example, the season of the year when the film is set is particularly prone to such East–West comparisons – the time of the Illuminations, when the whole town looks more colourful and vivid than usual, which is reminiscent of the Indian Diwali festival. The ease with which the two cultures, English and Indian, blend, is epitomized by the Punjabi version of Cliff Richard's 'Summer Holiday', sung by the women on their way to Blackpool and by the seasoning of chips with curry, practised by some of them. Even the climatic phenomenon of rain, regarded as quintessentially Northern, gains different connotations in Chadha's film. It is no longer a downpour that forces everyone to hide and makes them miserable, but warm rain, which refreshes the air and makes walking more pleasant. For the viewers who have no chance to relate Chadha's Blackpool with its earlier cinematic representations, the resort might seem lively and full of people. However, in comparison with the Blackpool of *Hindle Wakes* or *Sing As We Go*, where the streets and the Pleasure Beach were so crowded that at times it was almost impossible to pass, the town in *Bhaji on the Beach* looks much less populated, suggesting the relative decline of the resort, as conveyed in Ambrose's nostalgic outpouring.

Blackpool, as the film's protagonists experience, can be described as 'soft' in the sense defined by Jonathan Raban, as a place that does not force its inhabitants to conform to its rules, but 'awaits the imprint of identity': 'For better or worse, it invites you to remake it, to consolidate it into a shape you can live in. You, too. Decide who you are, and the city will again assume a fixed form round you. Decide what it is, and your own identity will be revealed, like a position on a map fixed by triangulation' (Raban 1975: 9–10).

However, the director of *Bhaji on the Beach* also acknowledges that there are some limits to Blackpool's softness and plasticity by pointing out that its hegemonic culture is English. Thus, those who publicly undermine Blackpool's Englishness risk conflict and rejection by the cultural mainstream. This opinion is best illustrated in the scene in which the Indian women visit a fish-and-chip shop. Two of them scorn the food offered there and instead start eating their samosas, which provokes an angry, racist reaction from the woman serving there. There are also limits to Blackpool's ability to free the visitors from their usual 'yokes'. Although Blackpool allowed the Indian women to get away

27. Tommy Fawkes in *Funny Bones* (1994),
dir. Peter Chelsom

from their everyday problems, caused by patriarchy, racism and Indian traditions, it has no power to change their values and their situation; it remains only a refuge, not a location of social and cultural revolution. Thus, it is suggested that after leaving Blackpool the unhappy Ginder will return to her brutal Indian husband and his sexist and intolerant family, and Asha will put up with her boring work and her family who neither appreciate her academic achievements nor understand her menopausal anxiety.

Motifs of escape and refuge are also to the fore in *Funny Bones*, the third part in a trilogy of films based loosely upon director Peter Chelsom's Blackpool childhood – a trilogy that also includes *Treacle* (1987) and *Hear My Song* (1991) (see Gray 1995: 49). Similar to *Bhaji on the Beach*, it encompasses two continents and two cultures; this time American and British. The main character of the film, Tommy Fawkes (Oliver Platt), the son of a famous American comedian, George Fawkes (Jerry

Lewis) and a stand-up comedian himself, comes to Blackpool from Las Vegas. For him, the trip to Blackpool is an escape from the humiliation caused by the failure of his stage performance, as well as a chance to 'buy' an act that can bring him success back home. It is also a sentimental journey, as he spent the first six years of his life in Blackpool and believes that his childhood was a time when everything was simpler and better than in America. Thus ingenuity (and lack of it) and nostalgia – two crucial concepts in postmodern discourse – are put at the centre of Chelsom's film.

There are two components to Tommy's attitude to Blackpool: on the one hand admiration, on the other disrespect mixed with cynicism. He believes that Blackpool is still genuine, in contrast to Las Vegas where everything is artificial and recycled, and he assumes that Blackpool will sell him its treasures cheaply, that he will be able to exploit it. Both assumptions essentially prove correct, although not everything turns out as Tommy hoped. His search for an 'act' is initially unsuccessful. Those who come to him with their jokes and tricks are not so much undiscovered artists as simply freaks living on the margin of society and thus confirming the marginal status of Blackpool. Many of them look old and withered, matching Blackpool's or perhaps even Britain's decay and fragility. The measure of their poverty and lack of dignity is their fight for some rather unappetizing sandwiches offered to them at the audition. Eventually, Tommy finds the comedians for whom he was looking. They are Jack Parker (real-life stand-up comedian Lee Evans), a man of about his own age, and Jack's father and uncle, Bruno and Thomas Parker. Although they all possess immense natural talents, their professional lives are very different from that of Tommy's less gifted father – Jack performs in a dingy, provincial-looking club, Bruno and Thomas work on the fairground ghost train as 'live horrors'. Tommy decides to buy the Parker brothers' act unseen. However, while watching their performance, he realizes that he knows their trick, as his own father performed it. Eventually he finds out that George Fawkes, who once worked with the Parkers, stole their act and destroyed their happiness by impregnating Bruno Parker's wife.

The Blackpool of Chelsom's narrative stands for integrity and true values, but also an inability to turn them into something profitable. The story of Jack Parker, who lost his career in the circus because he was too genuine, too honestly funny, suggests that honesty and talent are not necessarily helpful in art. On the other hand, Las Vegas embodies

28. Bruno and Thomas Parker in *Funny Bones* (1994), dir. Peter Chelsom

kitsch, pomposity and imitation, but also the success and prosperity that Blackpool does not enjoy and has no chance of achieving. Furthermore, Chelsom suggests that even the authenticity of Blackpool and, by the same token, of English culture, is relative, not absolute, as there is something more genuine than Blackpool and England – Paris and France. When a group of Frenchmen come to the Lancashire Riviera and see the Blackpool Tower, they comment, 'The English – what a bunch of thieves', which is an obvious reference to the fact that Blackpool's main attraction is an imitation of the Eiffel Tower. The English also try to steal from the French sailors some mysterious eggs containing a magic powder that secures eternal youth. Furthermore, it can be suggested that the genuineness and purity of Jack Parker's sense of humour have something to do with the fact that he is half-French.

Although Blackpool in *Bhaji on the Beach* was compared to Bombay, spectators could not actually judge for themselves the similarity of these two cities. In *Funny Bones*, on the other hand, Blackpool is not only discussed in comparison with Las Vegas, but also juxtaposed with its images. The main similarity stems from the fact that both towns live from and for spectacle. However, in Las Vegas the theatres and music-halls are multi-storey, brightly lit and omnipresent. It seems as if in the whole city there is nothing but the venues for shows and the carnival there lasts all the year round. The whole town appears flourishing and self-satisfied in its gaudy kitsch. Similarly, the people who frequent the shows, such as Tommy Fawkes's parents, look ostentatiously rich and self-satisfied, coming to the theatre in 'stretch' limousines and wearing shiny clothes. They seem to be entirely in tune with their flashy, pretentious surroundings. The success of Las Vegas is emphasized by the way in which the town is shot – low-angle framing makes the buildings look very tall, robust and overwhelming and night sequences accentuate the gaudiness and brightness of theatres, clubs, music-halls and cabarets.

There are two Blackpools that are compared with Las Vegas – the old and the contemporary. The old appears in flashbacks representing Tommy's memories of his childhood and is recollected by various other people, such as Jack Parker's French mother and the tourist manager who organizes Tommy's stay in the resort. All the memories are happy, although different people associate Blackpool with different features. For Tommy, the Blackpool of his childhood is a sunny, idyllic place full of happy, friendly people. The tourist manager recollects Blackpool as an artistic centre, where the most famous comedians and music-hall artists were proud to perform. He mentions Frank Sinatra and George Formby alongside Tommy's father, George Fawkes (who is, of course, a fictitious character). Similarly, Jack's mother remembers Blackpool from the times when it was flourishing and artistic, when thousands of people came to the music-halls to delight in their shows. She also associates the Blackpool of her youth with a communal spirit, thus conforming to the previously mentioned myth of the North as *Gemeinschaft*. She says: 'In the past we did everything together: we worked together, we loved together.' By contrast, contemporary Blackpool is a rundown, almost deserted place. The music-halls are empty, there are few tourists on the pier or on the promenade and only a handful of ordinary-looking people sit on the beach. The rest look like freaks transported to Blackpool from some surreal spectacle: poorly clothed, obese, strange. The illuminations are also more modest in Blackpool than in Las Vegas and only seasonal – when there are no lights, one sees more clearly the town's decline. The untouristy part of the resort looks even less appealing, with seedy districts, dirty streets, old cars, junk shops and drunken violence. While in Chelsom's film Las Vegas is looked at from below, Blackpool is often looked at from above – from the top of the Blackpool Tower or from a roller-coaster. From a bird's-eye view, streets look chaotic and houses seem very tiny and fragile, like pieces of Lego.

Even more poignant are the differences in lifestyle between George Fawkes and the Parker brothers. George lives like an archetypal superstar, in a large, spacious house complete with widescreen television and swimming pool. He has an attractive wife and generally seems to be well satisfied with life. Although he is ageing, he does not seem to be nostalgic – if it were not for Tommy, he probably would not come to Blackpool at all. The best measure of George's youthful spirit is his ability and willingness to overshadow the performance of his own son. George is a model American individualist and pragmatist – he sees nothing wrong in stealing ideas as long as they are effective. The Parker brothers, on the other hand, inhabit a shed beneath a rickety roller-coaster. In one scene they are framed beside an old gramophone, lit only from a solitary window. It looks as if they must 'borrow' from the past to nourish them in their twilight years. In contrast to George, who stopped using his/their act, they cling to old acts, old music and old memories. Their jobs working on the ghost train; their appearance – withered, pale faces, shabby clothes; their shy behaviour and the mute-ness of one of them epitomize Blackpool's decline and withdrawal from the world, its gradual death. Moreover, it seems as if the Parkers are trapped in decay for ever, as if they cannot be helped. This is suggested in the scene where they prepare for their last big show. They use an elixir of youth, hidden in a large, orange egg. However, when they put the magic powder on their faces, a miasma of dust gathers around them and their faces look even more pale and ghostly than before. The show itself is a repetition of performances that the group used to give in their better days. On the whole, it can be argued that all attempts to invigorate Blackpool only reaffirm its ultimate demise. Probably, the most accurate reflection of Blackpool's low status and decay is the way George Fawkes is treated by his old colleagues. He returns to Blackpool in a private jet, bringing dozens of suitcases, carried by his servants, then walks on a red carpet, laid out especially for him. He is presented with the symbol of the city, a miniature Blackpool Tower, and special lights spell out his name. This regal reception offered by Blackpool to George Fawkes, who comes back as a foreigner, com-bined with the neglect of the Parker brothers, can be interpreted as a symbol of Britain's willingness to exalt America and degrade itself, an attitude typical of the 1980s and 1990s.

In *Funny Bones*, Blackpool Tower is used not only as an element of the setting, but plays an important narrative function. First, Jack climbs the tower and refuses to go down, in spite of the persuasion of his father, his uncle, the local policemen and a psychologist. The tower seems to provide him with shelter and a refuge from the world, which neither understands nor accepts him. He climbs down only after the intervention of his mother. While still at the top of the building, Jack looks up at a plane. From the plane's perspective, the tower looks small and fragile, more like a toy than a symbol of man's power over nature. The words of John Urry, 'Towers connecting the land and the sky are now dwarfed by skyscrapers, hotels, space capsules, and of course by aircraft, all of which are much more obviously "modern" and extra-ordinary' (Urry 1990: 34), are particularly appropriate to this episode. There is also something camp in the image of the tower reduced to a toy – a seriousness that failed and thus gave way to kitsch. The Blackpool Tower is also regarded as a phallic symbol. Chelsom does not particularly emphasize this association, yet it could be argued that George's holding a miniature tower in his hands accentuates his virility.

Jack's eccentricity, his shyness and stubbornness and the fact that he only responds to a woman, likens him to King Kong; he seems to be a rare and precious species, doomed to extinction. There is another part of the film that bears associations with King Kong – the previously mentioned scene in which George Fawkes is presented with a miniature Blackpool Tower. He pretends to be a clumsy ape, clutching on to the tower and making ape-like faces. George Fawkes's King Kong seems to be more powerful than when Jack plays this role. George commands the tower and the whole city of Blackpool; Jack is dwarfed by his surroundings.

The metaphor of the 'soft city' as a place that can be moulded according to individual desires and that 'awaits the imprint of an identity', is no less appropriate to Blackpool in *Funny Bones* than it was to *Bhaji on the Beach*. In *Funny Bones*, Blackpool receives the imprint of an American visitor, as is apparent in the 'King Kong scene', but also in Tommy's first car journey through Blackpool. With its almost empty beaches, people hiding from the wind behind windbreaks, Blackpool looks like the Florida in Jim Jarmusch's *Stranger than Paradise* (1984). The blues music accompanying the images adds to the American road movie atmosphere. On other occasions – particularly in the scene in which a boy finds a human foot on the beach (which was supposedly based on a real event); in the episode in a mortuary where Jack teaches Tommy the secrets of being a successful comedian; and in the audition scene

– Blackpool unfolds itself as a quintessentially surreal city. When Chelsom reveals the interior of the Parker brothers' 'home' and the fairground ghost train on which they work, Surrealism blends with Expressionism. Strange objects are revealed, which look as if they were borrowed from Frankenstein's laboratory: jars with body parts in formalin, a pig's head, old kettles and very old kitchen utensils. We also see huge shadows on the walls. Moreover, in the scenes shot in the Parkers' surroundings, low-angle and canted framing is used, which result in disquieting compositions reminiscent of Roger Corman's adaptations of works of Edgar Allan Poe. Raban's 'soft city' contains positive connotations: it is a friendly, tolerant, democratic and 'human' place. However, there is another side to the 'soft city' that is explored by the director of *Funny Bones*. This is 'weak city' – a place that can easily be submitted to the power of the visitors' gaze and tastes, that has no self-confidence or power of its own, that is like a palimpsest, from which old words can be erased to make room for the new text. It looks as if Blackpool 'goes soft' more easily than Las Vegas.

The title of the film refers to the difference between two types of comedian: those who are funny and those who talk funny. The first, superior, type has funny bones. George Fawkes, who refers to this categorization in a conversation with his son, tells Tommy that he does not belong to any of these categories – he is simply not funny. Characteristically, George also is not particularly funny, either in his appearance or in his talk. In contrast, Jack and the Parker brothers are genuinely and sublimely funny – they have funny bones. Andy Medhurst suggests that the concept of 'funny bones' can be applied to Blackpool itself. He writes: 'Blackpool still has its carnival roots showing, its dark side still visible, its Victorian grotesqueness still there for those who know where to look. It's a funny-bones resort, belching excess from every pore, while Las Vegas can put on show but has no heart' (Medhurst 1995: 10). However, it is worth recollecting that Chelsom equally demonstrates that heart, commitment and past glory are not enough to secure an everlasting success. Although nostalgia is one of the key issues in *Funny Bones*, the film does not actually promote nostalgia. On the contrary, it denounces it by showing that the yesterdays for which we nostalgically yearn and which we extol never existed in reality. Chelsom seems to agree with Fred Davis's opinion that we invent an idyllic past to cope with current problems and disappointments (see Davis 1979). Interestingly, both Jack Parker and Tommy Fawkes achieve their greatest success not by imitating, repeating or recycling old acts, but by learning new skills and inventing a new act.

The difference between welcoming Blackpool and unfriendly Las Vegas, as noted by Medhurst, might have something to do with the relation between the private and the public lives of the inhabitants of the respective towns. In Blackpool, as represented by Chelsom, the public and private spaces intermingle and the difference between public and private lives is blurred. Jack and the Parker brothers practically live in a public place – under the roller-coaster, only inches from the tourists – and when they do not work as horrors in the funfair, they practise their tricks. Their commitment to the circus art is particularly worthy of attention as they have lost almost all hope that they will ever again perform their acts in public. In their dedication to performance the Parkers are reminiscent of Ambrose in *Bhaji on the Beach*, who describes himself as a man who devoted his entire life to spectacle and magic and claims that theatre is his true home. The Fawkes, on the other hand, treat their work in the entertainment industry simply as a means to earn a living and as a vehicle for social advancement. They always know very well when the spectacle finishes and true life starts. On the whole, if we assume that artificiality, superficiality and imitation are characteristics of postmodernism, and genuineness and naivety the features of earlier epochs, Blackpool is less postmodern than its American sister town. On the other hand, its nostalgic aura, openness and adaptability to international influences make it a typical postmodern place, more so than Las Vegas, which is quintessentially American.

References to films about the art of comedy and performance abound in Chelsom's movie. As Louise Gray observes: 'As George, the big shot American comedian whose lopsided charisma induces standing ovations across middle America, Jerry Lewis recapitulates elements of his role in Martin Scorsese's *King of Comedy*' (Gray 1995: 49). Another film that bears strong associations with *Funny Bones* is Marcel Carné's *Les enfants du paradis* [Children of Paradise, 1945]. These references not only add to the postmodern style of Chelsom's film, but reinforce its message about the power of art over life and the close connection between the two – a message that is an important element, if not the essence, of postmodern ideology.

Against the backdrop of the bulk of British films made in the 1980s and 1990s, including those discussed in this book, in which cities are typically neutered, erased, reduced to tiny fragments or portrayed as 'any towns' or as media-constructed representations of cities, *Bhaji on the Beach* and *Funny Bones* could be described as proper 'city films'. First, the majority of their scenes are set in the public spaces of Blackpool: on the beaches and piers, on the Pleasure Beach, in the streets, in the clubs, and inside and outside the Blackpool Tower. The majority of the places are easily recognizable as Blackpool locations and cannot be found in any other part of Britain. It is suggested that life in Blackpool is lived in public (in contrast to the stereotype of British life as led in private). Second, apart from giving us images of various conspicuous objects and districts of the town, the films' directors, mainly through the use of bird's-eye-view shots, give us a portrait of the whole of Blackpool. These portraits typically belong to the people who look at the town from the Tower or from a roller-coaster, rather than to the impersonal camera. Accordingly, one gets the impression that everybody can know Blackpool intimately. Third, geographical location plays a crucial role in Chadha's and Chelsom's narratives. To put it crudely, it would hardly be possible to move the characters to any other town and preserve even the basic storyline of the films. Moreover, apart from showing visitors to Blackpool, *Bhaji on the Beach* and *Funny Bones* are films about idiosyncratic Blackpool people, who cannot live in any other place; they provide their town with their unique character and Blackpool in return nourishes their eccentricities. The filmmakers also suggest that Blackpool, as a town built on spectacle and a locus of 'eternal post-modernity', is under severe threat. The danger comes primarily from the new forms of entertainment, particularly the cinema and television. Indeed, considering the rich and multi-layered image of Blackpool that is presented in *Bhaji on the Beach* and *Funny Bones*, one may wonder if there is any need to see the real thing.

Conclusion

The problem for Europe, then, is to learn how to marginalise itself, to see its present in its historical particularity and its *limitedness*, so that Europeans can start relating to cultural 'others' in new, more modest and dialogic ways. (Ien Ang 1992)

'*Les grandes villes n'ont rien de vrai*' ('The great cities are false'), as Godard says in his 1985 film *Détective*. Godard is to be taken as an authority on cinematic representations of cities. Much of his work can be read, on the one hand, as a commentary on the evolution and decay of the modern urban cityscape and life in it, and of those of its cinematic representation on the other. His debut feature, *A bout de souffle* [Breathless, 1959], immediately provided us with one of the archetypal images of Nouvelle Vague Paris, a true black and white *carte postale* image, which mythologized the city centre. A similar image of Paris as a tangle of lively streets and cafés, albeit shot in colour, can be found in *Une femme est une femme* [A Woman is a Woman, 1961]. Chris Darke has pointed to how this dream Paris soon turned into a nightmare with Godard's *Alphaville* (1965): 'Paris 1965 is Alphaville, a modernist nightmare of post-Bauhaus functionalism where the curtain-walled skyscraper becomes the simultaneous symbol of progress and apocalypse' (Darke 1997: 11). Later, Godard began to show less and less of Paris in his films and then, as in *Détective*, to show it as a fragmented and almost unrecognizable urban environment; finally, he left it altogether, as if disappointed with what had happened both to Paris and to the cinematic city.

Pierre Sorlin (1994) maintains that the evolution in Godard's depiction of the city is part of a more general trend. For Sorlin, in fact, in the 1960s the image of towns in European cinema began to lose focus. De Sica's *Il tetto* [The Roof, 1956] marks, according to the author, the passage to a new, blurred image of the cinematic city: 'The strong system which associated the centre and the outskirts, presented as complementary entities, vanished ... and [many filmmakers] moved from the classic polarization towards less structured and even towards destructured visions of cities' (Sorlin 1994: 126–7). One aspect of this evolution in the representation of the city is the sharp increase in the number of films set in shantytowns, which were represented as disconnected and totally isolated from the centre, thus as an imaginary 'outer-world' or even 'third world'. The other aspect is called by Sorlin 'the cinematic destruction of towns', and consists of the annihilation of urbanized areas, which began to be reduced to 'ugly rows of blind walls' (p. 130). Towns ceased to be a self-evident and solid presence in films, and became instead anonymous places. In films such as Antonioni's *Blow-Up* (1967) and Godard's *Deux ou trois choses que je sais d'elle* [Two or Three Things I Know about Her, 1966], London and Paris are almost un-recognizable.

> Instead of being played as a counterpoint, as a supplementary delight, cities were flattened, reduced to prosaic clichés. There was surely a 'message' underlying the pictures, something like: towns become increasingly humdrum expanses crossed by indifferent drivers and damaged by greedy property developers. Spectators either caught these implications or they did not but they could not miss the dullness, the anonymity of the urbanized areas. (Sorlin 1994: 133)

Sorlin's is, unfortunately, a limited study of the cinema of selected European countries (Great Britain, Italy, France and Germany), and refers to a small sample of films, so that its conclusions run the risk of being generic and partial. It is nevertheless safe to argue that, at least in the case of European modernist cinema (and with reference to selected filmmakers including Antonioni, Godard, Resnais, Pasolini and Wenders), the films of the 1960s reacted to the transformations of the city fabric and lifestyle by constructing a disjointed, unconnected and almost unidentifiable urban space. This tendency is still recognizable in much current European cinema. In many of the films studied in this book, the city is represented as a fragmented, anonymous environment.

Although this recurrent way of filming the European city superficially looks like a mere prolongation of modernism, the result achieved by contemporary films is very different – in tune with the spirit of the times, no apocalyptic, dystopian vision of modern city life is produced today, but a distinctly postmodern urban environment, which more than once in this book we have described by the phrase 'any-town'. Among our chosen films, even those which most clearly try to define and characterize the local urban environment – by paying attention to the place's particular accent, traditions and locales – end up conveying the image of a city that clearly belongs to postmodernity.

One element that has become clear in the course of our work is the difference that exists between representations of big and small cities. Whereas European metropolises such as London, Moscow, Berlin, Madrid and Warsaw tend to be represented as homogenized and standardized, smaller places like Estaque (Marseilles), Blackpool and Swansea preserve in the films that depict them a more genuine local character, despite their evident belonging to a postmodern and late-capitalist society. This observation takes us back to Godard's motto that 'All big cities are fake'. The question at stake here is not the contrast between 'reality' and 'representation', since all cities are representations, and it is as representations that we know them. What else is a city to us, if not a stratification and a combination of meanings, memories and perceptions, both private and shared, journalistic and fictional, geographical and historical? The problem, then, no longer is to understand whether the city in a film is 'authentic' (or less false), but whether it is in tune with a certain (hegemonic, privileged) representation. In each of the cases that we studied, we have tried to establish precisely whether the cinematic city corresponds or conflicts with its hegemonic, privileged representation, a representation that partly derives from historical, economic, journalistic and geographical documents, partly from an imagery linked to mainstream fictions.

One way of reading Godard's motto is by equating falseness with standardization, and authenticity with the preservation of local character and traditions. It is obvious that in the case of a metropolis like London, with its 14 million inhabitants, it is hardly possible to talk of 'local traditions'. From this perspective, a metropolis presenting a very varied and mixed population is inevitably more 'fake' than a smaller and more homogeneous town. The general impression that results from our work is that each European town has developed its own form of postmodernity, by combining local traditions and global culture, whereas European big cities and metropolises seem more standardized, and consequently their filmic representations are often less interesting and original. This impression confirms Ien Ang's suggestion that the postmodern 'end of the meta-narratives' heralded by Baudrillard has opened up, in European film as well, the possibility of looking at smaller, local narratives (Ang 1992: 28). Many of the city films that we discussed are such local narratives, a tendency that clearly contrasts with the old city-film genre, and especially with the city symphonies, which endeavoured to be grand and totalizing narratives. Accordingly, the old, prevalent way of inscribing city-films within the dichotomy utopia/dystopia has not been a useful instrument of analysis, as these categories seem better to pertain to modernism. Similarly, the contrast between centre and periphery is no longer a viable tool for reading the contemporary European cinematic city. The fragmentation of the postmodern urban environment wipes away the distinction – the city is mostly represented as an undistinguished and practically unreadable collage of sections of areas, streets and buildings; routes through the town are not clearly marked, so that our sense of space and time are challenged. This collage is mostly alienating (*Nenette et Boni, Wonderland*), but can sometimes even be elating (*Beautiful People*). City and country are represented as contrasting ways of living in some of our films – for instance, in *The Flower of My Secret, Beautiful People, Notting Hill* and *Luna Park*. Nevertheless, the countryside does not represent a true alternative to urban life – either because it does not truly differ from it (as in *Luna Park*), or because characters display a postmodern cynicism towards the benefits of country life and they see it as belonging to an inevitably lost past.

A second general impression that emerges from our work is that of a certain void resulting from change, from the fragmentation of the environment and from the loss of prior contents – nothing or at best unappealing substitutes replaced forgotten traditions as well as demolished old buildings. Accordingly, many of the films studied show people who, in various ways, try to deal with this void: they can attempt to escape (as in *Trainspotting, Twin Town* and *Bye-Bye*); to 'clean' the city (*Taxi Blues* and *Luna Park*); to withdraw to the safety of the home (*Nenette et Boni*); or, at the other extreme, to reclaim the urban space (*Marius et Jeannette*). There does not seem to be a great difference from this point of view between cities of Eastern and Western Europe – the experience of a void and rootlessness is widespread and pervasive. One factor that does distinguish representations of cities in Old Europe and in postcommunist Europe is immigration. Western European cities, both big and small, are represented in many films as increasingly cosmopolitan – life in London, Naples, Marseilles, Blackpool, as described in the films that we analysed, is marked by the presence of immigrants, both from Eastern Europe and from the former European colonies. In some cases, the friction between locals and immigrants is strong, as seen in particular in *Beautiful People* and in *Bye-Bye*. In other cases, the mix of peoples and cultures seems less problematic, as in the films set in Blackpool and in Naples, as well as in two of the films set in Marseilles (*Marius et Jeannette*, in which Jeannette has two children, one black and Muslim, one white and Christian; and *Nenette et Boni*, in which, though cohabitation is not highlighted, conflict does not feature), possibly because these cities are near the sea, and the sea is an element of fluidity that often favours the crossing of barriers. In any case, immigration is frequently presented in recent city-films as a crucial element in the definition of new European identities. In fact, cinematic representations of cities serve also as a mirror of general issues that are at stake in European society at large.

In 'European Cinema on the Verge of a Nervous Breakdown', Stuart Hall notes how many recent European films concentrate on immigration and dislocation. After all, as he reminds us:

> Paris, Rome, London, Barcelona, Naples, Frankfurt, like Miami, Los Angeles and New York, are, as someone remarks in Tom Wolfe's *Bonfire of the Vanities*, Third World or 'global' cities. The one-way ticket and the charter flight have brought Europe (which for so long dealt with its colonial outposts at arm's length) within reach of its 'others'. In the age of global production and capital flows and liberalised markets and information systems that exchange messages of their own accord, we are all 'economic migrants' now. The barbarians are already within the gate. (Hall 1992: 47)

Hall wonders whether in contemporary European cinema this 'dislocation' is represented as productive and leading to the possible formation of new identities and to a true dialogue between the margins, as opposed to announcing the recovery of old centres or the replacement of one centre with another. According to Hall, most films seem to recognize the 'deep but as yet impassable barriers before which Europe finds itself' (p. 53). Similarly, the films that we analysed emphasize, for the most part, the new problems and obstacles that European citizens of most nationalities and classes are experiencing in their lives. Identities are widely represented as shifting between old traditions and new lifestyles, between acquired beliefs and new challenges; Europe is changing, European identities are also changing, but we usually fail to respond and find new, satisfactory ways of perceiving ourselves. We no longer are what we used to be, we have all become 'economic migrants', the barbarians are already here (indeed, some of us have now become the barbarians, namely the travellers and peoples from Eastern Europe and from Southern Europe). This loss of the centres (both physical and ideal) has produced a mix of scepticism and nostalgia, and sometimes even a blind rejection of the evidence of change. Cohesion and centrality belong to the past, and we are now left to learn how to marginalize ourselves.

Notes

Introduction

1. See, for instance: Bruno (1993); Anne Friedberg, *Window Shopping: Cinema and the Postmodern* (Berkeley and Los Angeles: University of California Press, 1993); James Donald, 'The City, the Cinema: Modern Spaces', in Chris Jencks (ed.), *Visual Culture* (London: Routledge, 1995); Clarke (1997); François Penz and Maureen Thomas (eds), *Cinema and Architecture. Méliès, Mallet-Stevens, Multimedia* (London: BFI, 1997); special issue on 'Cityscapes', *Wide Angle*, vol. 19, no. 4 (1997); special issue on 'Space/Place/City', *Screen*, vol. 40, no. 3 (1999); Myrto Konstantarakos (ed.), *Spaces in European Cinema* (Exeter and Portland, OR: Intellect, 2000).

2. Among the recent literature, see Frank Krutnik, 'Something More than Night: Tales of the Noir City', in Clarke (ed.), *The Cinematic City*.

3. For a more detailed account of Sorlin's theory see both Chapter 8 and the Conclusion.

4. For a discussion of cinematic representations of war-torn Sarajevo, see Dina Iordanova, *Cinema of Flames: Balkan Film, Culture and the Media* (London: BFI, 2001).

5. Examples of postmodern readings of American cinematic cities are: Giuliana Bruno, 'Ramble City: Postmodernism and *Blade Runner*', in Annette Kuhn (ed.), *Alien Zone* (London and New York: Verso, 1990); the chapter 'Space on Flat Earth: *Blade Runner*', in Neville Wakefield, *Postmodernism. The Twilight of the Real* (London: Pluto, 1990); Peter Wollen, 'Delirious Projections', *Sight and Sound*, no. 4 (1992), pp. 25–6. Examples of modernist readings of European cinematic cities are: Penz and Thomas (eds), *Cinema and Architecture*; Antony Easthope, 'Cinécities in the Sixties', in Clarke (ed.), *The Cinematic City* (this essay tries to trace the passage from modernity to postmodernity in films by Godard and Antonioni); Darke (1994); the chapter 'Light in Dark Spaces. Cinema and City', in Donald (1999).

6. See, for instance, Hans Bertens, *The Idea of the Postmodern. A History* (London and New York: Routledge, 1995).

7. 'European cinema' is, of course, yet another problematic expression. Here we simply want to point to the existence of a debate on what European cinema is, without getting into the merits of the discussion. In our work we will straightforwardly consider as European films produced by (or co-produced by) and filmed in the countries that we decided to include in our broad definition of Europe.

8. See, for instance: Mike Davis, *City of Quartz: Excavating the Future in Los Angeles* (London: Verso, 1990); David Harvey, 'Flexible Accumulation Through Urbanisation: Reflections on Post-modernism in the American City', in Ash Amin (ed.), *Post-Fordism. A Reader* (Oxford: Blackwell, 1994); Charles Jencks, 'Hetero-architecture and the L.A. School', in Allen J. Scott and Edward W. Soja (eds), *The City. Los Angeles and Urban Theory at the End of the Twentieth Century* (Los Angeles: University of California Press, 1996).

3 A Present and a True City?

1. The Italian expression *'speculazione edilizia'* does not have a direct translation and refers to the practice, widespread in Italy, of erecting houses and apartment blocks without regard for planning or building regulations.
2. Literal translation from the Italian *'caschi blu'*, which stands for UN troops.
3. Literal translation from the Italian *'croce uncinata'*, another name for a swastika.

5 Any Town?

1. As the majority of Polish films made before 1945 were set either in a studio or on location in rural Poland, Warsaw hardly featured in the cinema till the end of the Second World War.
2. Condee and Padunov (1995) limit their discussion to Russia, but many of their observations and conclusions can be applied to the countries of the Eastern bloc.
3. In Polish, *'Pisarka'* means 'Scribbler'.
4. In some films made in the 1990s, most importantly in *Rozwowy kontrolowane* [Controlled Conversations, 1992] by Sylwester Checinski, which was the first Polish comedy about martial law, the Palace of Culture was actually destroyed, suggesting that this idea was deeply rooted in social consciousness and/or subconsciousness.
5. After *Kiler*, Machulski directed its sequel, *Kilerow dwoch* [Two Kilers, 1999], which uses postmodern aesthetics more extensively than the films discussed in this chapter.

British Cities since the 1980s

1. See Peter Hall, 'The City of Capitalism Rampant. London 1979–1993', in his *Cities in Civilisation* (London: Phoenix Giant, 1999), pp 888–931; Jon Bird, 'Dystopia on the Thames', in Jon Bird et al. (eds), *Mapping the Futures. Local Cultures, Global Change* (London and New York: Routledge, 1995), pp. 120–35.

8 London: Fragments of a Metropolis

1. The interest in Dickensian London might have something to do with the writer's talent for portraying London vividly and accurately. The architect Kevin Lynch once observed: 'Dickens helped to create the London which we experience as surely as its actual builders did.' See Donald (1999: 2).
2. For a further discussion of Sorlin's theory, see the Conclusions.

9 Escape from a Celtic City

1. The director of *Trainspotting*, Danny Boyle, whose roots are in the North of England, does not hide the fact that his personal experience to a certain degree res-

embles that of his protagonist Mark Renton. As does Renton, he felt that in order to achieve anything in life, he had to leave his home town and move south. Those who stayed in their old place were also left behind in terms of their careers and personal achievements (see Macnab 1996: 11).

2. The importance of male bands in working-class communities was also conveyed in English films, such as New Wave classic *A Kind of Loving* (1962), directed by John Schlesinger, and, more recently, by *Brassed Off* (1996), directed by Mark Herman.

3. Such a pessimistic vision of Thatcherite urban reality is also conveyed in Ken Loach's films of the 1990s, such as *Raining Stones* (1993) and *My Name is Joe* (1998) (see Hill 2000). However, the motif of escape seems to appear only in 'Celtic' films.

10 The Eternal Postmodernity of Blackpool

1. The term 'Northern' refers here not so much to a precise geographical location as to the 'spatial mythology' surrounding the North of England. See Rob Shields, 'The North–South Divide in England', in his *Places on the Margin* (1991).

Bibliography

Almodóvar, Pedro (1991) *The Patty Diphusa Stories and Other Writings* (London and Boston: Faber and Faber).

Amendola, Giandomenico (1997) *La città postmoderna. Magie e paure della metropoli contemporanea* (Rome and Bari: Laterza).

Ang, Ien (1992) 'Hegemony-in-trouble', in Duncan Petrie (ed.), *Screening Europe* (London: BFI).

Armogathe, Daniel and Pierre Echinard (1995) *Marseille, port du 7ᵉ Art* (n.p.: Jeanne Laffitte).

Aronica, Daniela (1993) *Pedro Almodóvar* (Rome: Il Castoro Cinema).

Bachelard, Gaston (1969) *The Poetics of Space* (Boston: Beacon Press).

Bagnasco, Arnaldo and Patrick Le Galès (eds) (2000) *Cities in Contemporary Europe* (Cambridge: Cambridge University Press).

Bakhtin, Mikhail (1984) *Rabelais and His World*, trans. Helene Iswolsky (Bloomington and Indianapolis: Indiana University Press).

Baudrillard, Jean (1981) *Simulacres et simulation* (Paris: Galilée).

Benjamin, Walter (1986) *Reflections*, trans. Edmund Jephcott (New York: Schoken Books).

Benjamin, Walter and Asja Lacis (1992) 'Naples' (1924), in Walter Benjamin, *One Way Street and Other Writings* (London and New York: Verso).

Berent, Jolanta (1996) 'Girl Guide', *Film*, 3, p. 74.

Berry, David (1994) *Wales and Cinema* (Cardiff: University of Wales Press).

Bianchini, Franco and Hermann Schwengel (1991) 'Re-imagining the City', in John Corner and Sylvia Harvey (eds), *Enterprise and Heritage* (London: Routledge).

Bouquet, Stéphane (1995a) 'Les enracinés', *Cahiers du cinéma*, 494 (September), pp. 36–41.

— (1995b) 'Marseille: les lois de l'attraction', *Cahiers du cinéma*, 495 (October), pp. 35–41.

— (1996) 'Claire Denis, les années sauvages de Nénette et Boni', *Cahiers du cinéma*, 501 (April), pp. 55–8.

Boym, Svetlana (1993) 'Carnivals Bright, Dark and Grotesque in the *glasnost* Satires of Mamin, Mustafayev and Shakhnazarov', in Andrew Horton (ed.), *Inside Soviet Film Satire* (Cambridge: Cambridge University Press).

Brooks, Peter (1995) *The Melodramatic Imagination. Balzac, Henry James, Melodrama and the Mode of Excess* (New Haven and London: Yale University Press).

Bruce, David (1996) *Scotland the Movie* (Edinburgh: Polygon).

Bruno, Giuliana (1993) *Streetwalking on a Ruined Map. Cultural Theory and the City Films of Elvira Notari* (Princeton, NJ: Princeton University Press).

Chambers, Iain (1994) *Migrancy, Culture, Identity* (London and New York: Routledge).

Champion, Edward (2000) *Interview: Jasmin Dizdar* http://24framespersecond.com/offcamera/interviews/jdizdar.html

Chiacchiari, Federico (1996) 'Pianese Nunzio 14 anni a maggio', *Cineforum*, 357 (September), pp. 74–5.

Clarke, David B. (ed.) (1997) *The Cinematic City* (London and New York: Routledge).

Claus, Horst (1999) 'Rebels with a Cause: The Development of the "Berlin-Filme" by Gerhard Klein and Wolfgang Kohlhaase', in Sean Allan and John Sandford (eds), *DEFA* (New York: Berghahn Books).

Combs, Richard (1995) 'New British Cinema: A Prospect and Six Views', *Film Comment* (November–December), pp. 52–9.

Condee, Nancy and Vladimir Padunov (1995) 'The ABC of Russian Consumer Culture', in Nancy Condee (ed.), *Soviet Hieroglyphics. Visual Culture in Late Twentieth Century Russia* (Bloomington and Indianapolis: Indiana University Press; London: BFI).

Conti, Sergio and G. Spriano (eds) (1990), *Effetto città*, Vol. I: *Sistemi urbani e innovazione: prospettive per l'Europa degli anni novanta* (Turin: Fondazione G. Agnelli).

Corner, John and Sylvia Harvey (eds) (1991) *Enterprise and Heritage* (London: Routledge).

Craig, Cairns (1982) 'Myths against History: Tartanry and Kailyard in 19th-Century Scottish Literature', in Colin McArthur (ed.), *Scotch Reels* (London: BFI).

Darke, Chris (1997) 'It All Happened in Paris', *Sight and Sound*, 7 (July), pp. 10–12.

Davis, Fred (1979) *Yearning for Nostalgia* (New York: Free Press).

de Lauretis, Teresa (1987). *Technologies of Gender* (London: Macmillan).

Deleuze, Gille and Felix Guattari (1988) *A Thousand Plateaus: Capitalism and Schizophrenia* (London: Athlone Press).

Denzin, Norman (1988) *'Blue Velvet*: Postmodern Contradictions', *Theory, Culture and Society*, 5 (2–3), pp. 461–73.

D'Lugo, Marvin (1995) 'Almodóvar's City of Desire', in Kathleen Vernon and Barbara Morris (eds), *Post-Franco, Postmodern. The Films of Pedro Almodóvar* (Westport, CT: Greenwood Press).

Donald, James (1992) 'Metropolis: The City as Text', in Robert Bocock and Kenneth Thompson (eds), *Social and Cultural Forms of Modernity* (Cambridge: Polity Press).

— (1999) *Imagining the Modern City* (London: Athlone Press).

Durgnat, Raymond (1967) *Films and Feelings* (London: Faber and Faber).

Eagle, Herbert (1992) 'Socialist Realist and American Genre Film: The Mixing of Codes in *Jazzman*', in Anna Lawton (ed.), *The Red Screen. Politics, Society, Art in Soviet Cinema* (London: Routledge).

Eleftheriotis, Dimitris (2000) 'Cultural Difference and Exchange: A Future for European Film', *Screen*, 41 (1), pp. 92–101.

Elseasser, Thomas (1989) *New German Cinema* (London: BFI).

Elseasser, Thomas with Michael Wedel (eds) (1999) *The BFI Companion to German Cinema* (London: BFI).

Enyedi, Gyorgy (1996) 'Urbanization Under Socialism', in Gregory Andrusz, Michael Harloe and Ivan Szeleney (eds), *Cities After Socialism* (Oxford: Blackwell).

Fishman, Robert (1987) *Bourgeois Utopias: The Rise and Fall of Suburbia* (New York: Basic Books).

Fuentes, Víctor (1995) 'Almodóvar's Postmodern Cinema: A Work in Progress ...', in Kathleen Vernon and Barbara Morris (eds), *Post-Franco, Postmodern. The Films of Pedro Almodóvar* (Westport, CT: Greenwood Press).

Gablik, Suzi (1984) *Has Modernism Failed?* (London: Thames and Hudson).

Gariazzo, Giuseppe (1995) 'Napoli corpi e luoghi', *Sentieri Selvaggi*, 8, pp. 38–45.

Goyomarch, Alain (1999) 'France', in Max-Stephan Schulze (ed.), *Western Europe: Economic and Social Change Since 1945* (London and New York: Longman).

Gray, Louise (1995) 'Funny Bones', *Sight and Sound*, 10 (October), p. 49.

Greuner, Suzanne (1993) 'Luna Park', *Epd Film* (February), p. 32.

Hall, Stuart (1992) 'European Cinema on the Verge of a Nervous Breakdown', in Duncan Petrie (ed.), *Screening Europe* (London: BFI).

Hall, Tim (1997) '(Re)placing the City. Cultural Relocation and the City as Centre', in Sallie Westwood and John Williams (eds), *Imagining Cities* (London: Routledge).

Hannigan, John (1998) *Fantasy City. Pleasure and Profit in the Postmodern Metropolis* (London and New York: Routledge).

Harloe, Michael (1996) 'Cities in the Transition', in Gregory Andrusz, Michael Harloe and Ivan Szeleney (eds), *Cities After Socialism* (Oxford: Blackwell).

Harvey, David (1990) *The Condition of Postmodernity: An Inquiry into the Origins of Cultural Change* (Oxford and Cambridge, MA: Blackwell).

Haussermann, Hartmut (1996) 'From the Socialist to the Capitalist City: Experiences from Germany', in Gregory Andrusz, Michael Harloe and Ivan Szeleney (eds), *Cities After Socialism* (Oxford: Blackwell).

Haussman, Leander (1999) 'Sonnenallee', *Kino* (Germany) (January), p. 15.

Higson, Andrew (1993) 'Re-presenting the National Past: Nostalgia and Pastiche in the Heritage Film', in Lester Friedman (ed.), *British Cinema and Thatcherism* (London: UCL Press).

— (1995) *Waving the Flag* (Oxford: Clarendon Press).

Hill, John (1997) 'British Cinema as National Cinema', in John Murphy (ed.), *The British Cinema Book* (London: BFI).

— (1999) *British Cinema in the 1980s* (Oxford: Clarendon Press).

— (2000) 'Failure and Utopianism: Representation of the Working Class in British Cinema of the 1990s', in Robert Murphy (ed.), *British Cinema of the 90s* (London: BFI).

Hoberman, J. (1998) *The Red Atlantis. Communist Culture in the Absence of Communism* (Philadelphia: Temple University Press).

Horton, Andrew (1993) 'Quick Takes on Yuri Mamin's *Fountain* from the Perspective of a Romanian', in Andrew Horton (ed.), *Inside Soviet Film Satire* (Cambridge: Cambridge University Press).

Hutchings, Peter (1986) '*Frenzy*. A Return to Britain', in Charles Barr (ed.), *All Our Yesterdays* (London: BFI).

Jaehne, Karen (1991) 'Taxi Blues', *Film Quarterly* (Spring), p. 52.

James, Nick (1999) 'Farewell to Napoli', *Sight and Sound*, 5 (May), pp. 20–2.

Jameson, Fredric (1985) 'Postmodernism and Consumer Society', in Hal Foster (ed.), *Postmodern Culture* (London: Pluto Press).

— (1991) *Postmodernism, or, The Cultural Logic of Late Capitalism* (London and New York: Verso).

Jencks, Charles (1981) *The Language of Postmodern Architecture* (London: Academy).

Jesinghausen, Martin (2000) 'The Sky Over Berlin as Transcendental Space: Wenders, Doblin, and the "Angel of History"', in Myrto Konstantarakos (ed.), *Spaces in European Cinema* (Exeter, UK and Portland, OR: Intellect).

Jousse, Thierry and Jean-Marc Lalanne (1995) '*Bye-Bye*. Propos de Karim Dridi', *Cahiers du cinéma*, 494 (September), pp. 39–41.

Kaes, Anton (1996) 'Sites of Desire: The Weimar Street Film', in Dietrich Neumann (ed.), *Film Architecture: Set Designs from Metropolis to Blade Runner* (Munich and New York: Prestel).

Kemp, Philip (1996) 'Trainspotting', *Sight and Sound*, 3 (March), p. 52.

King, Anthony D. (ed.) (1996) *Re-Presenting the City* (New York: New York University Press).

Knoben, Martina (2000) 'Plus-Minus Null', *Epd Film* (April), p. 45.

Kolodynski, Andrzej (1997) 'Kiler i inni', *Kino* (Poland), 12, pp. 33–5.

Kreimeier, Klaus (1987) 'Der Schlafwandler. Fritz Lang und seine deutschen Filme', in Uta Berg-Ganschow und Wolfgang Jacobsen (eds), … *Film … Stadt … Kino ; Berlin …* (Berlin: Argon Verlag).

La Capria, Raffaele (1992) 'Morte di un matematico napoletano', *Il Mattino*, 25 September.

Lawton, Anna (1992) *Kinoglasnost. Soviet Cinema in Our Time* (Cambridge: Cambridge University Press).

Ledochowski, Aleksander (1990) '1:0 dla Pawla Lungina', *Film*, 36, p. 24.

Lefebvre, Henri (1974) *La production de l'espace* (Paris: Anthropos).

Lever, William (1999) 'Urbanization', in Max-Stephan Schulze (ed.), *Western Europe. Economic and Social Change Since 1945* (London and New York: Longman).

Lewis, Robert A. and Richard H. Rowland (1976) 'Urbanization in Russia and the USSR, 1897–1970', in Michael F. Hamm (ed.), *The City in Russian History* (Lexington: University Press of Kentucky).

Lis, Piotr (1989) 'Prowincja i metropolia w polskim filmie wspolczesnym', in J. Trzynadlowski (ed.), *Studia filmoznawcze VIII. Dzielo filmowe – teoria i praktyka* (Wroclaw: Wydawnictwo Uniwersytetu Wroclawskiego).

Luckett, Moya (2000) 'Image and Nation in 1990s British Cinema', in Robert Murphy (ed.), *British Cinema of the 90s* (London: BFI).

Lury, Karen and Doreen Massey (1999) 'Making Connections', *Screen*, 40 (3), pp. 229–38.

McArthur, Colin (1982) 'Scotland and Cinema: The Iniquity of the Fathers', in Colin McArthur (ed.), *Scotch Reels* (London: BFI).

— (1997) 'Chinese Boxes and Russian Dolls: Tracking the Elusive Cinematic City', in David B. Clarke (ed.), *The Cinematic City* (London and New York: Routledge), pp. 19–45.

MacDonald, Scott (1997–98) 'The City as the Country. The New York City Symphony from Rudy Burckhardt to Spike Lee', *Film Quarterly* (Winter), pp. 2–20.

Macnab, Geoffrey (1996) 'Geoffrey Macnab Talks to the Team that Made *Trainspotting*', *Sight and Sound*, 2 (February), pp. 8–11.

Martone, Mario (1997) *L'amore molesto* (Mantova: Circolo del Cinema – Comune di Mantova).

— (1998) *Teatro di guerra. Un diario* (Milan: Bompiani).

Matthews, Peter (1996) 'The Flower of My Secret', *Sight and Sound*, 2 (February), p. 40.

— (1998) 'Sliding Doors', *Sight and Sound*, 6 (June), pp. 55–6.

Medhurst, Andy (1995) 'Unhinged Invention', *Sight and Sound*, 10 (October), pp. 6–10.

Mira, Alberto (2000) 'Transformations of the Urban Landscape in Spanish Film Noir', in Myrto Konstantarakos (ed.), *Spaces in European Cinema* (Exeter, UK and Portland, OR: Intellect).

Morley, David and Kevin Robins (1993) 'No Place like *Heimat*: Images of Home-(land) in European Culture', in Erica Carter, James Donald and Judith Squires (eds), *Space and Place. Theories of Identity and Location* (London: Lawrence and Wishart).

Murphy, Robert (2001) 'Citylife: Urban Fairy-tales in Late 90s British Cinema', in Robert Murphy (ed.), *The British Cinema Book*, 2nd edn (London: BFI).

Neumann, Dietrich (1996) 'Before and After *Metropolis*: Film and Architecture in Search of the Modern City', in Dietrich Neumann (ed.), *Film Architecture: Set Designs from Metropolis to Blade Runner* (Munich and New York: Prestel).

O'Hagan, Andrew (1996) 'The Boys are Back in Town. Andrew O'Hagan on *Trainspotting* and *Heartless Midlothian*', *Sight and Sound*, 2 (February), pp. 6–8.

O'Healy, Áine (1999) 'Revisiting the Belly of Naples: The Body and the City in the films of Mario Martone', *Screen*, 40 (3), pp. 239–56.

Orr, John (1993) *Cinema and Modernity* (Cambridge: Polity Press).

Paton, Maureen (1999) 'The Man Who Got Julia to Ditch the Make-up', *Guardian*, 19 May, pp. 12–13.

Plachov, Andrei (1990) 'Czarniucha i czarna otchlan', trans. Jerzy Plazewski, *Kino* (Poland), 10, pp. 35–6.

Ponarin, Teimuraz (1990) 'Raskvitatsia s epokoi' (interview with Pavel Lungin), *Sovietskij Ekran*, 13, pp. 18–19.

Raban, Jonathan (1975) *Soft City* (Glasgow: Fontana).

Ranucci, Georgette and Stefanella Ughi (eds) (n.d.) *Mario Martone* (Rome: Script/ Leuto, Dino Audino Editore).

Richards, Jeffrey (1984) *The Age of the Dream Palace. Cinema and Society in Britain 1930– 1939* (London: Routledge and Kegan Paul).

— (1997) *Films and British National Identity* (Manchester: Manchester University Press).

Richie, Alexandra (1998) *Faust's Metropolis* (London: HarperCollins).

Roddick, Nick (1995) 'Four Weddings and a Final Reckoning', *Sight and Sound*, 1 (January), pp. 13–15.

Roma, Giuseppe and Gianni Dominici (eds) (1997) *Municipia. Rapporto sulle città italiane* (Rome: Franco Angeli).

Ross, Anthony (2000) *Interview with Writer/Director Jazmin Dizdar* wysiwyg://15/ http://www.rossanthony.com/interviews/dizdar.shtml

Roth, Wilhelm (1999) 'Filme aus Berlin', *Epd Film* (April), pp. 14–15.

Sadowska, Malgorzata (1997) 'Chodzi o to, zeby bylo smiesznie' (interview with Juliusz Machulski), *Kino* (Poland), 10, pp. 23–4.

Secchi, Bernardo (1999) *Immagini della città contemporanea* www.iuav.unive.it/urbanlab/ lez2a.htm#1A

Shields, Rob (1991) *Places on the Margin. Alternative Geographies of Modernity* (London: Routledge).

Sitbon, Guy (1991) 'Ostatnia czerwona taksowka', trans. Maria Oleksiewicz, *Kino* (Poland), 2, pp. 44–5.

Smith, Paul Julian (1992) *Laws of Desire. Questions of Homosexuality in Spanish Writing and Film 1960–1990* (Oxford: Clarendon Press).

— (1994a) *Desire Unlimited. The Films of Pedro Almodóvar* (London: Verso).

— (1994b) 'Future Chic', *Sight and Sound*, 1 (January), pp. 6–10.

— (1996) 'Almodóvar and the Tin Can', *Sight and Sound*, 2 (February), pp. 24–7.

Soja, Edward W. (1997) 'Six Discourses on the Postmetropolis', in Sallie Westwood and John Williams (eds), *Imagining Cities* (London and New York: Routledge).

Sorlin, Pierre (1994) *European Cinemas, European Societies 1939–1990* (London and New York: Routledge).

Stiszowa, Jelena (1997) 'Krotka historia kina postradzieckiego', trans. Jerzy Plazewski, *Kino* (Poland), 6, pp. 12–15.

Strauss, Frédéric (ed.) (1994) *Almodóvar on Almodóvar* (London: Faber and Faber).

Street, Sarah (1997) *British National Cinema* (London: Routledge).

Stuart, Angela (1994) 'Blackpool Illumination', *Sight and Sound*, 2 (February), pp. 26– 7.

Taylor, Ronald (1997) *Berlin and Its Culture* (New Haven and London: Yale University Press).

Thompson, Ben (1997) 'Twin Town', *Sight and Sound*, 4 (April), pp. 53–4.

Triana Toribio, Núria (1996) 'Almodóvar's Melodramatic *mise-en-scène*: Madrid as a Setting for Melodrama', *Bulletin of Hispanic Studies*, 73 (2), pp. 179–89.

Tuan, Yi Fu (1977) *Space and Place* (London: Edward Arnold).

Turim, Maureen (1991) 'Cinemas of Modernity and Postmodernity', in Ingeborg Hoesterey (ed.), *Zeitgeist in Babel* (Bloomington: Indiana University Press).

Urry, John (1990) *The Tourist Gaze* (London: Sage).

Valens, Grégory (1999) '*Wonderland*. Éloge de la fragmentation', *Positif*, 463 (September), pp. 40–1.

Venturi, Robert, Denise Scott Brown and Steven Izenour (1985) *Learning from Las Vegas: The Forgotten Symbolism of Architectural Form* (Cambridge, MA: MIT Press).

Vincendeau, Ginette (2000) 'In the Name of the Father. Marcel Pagnol's "Trilogy": *Marius* (1931), *Fanny* (1932), *César* (1936)', in Susan Hayward and Ginette Vincendeau (eds), *French Film: Texts and Contexts* (London and New York: Routledge).

von Thuna, Ulrich (1999) 'Nachtgestalten', *Epd Film* (August), p. 41.

Walton, John K. (1978) *The Blackpool Landlady* (Manchester: Manchester University Press).

— (1998) *Blackpool* (Edinburgh: Edinburgh University Press).

— (2000) 'Blackpool and the Varieties of Britishness', paper presented at the conference on 'Relocating Britishness', University of Central Lancashire, June 2000.

Walvin, James (1978) *Beside the Seaside* (London: Allen Lane).

Weihsmann, Helmut (1997) 'The City in Twilight: Charting the Genre of the "City Film" 1900–1930', in François Penz and Maureen Thomas (eds), *Cinema & Architecture: Méliès, Mallet-Stevens, Multimedia* (London: BFI).

Welsh, Irvine (1993) *Trainspotting* (London: Minerva).

Wenders, Wim (1999) *The Logic of Images*, trans. Michael Hoffman (London: Faber and Faber).

Wilson, Tony (1990) 'Reading the Postmodernist Image: a "Cognitive Mapping"', *Screen*, 31 (4), pp. 390–407.

Worschech, Rudolf (1997) 'Das Leben ist eine Baustelle', *Epd Film* (March), pp. 33–4.

Yampolsky, Mikhail (1995) 'In the Shadow of Monuments', in Nancy Condee (ed.), *Soviet Hieroglyphics. Visual Culture in Late Twentieth Century Russia* (Bloomington and Indianapolis: Indiana University Press; London: BFI).

Yates, Robert (1994) 'London', *Sight and Sound*, 6 (June), pp. 54–5.

Index

(page numbers in *italics* refer to illustrations)